The Appointed
State

Public Policy and Management

Series Editor: Professor R.A.W. Rhodes, Department of Politics, University of Newcastle.

The effectiveness of public policies is a matter of public concern and the efficiency with which policies are put into practice is a continuing problem for governments of all political persuasions. This series contributes to these debates by publishing informed, in-depth and contemporary analyses of public administration, public policy and public management.

The intention is to go beyond the usual textbook approach to the analysis of public policy and management and to encourage authors to move debate about their issue forward. In this sense, each book both describes current thinking and research, and explores future policy directions. Accessibility is a key feature and, as a result, the series will appeal to academics and their students as well as to the informed practitioner.

Current titles include:

Christine Bellamy and John A. Taylor: *Governing in the Information Age*
Tony Butcher: *Delivering Welfare*
John Ernst: *Whose Utility? The Social Impact of Public Utility Privatization and Regulation in Britain*
Christopher D. Foster and Francis J. Plowden: *The State Under Stress: Can the Hollow State be Good Government?*
Lucy Gaster: *Quality in Public Services: Managers' Choices*
Patricia Greer: *Transforming Central Government: The Next Steps Initiative*
Steve Leach, Howard Davis and Associates: *Enabling or Disabling Local Government: Choices for the Future*
David Marsh (ed.): *Comparing Policy Networks*
O. Morrissey, B. Smith and E. Horesh: *British Aid and International Trade*
R.A.W. Rhodes: *Understanding Governance: Policy Networks, Governance, Reflexivity and Accountability*
Chris Skelcher: *The Appointed State: Quasi-Governmental Organizations and Democracy*
Gerald Wistow, Martin Knapp, Brian Hardy and Caroline Allen: *Social Care in a Mixed Economy*
Gerald Wistow, Martin Knapp, Brian Hardy, Julien Forder, Jeremy Kendall and Rob Manning: *Social Care Markets: Progress and Prospects*
Spencer Zifcak: *New Managerialism: Administrative Reform in Whitehall and Canberra*

The Appointed State

Quasi-Governmental Organizations
and Democracy

Chris Skelcher

Open University Press
Buckingham · Philadelphia

Open University Press
Celtic Court
22 Ballmoor
Buckingham
MK18 1XW

email: enquiries@openup.co.uk
world wide web: http://www.openup.co.uk

and

325 Chestnut Street
Philadelphia, PA 19106, USA

First Published 1998

A catalogue record of this book is available from the British Library

ISBN   0 335 19882 1 (hb)   0 335 19881 3 (pb)

Library of Congress Cataloging-in-Publication Data
Skelcher, Chris, 1951–
    The appointed state : quasi-governmental organizations and
democracy / Chris Skelcher.
        p.   cm. – (Public policy and management)
    Includes bibliographical references and index.
    ISBN 0-335-19882-1 (hb) – ISBN 0-335-19881-3 (pbk.)
    1. Executive advisory bodies – Great Britain.   2. Patronage.
Political–Great Britain.   3. Democracy–Great Britain.   I. Title.
II. Series.
JN409.S55   1998
352.2'5'0941–dc21   97–45701
                                                          CIP

Typeset by Dorwyn Ltd, Rowlands Castle, Hants
Printed in Great Britain by Biddles Ltd, Guildford and King's Lynn

Contents

Preface

This book provides an analysis of a fundamental change in the governance of Britain. It is the transfer of power from directly elected and relatively transparent central and local government to the closed world of quasi-government – the appointed boards or *quangos*. I focus particularly on those quangos having executive power – weighing values, making decisions and allocating resources for public purpose. These executive quangos – unlike their advisory and quasi-judicial counterparts – perform an essentially governmental role. I set out to understand the development of this sector, the nature of the appointees, their modes of operation and the possibilities for reform.

I develop four main arguments. The first is that the recent growth of quasi-government is a highly significant development that contradicts the conventions of democratic practice and good governance. Second, that the exercise of patronage which is inevitably associated with appointment is a much more complex phenomena than is reflected in recent attempts to 'find the Tory on the board'. Third, that the problem of quangos raises wider questions about the nature of the British governmental system and the relationship between the citizen and the state. And, finally, that the declining impetus for quango reform following the change of political power at national level in 1979 should be taken as a warning of what may happen in the current period. The issues are too important to be dismissed as an irrelevance following the removal of the Conservative Government in May 1997.

In writing this book I owe a particular debt of gratitude to Liz and Tom Skelcher and Barbara Webster for permitting me to monopolize the household computer for the past nine months, and for accepting delays to their suppers when I was both cook for the day and striving to finish a chapter. Thanks also to colleagues in the School of Public Policy at the University of Birmingham. Chapters 2, 4 and 6 draw on the survey of local appointed body members undertaken by Howard Davis and myself in 1995. Howard also provided ideas and material that contributed in various ways to the development of the book, which I greatly appreciate. Teresa Payne (now at Merton Council) and I wrote a paper for *Public Administration*, elements of which appear in revised form in Chapter 5. I also greatly valued discussions arising from her doctoral research into decision making in local quangos, together with her many and very helpful comments on the draft of this book – an interesting role reversal since at the time I was supervising her PhD! Vivien Lowndes (now at De Montfort University) provided particular help with the question of patronage and also, through our other work together, the impact of new modes of governance. Simon Baddeley, Michael Clarke, Andrew Coulson, Mary Furamera, Chris Game, David Mullins, Janet Newman, John Raine, Moyra Riseborough, Mike Smith and John Stewart also offered ideas, thoughts, observations and support in a variety of ways.

Beyond the University my particular thanks go to Wendy Hall and Stuart Weir for their detailed investigation of the field, on which I have drawn, and to Roger Bennett and Fraser Mitchell for their insights. John Skelton and Linda Watkins from the Open University Press and Rod Rhodes, the series editor, offered timely advice, encouragement and criticism, for which many thanks. Responsibility for the final result is, of course, mine!

Chris Skelcher
Kings Heath
Birmingham

Abbreviations

AMA	Association of Metropolitan Authorities
BBC	British Broadcasting Corporation
DE	Department of Employment
DfEE	Department for Education and Employment
DNH	Department of National Heritage (now Department of Culture, Media and Sports)
EGO	extra-governmental organization
FAS	Funding Agency for Schools
FEC	further education college
FHSA	family health service authority
FMI	Financial Management Initiative
GM school	grant-maintained school
HA	health authority
HAT	housing action trust
LDDC	London Docklands Development Corporation
LEA	local education authority
LEC	local enterprise company
LMS	local management of schools
MSC	Manpower Services Commission
NAO	National Audit Office
NDPB	non-departmental public body
NHS	National Health Service
NPM	new public management
NVQ	National Vocational Qualification

PAC	Public Accounts Committee
PAU	Public Appointments Unit
QUALGO	quasi-autonomous local government organizations
QUANGO	quasi-autonomous non-governmental organization
TEC	training and enterprise council
TFW	Training for Work
UDC	urban development corporation
YT	Youth Training

1

Understanding quasi-government

Ideology and pragmatism have combined to reshape the British governmental system by introducing a class of organizations having considerable public significance yet remaining largely outside democratic political activity. These are the *quangos* – quasi-governmental bodies that are appointed rather than elected and have responsibility for shaping, purchasing, delivering and adjudicating across the arenas of public policy. Quangos are to be found playing a key role in almost every area of public policy and service delivery. Whether in health, education, agriculture or science policy, they are now an integral part of the British state and have replaced elected authorities as the natural home for the governance and management of public purpose. The 70,000 women and men appointed to their boards are found not only in the interstices of the governmental machine – in areas of low political salience where minimal democratic accountability could arguably be tolerated – but also at the heart of major public services and areas of intense political debate. It is they, rather than elected politicians, who take decisions on the nature, distribution, funding and prioritizing of many public services. In the process, they negotiate the inevitable tensions and contradictions involved in resolving complex value choices. Sometimes these judgements become a matter of public debate: in 1995, the decision of Cambridge and Huntingdon Health Commission not to fund an expensive and controversial treatment for one individual was contested through the courts in what came to be known as the 'Child B' case. More often than not, these choices remain in the quango's boardroom, an arena to which the public have few opportunities of access.

There has been a spectacular growth in this appointed sector of government since the late 1980s. The creation of new types of public body and the transfer of activities from elected local government to appointed quangos has substantially increased both their number and the range of policy areas in which they operate. The growth has been most marked at the local level, where 80 per cent of the UK's 6500 appointed bodies are found. The introduction of a quasi-market in the NHS, for example, involved separating the purchasers of services from the hospitals and other public providers. This process spawned several hundred new local organizations – the NHS trusts. In education, the recent Conservative Government's policies resulted in one thousand schools leaving local authority control to become grant maintained, overseen by a new quango – the Funding Agency for Schools (FAS). And in the regeneration field, the appointed boards of urban development corporations (UDCs) and housing action trusts (HATs) manage major public investment programmes intended to revitalize local communities.

The recent growth of quangos is also a manifestation of the new public management which has had so much impact on the UK public service (Clarke and Newman 1997). The deconstruction of large public bureaucracies and their re-emergence as a multiplicity of smaller bodies in contractual and market-type relationships to each other has been mirrored by the corralling of elected politicians into the role of strategic policy makers. The interpretation of their wishes, reconciliation of choices and purchasing and delivery of services is interpreted as a managerial task undertaken by an appointed board recruited principally for their business-oriented expertise. In the conventional wisdom, quangos provide an appealing and managerially efficient solution to the problems of governing a complex society.

The creation of appointed governmental bodies is not a new idea. *Ad hoc* boards were created at the local level during the period of urbanization and industrialization in the eighteenth and nineteenth centuries. The legacy of earlier administrative arrangements combined with the promotion of Acts of Parliament by individual localities and interests resulted in a proliferation of turnpike trusts, boards of improvement commissioners, poor law boards and other local non-elected bodies. Their inefficiency, lack of coordination and interweaving of public purpose with private gain stimulated a process of administrative reform, centralization and democratization (Keith-Lucas 1980). For example, a national system of Boards of Guardians elected on a restricted franchise was introduced following Chadwick's Poor Law Amendment Act 1834. Other *ad hoc* non-elected bodies were incorporated into the elected municipal councils created in 1835, the county councils formed in 1888 and the multipurpose district councils introduced several years later.

Governments, however, continued to view quangos as a legitimate means to achieve policy objectives. Their arm's-length status enabled ministers to set objectives and allocate finance and then, in theory at least, leave the appointed body to manage the process of implementation. This relative independence of quangos can be advantageous to government when its policy is being applied in a contentious area, as was the case with the Local Government Commission's assessments of the competing claims of county and district councils in the mid-1990s review of local authority structure. Independence is also important in seeking agreements between parties. The Parades Commission in Northern Ireland, for example, has a role in negotiating the political complexities of the marching season, the point at which relationships between communities in the province are often tense. Quangos, however, are not remote from government. Ministers are able to determine the structure of a quango board in order to increase the legitimacy and acceptability of its decisions. This is the intention behind the new Labour Government's decision to create a Low Pay Commission composed of relevant stakeholders, including employers, the trade unions and others with expertise on the issue. The appointment process can also be used to create a board sympathetic to the Government's policies – a tendency of the pre-1979 Labour Government as well as subsequent Conservative administrations.

Some quangos have an advisory rather than executive role. This may imply that they can be dismissed as marginal bodies, and indeed some operate in relatively obscure areas with limited political salience. Others, however, play a central role in shaping government policy and legislation by virtue of the weight of authoritative opinion they contain and expert evidence they offer. They also deal with major issues of public concern having consequences into the distant future. During the 1990s, for example, the Ministry of Agriculture, Fisheries and Food's Spongiform Encephalopathy Advisory Committee provided regular briefings and opinions to government on control strategies in relation to the BSE outbreak amongst cattle – although, as Hall and Weir (1996) discovered, this advice may be re-presented in a way that more conveniently fits the political needs of the government of the day. Less well-known but equally important advisory non-departmental public bodies (NDPBs) deal with issues ranging from the safety of nuclear-powered warships to the impact of releasing genetically modified organisms into the environment. These advisory bodies have not been exposed to public scrutiny to the same extent as executive quangos, partly because of the secrecy which surrounds their activities. They are, however, of major significance to an understanding of the way in which government is informed and policy is shaped.

The use of appointed bodies for public purpose leads to the problem of the *democratic deficit* – the absence of both an electoral process and other mechanisms through which the public can influence the body and hold it to account. Board accountability through ministers to Parliament is weak. There are also a large number of local quangos where ministers play no part in board appointment – new members are selected by the board itself or outside interests, including other quangos. The statutory requirements to ensure transparency in decision making, facilitate public access to meetings and information and avoid members' conflict of interest are less stringent in the case of quangos than elected central and local government. Quangos sometimes do not come within the jurisdiction of one of the ombudsmen, thus reducing the opportunity for citizens to obtain an independent investigation into a grievance. Audit requirements are also less rigorous for some quangos than for elected bodies, leading their stewardship of public funds to be called into question. Since almost one-third of UK public expenditure is controlled or channelled through appointed bodies, this is a matter of some public concern. Almost all of the National Health Service's (NHS) £35 billion annual expenditure, for example, is allocated by locally-based but centrally-appointed health authorities.

The fact of appointment results in a degree of opacity between board members and citizens. Unlike elected politicians, they do not have to undergo the public process of canvassing, election, lobbying and responding to constituents' problems. They seldom become visible figures either nationally or in the locality. Their process of appointment is one of private patronage. Individuals who are known by existing board members, ministers or their advisors and thought to be fit for the job are approached and invited to join. Patronage has also involved appointing individuals who are politically sympathetic to the government of the day. Advertisements inviting citizens to nominate themselves have only recently started to appear, and then only for some classes of quango. This process leads to a board of individuals who tend to be of like-mind and like-background – middle class, business-oriented, white and male. Yet the communities quangos serve will have greater diversity in terms of age, ethnicity, class and other characteristics.

The recent extensive growth of appointed bodies raises the question of their implications for the debate about the good government of public affairs. Quangos weaken the link between elector and government, a link that is already tenuous by virtue of a 'first-past-the-post' voting system, limited freedom of information and open government and a constitution built on convention rather than conviction. At the very time when transparency, standards in public life and effective corporate governance are on the agenda, appointed bodies as they are currently constituted impose barriers and constraints to a new relationship between citizen and state. The benefits, however, are argued to be in organizational performance. The managerialist philosophy of *Reinventing Government* (Osborne and Gaebler 1992) proposes that gains arise from flexible, customer-oriented organizations with small corporate structures and a high degree of autonomy around a clearly defined mission. These characteristics fit many of the new types of quangos. The costs to citizens of reduced democratic involvement, therefore, are intended to be offset by improved performance to satisfy customer expectations.

The tensions generated by the democratic deficit have created a growth industry in proposals for the reform of quangos. Some changes are already taking place. A more open appointments process has been introduced in certain types of quango and there is official information appearing on members – including, in the case of NHS bodies, an indication of party political loyalty. Codes of practice are being introduced and audit arrangements improved. Yet are these significant reforms or merely a sleight of hand to conceal the fundamental contradictions between government by appointment and the principles of good public governance? There is a wider agenda of reform. It involves the introduction of an elected or competitive element into board composition, transfer of bodies to local authority or community control and a more funda-mental rethink of the way in which public agencies relate to their communities through innovations in democratic practice (Stewart 1995b). The debate about quango reform is also intrinsic to the wider discussion about the constitutional and democratic framework of the UK. Democratic renewal involves appointed bodies as much as the elected sector. The future of quangos is part of this bigger picture.

This, then, is quasi-government. From one perspective it is the weighing of public values and exercise of judgement – an essentially political activity – undertaken by a group of individuals appointed through a process of patronage and having no accountability to or legitimacy with citizens. From another perspective it is an efficient and politically astute way of governing and manag-ing public services by drawing on the skills and experience of experts who, by virtue of being insulated from public view and party competition, are able to reach the best decisions for the community. This opaque world of quasi-government is explored and evaluated in the following chapters, with the aim of understanding why it has arisen, how it operates, who the appointees are, what political processes are involved and – ultimately – whether it is compat-ible with the values of a democratic society. The starting point is to identify the characteristics of quangos.

Defining quangos

The term 'quango' has been widely used during the last two decades, but with considerable variation and confusion as to its meaning. The term emerged at the end of the 1960s from an Anglo-American conference at Ditchley, Oxfordshire. Quasi-non-governmental (QNG) organizations were a new genus of agency observed on the American scene. They were private sector bodies created as a result of legislation or executive action to fulfil public purposes and dependent on public funding for their existence. Their programmes were influenced by political priorities set by government, and accountability was assured through auditing and other regulatory devices such as contracts (Pifer 1975). In their UK context QNG organizations became known by the acronym QUANGO, a term coined by Anthony Barker and subsequently interpreted either as quasi-autonomous *non-*governmental organization or quasi-autonomous *national* governmental organization – depending on the author in question.

Barker and his colleagues saw quangos as a fourth sector, set against government itself, the market and the public corporations responsible for nationalized industries. They adopted a broader definition than their American colleagues, seeing them as something of a catch-all within which to locate the various bodies created for public purpose that did not sit comfortably within either of the other three categories (Hague *et al.* 1975). The spirit of this definition has remained ever since, especially in the way quangos are some-times defined by what they are *not* (not elected, not accountable, and so on)

Table 1.1 Characteristics of selected executive quangos

Type of body	Purpose	Status
Careers service companies	From 1993–4 onwards, to compete for and deliver contracts to provide former local authority careers services	Company limited by guarantee; normally created from partnership of local authority, TEC (see below) and chamber of commerce; partners or board itself appoint new chair and members
Funding Agency for Schools	From 1994, to fund and plan GM school sector	NDPB whose chair and members are appointed by Secretary of State
Further education corporations	Corporations established 1993 by transfer from local education authority	Statutory corporation (exempted educational charity); specified classes of board members; new chair and members appointed by existing board, sometimes on recommendation of outside interests (e.g. employers bodies)
Health authorities	New authorities created in 1996 from merger of district health authorities and family health service authorities; they have responsibility for commissioning and purchasing health services to meet needs of their locality	NHS bodies; board includes non-executive and executive members; chair and non-executives are government appointments, who may be recruited after public advertisement or on recommendation of board itself
Scottish Enterprise	Responsibilities for development of Scottish economy, including oversight of local enterprise companies (Scottish equivalent of TECs)	NDPB whose chair and members are appointed by Secretary of State for Scotland
Training and enterprise councils	During 1990–1 in England and Wales, to manage delivery of government training programmes under contract to Department for Education and Employment	Company limited by guarantee; normally created through partnership involving chamber of commerce, business leaders and local authority. Partners or board appoints new chair and members subject to conditions required by Secretary of State for Education and Employment
Urban development corporations	Twelve created in England and Wales in four phases from 1981, with expected life of 5–17 years; role is to undertake urban regeneration in specific localities	NDPB whose chair and members are appointed by Secretary of State, sometimes after consultation with local authority and other local interests

Source: Adapted from Hall and Weir (1996).

rather than what they *are*. Other acronyms have emerged, including EGOs (extra-governmental organizations), QUALGOs (quasi-autonomous local government organizations) and NDPBs (non-departmental public bodies). Despite this alphabet soup, 'quango' has remained in constant usage. If not exactly a definitive concept, it at least has the virtue of providing a broad umbrella under which a wide array of organizations can cluster and be examined (Table 1.1). It is in this spirit that the term is used in this book – more as a symbol of the field than as an acronym. 'Appointed body' is used synonymously in order to avoid excessive repetition and the pejorative associations that the term 'quango' has accrued.

The search for a definition is an intensely political activity since it reveals what Weir has referred to as 'the absence of any stable statutory and constitutional underpinning for the whole ramshackle apparatus'. He observes that 'government bodies float in and out of 'quangodom', change shape or size, die and sometimes resurrect themselves, sometimes in multiple form' (Weir 1996: 23). The definitions employed by Conservative Governments between 1979 and 1997, for example, conveniently ignore a whole class of local appointed bodies created as a result of their legislative activity. Equally, there is confusion about whether training and enterprise councils (TECs) which are constituted as private companies for public purpose, truly quasi-non-governmental bodies in the original American sense of the term, should be regarded as quangos at all.

Public bodies

The Conservative Governments of 1979 to 1997 derived their official definition of appointed bodies from Sir Leo Pliatzky's report (1980). He argued that the term quango was misleading and proposed instead *non-departmental public body* (NDPB) – a public body that is not organizationally part of a government ministry. The Government adopted this terminology and it is to such bodies that official statements usually refer. They recognize three types of NDPB:

1 *Executive bodies*: These have direct responsibility for the execution of a particular function or activity, and consequently have their own budget and staff. Their powers may be defined in statute, but equally many are created by administrative action. Some operate nationally, for instance the Commission for Racial Equality which has statutory responsibilities in relation to countering and overcoming racial discrimination and disadvantage. Others are only found in specific localities, an example being the six housing action trusts (HATs) each of which undertakes regeneration in a small area of public housing.

2 *Advisory bodies*: These bodies exist to provide advice to government on matters requiring external expertise. In general, they do not incur expenditure on their own behalf and only have a small secretariat. Examples include the Advisory Committee on NHS Drugs and the Government Hospitality Fund Advisory Committee for the Purchase of Wine.

3 *Tribunals*: These NDPBs have a quasi-judicial role in the exercise of their licensing or appeal functions. Expenditure is related to servicing the board's activities and staffing is provided by the relevant government department. Examples include the Industrial Tribunals who hear cases related to employment law and the Rent Assessment Panel for Scotland.

NHS bodies such as health authorities and trusts are regarded as *departmental* rather than *non-departmental* public bodies since they operate within a hierarchical structure. Health ministers exercise authority through the NHS Executive and its regional outposts, formerly the regional health authorities, to influence and structure the commissioning and purchasing activities of health authorities in their contracting with NHS trusts and other providers. *Public corporations*, the device created to take managerial responsibility for nationalized industries, are also sometimes identified separately from NDPBs in official pronouncements. The Conservative Government's privatization programme has removed many of these bodies. Those remaining include the British Waterways Board, with its responsibilities for managing the nation's canal network, together with cultural bodies including the BBC and the British Council. Public corporations follow the pattern of NDPBs in having appointed boards with executive and financial authority operating at arm's length to ministers. The distinctions between NDPBs, NHS departmental public bodies and public corporations are fine ones and have more to do with a political game over the number of quangos than any solid intellectual justification. They are collectively termed *public bodies*.

The non-recognized bodies

From the late 1980s until the mid-1990s, the Conservative Government facilitated the creation of several new classes of quango as a means to achieve its restructuring of the governance and provision of public services at the local level. These are what Weir and Hall (1994) refer to as the *non-recognized* bodies – quangos that are excluded from government definitions yet are highly significant in numerical and constitutional terms. These bodies include further education and sixth-form colleges, grant-maintained (GM) schools who have chosen to leave the local education authority, TECs who manage the delivery of government training programmes and careers service companies who provide careers advice under contract. Housing associations are sometimes treated as non-recognized quangos because of their central role in spending public money to secure the provision of social housing, despite their philanthropic and charitable origins. They, together with TECs, further education colleges (FECs) and GM schools, were the 'local public spending bodies' considered in the Nolan Committee's second report (Committee on Standards in Public Life 1995b).

The emergence of non-recognized appointed bodies has had a major impact on the governance of local communities, redistributing power away

---

Box 1.1   The growth of the new magistracy

- Local authority representatives removed from DHAs and FHSAs; post-1990 health authorities have no local authority representatives as of right.
- NHS trusts created to manage delivery by hospitals and community services.
- TECs and LECs created to exercise functions at local level, incorporating or overlapping with some local authority activities.
- Careers service companies, formed by partnership of local authorities, business and others, bid for contract to deliver careers service in each locality. Service formerly part of local government.
- Self-appointing boards of governors take responsibility from local education authorities for further education colleges and sixth-form colleges. They are subject to the requirements of various funding councils, themselves non-departmental public bodies.
- Schools encouraged to opt out of local authority control and become grant-maintained, funded and regulated by new national non-departmental public bodies.
- Housing associations gain increased responsibility for social housing.
- HATs and UDCs created to undertake urban regeneration in specific localities, with some transfer of responsibility from local authorities.
- Police authorities with majority local authority membership abolished. New police authorities have seventeen members – five appointed by minister after local consultation, nine by local authorities and three by magistrates.

Source: Adapted from Stewart and Davis (1994).

---

from elected and multipurpose local authorities towards appointed or self-appointing single purpose boards (Box 1.1). This has been compounded by the creation of new local NDPBs such as UDCs and HATs, the NHS reforms leading to the formation of trusts and the transfer of policing responsibilities to new appointed police authorities. The members of these bodies have become known as the 'new magistracy', a term coined by Morris (1990) in drawing parallels with shire county government under the *ancien régime* which was undertaken by local justices of the peace meeting in quarter sessions. The 1888 reforms transferred power from this appointed lay élite to elected county councillors. Now, in the 1990s, the reverse process is taking place.

The appointed nature of such bodies and an emphasis on the idea of a new magistracy nevertheless conceals a variety of relationships with local government. The way in which bodies are perceived by local authorities and operate in relation to them is likely to be considerably affected by the circum-stances of their creation and the nature of their board structure, for example whether local authority officers or members are included on the board – either as of right or by local discretion. More importantly, however, is likely to be the strategy of the new appointed body and the extent to which it has to engage in domain invasion as a means of gaining legitimacy and being treated as a serious player in the increasingly complex and congested organizational arena for public policy (Painter *et al.* 1997).

The appointed world of local government

Local authorities themselves have created and are participants in a wide range of non-elected bodies. These include public–private–community partnerships built around single regeneration budget, intergovernmental forums to liaise on strate-gic planning issues and companies such as the enterprise boards. Stoker (1991) observes that the growth in such non-elected local government has been stimu-lated as much by local authorities' innovation and experimentation as central government policy, partly because they offer the advantages of greater flexibility and speed of reaction than is generally possible in the elected sector. However local government reorganization in Scotland, Wales and England over the last two decades has also left its legacy in a range of single-purpose bodies with their own legal identity whose memberships are appointed by the local councils within their area. These joint boards were created to provide services over an area larger than a single local authority, the majority being found in the metro-politan areas as a result of county council abolition in 1986. They typically cover fire and civil defence, public transport, waste disposal (prior to reforms of the early 1990s), police (although the board's composition was changed by the Police and Magistrates' Court Act 1994) and occasionally other functions. New joint boards for fire and civil defence are now being created as a result of local government reorganization. Joint board memberships are made up entirely or largely of elected local councillors nominated by the constituent local authorities and therefore it may be argued that by virtue of such *indirect* election they are different in kind from the NDPBs and other types of quango discussed above.

The fact of appointment, however, breaks the direct accountability link. Leach (1996: 74) perceives such bodies as being located 'in an intermediate position between the direct accountability of local authorities and the opaque accountability processes' of quangos. He argues that joint boards offer greater formal mechanisms of accountability than is typically found in the quangos discussed above, especially due to the comprehensive access to information requirements of local government. The nominating local authority also has the ability to mandate its members and curtail their tenure should performance not be satisfactory or political control change, although this seldom occurs in practice. The single-purpose nature of such bodies also reduces political choice in resource allocation and increases the complexities of inter-agency coordina-tion and collaboration.

Although such joint boards are appointed, they retain their roots in the world of elected local government and thus operate to different conventions and rules of conduct and accountability than the NDPBs, NHS bodies and non-recognized quangos discussed above. Consequently, they are largely excluded from the material presented in the remainder of the book. However, they do reappear in Chapter 8 since one of the ways to reform quangos and increase their accountability is to develop mechanisms for indirect election. Here the experience of joint boards provides a basis against which to evaluate this proposal.

The terminology of quangos

If determining the boundaries of the quango state is a difficult issue, the titles given to such bodies add to the confusion. The term 'trust' – as in housing action trust and NHS trust – suggests a charitable status that does not match the reality of these bodies. Similarly the education associations which have been appointed to take over the running of poorly performing schools are not the voluntary associations that their titles imply but bodies of individuals appointed by the minister. The terminology occludes the nature of the body and hence the standards and principles to which it should conform. If it can be argued that an activity is or is not within the public sector then different modes of governance may apply, for example in relation to accountability and selection of members. This issue was noted by the Nolan Committee when setting out their agenda for the examination of local public spending bodies:

> They operate at the boundary of the public and private sectors. They have considerable freedom to set their own priorities, yet their decisions are in many respects part of public policy. Their actions may have a significant impact upon their local communities, going beyond those who are directly involved in the organisations themselves.
>
> (Committee on Standards in Public Life 1995a: 5)

Some of these issues are illustrated where quangos have established or become partners in companies. Incorporation under the Companies Acts has become a noticeable trend because of the additional flexibility such structures permit – for example, in the raising of capital funds and minimizing of tax liabilities on commercial activities. Companies are also familiar territory to the business people who comprise a substantial proportion of quango members. Birmingham TEC, Birmingham City Council and Birmingham Chamber of Commerce, for example, are partners in a registered company established for economic development purposes. The Sports Council provides a more complex example, and one which illustrates the problems of control and accountability in this area.

The Sports Council is a NDPB established by Royal Charter in 1972 and receives the majority of its income through a grant-in-aid from the Department of Culture, Media and Sports (formerly the Department of National Heritage). In 1990, the Sports Council decided to strengthen its commercial

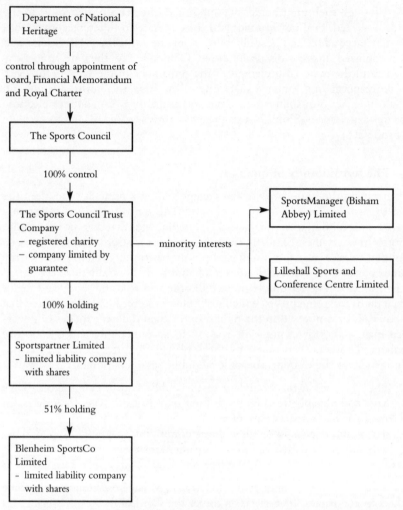

Figure 1.1   Department of National Heritage and the Sports Council Group of Companies at 1994.
Source: Adapted from National Audit Office (1994).

operations by creating a charitable company – the Sports Council Trust Company. This acquired Sportspartner Limited, a sports and architectural consultancy. Sportspartner Limited formed a joint venture company – Blenheim SportsCo Limited – with Blenheim Exhibitions plc. This company's purpose was to undertake exhibition and seminar activities for the sports and leisure industry. Additionally the Sports Council Trust Company took minority interests in two management buy-out companies formed following competitive tendering for the management of the national sports centres. One of these companies – Lilleshall Sports and Conference Centre Limited – in turn had an interest in Crystal Palace Sports and Leisure Limited, another management buy-out responsible for the management of Crystal Palace National Sports Centre (Figure 1.1). The National Audit Office concluded that:

> The arrangements put in place by the Council to strengthen their commercial activities have weakened accountability for and control over publicly funded assets and services. The position has been made more serious by the lack of a clear arm's-length relationship between the bodies forming the Sports Council Group and inadequate arrangements to prevent potential conflicts of duty of interest or the appearance of such conflicts.
>
> (NAO 1994: 5)

These problems of accountability and probity are found more generally across the appointed sector, as later discussion illustrates. However, the example of the Sports Council Group does highlight the issue of where to delimit the world of quangos and at what point the activities of their boards and expenditure of public money ceases to be a matter for public accountability. Clarity of definition, therefore, is important in ensuring appropriate standards of governance and in paving the way for a programme of reform. A broad definition of quango is employed in this book, including NDPBs, NHS bodies and Weir and Hall's non-recognized bodies. Whatever their formal status, all are treated as being part of the public sector by virtue of their collective purpose, underlying accountability to governmental authority, lack of direct and indirect board election and primary resourcing from the public purse.

The arithmetic of the quango state

The activities of Britain's quangos involve large numbers of appointees. Hall and Weir's count of the quango population includes executive and advisory recognized and non-recognized NDPBs, but excludes tribunals (Table 1.2).

Table 1.2   Executive and advisory quangos in the UK, 1996

Type of body	Number
Executive	
NDPBs	301
Non-recognized Northern Ireland NDPBs	8
NHS bodies	788
Non-recognized local quangos	4653
Total executive bodies	5750
Advisory	
Advisory NDPBs	674
Total of all executive and advisory bodies	6424

Source: Hall and Weir (1996).

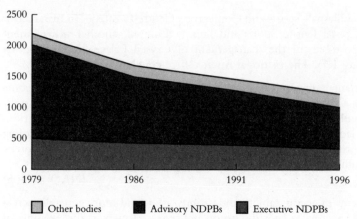

Figure 1.2   Numbers of non-departmental public bodies, 1979–96
Source: Cabinet Office (1996).

They identify approximately 6500 bodies of which 5166 operate at local level – 90 per cent being in the non-recognized category. Their analysis reinforces the significance of local appointed executive bodies in the total picture and further challenges the Conservative Government's decision to maintain the limited definition arising from the Pliatzky review and which pre-dated most of this growth. It also puts into perspective the declining number of NDPBs identified in *Public Bodies* and used by the Conservative Government's ministers as the basis from which to claim that the quango was being hunted (Figure 1.2). Even these government figures need qualification since the reduction in executive NDPBs by 183 is far outweighed by the loss of 811 advisory bodies.

Table 1.3   Numbers of appointments by type of quango, 1996

Type of body	Number of board members
Executive NDPBs	3,733
Advisory NDPBs	8,125
Nationalized industries	110
Public corporations	113
NHS bodies	4,292
Non-recognized local executive quangos	60,000
Total number of executive and advisory appointments	76,373
Tribunals	21,906
Board of Visitors	1,777
Total of all appointments	100,056
Total number of ministerial appointments	34,564

Source: Cabinet Office (1996); figures for non-recognized local executive quangos are the midpoint of range calculated by Hall and Weir (1996) and assumes a mean board size of 13.

The six-and-a-half thousand executive and advisory quangos translate into approximately 76,000 appointments, of which approximately 60,000 are to the non-recognized bodies (Hall and Weir 1995). When tribunals and Boards of Visitors are included this gives a grand total of just over 100,000 appointments (Table 1.3). Significantly, only 35 per cent of all appointments and 51 per cent of those to executive quangos are made by a minister. This contradicts the conventional view that the power to appoint enables government patronage to run rampant across the world of quangos. The majority of appointments to the other 49 per cent of board positions are made by the non-recognized bodies themselves, raising important issues about the nature of the process, selection criteria employed and the members' perception of their accountability (see Chapter 4).

The significance of local quangos becomes apparent when their membership numbers are compared with those for local councils. In the UK as a whole there are now about two-and-a-half times as many members of local appointed executive bodies as there are local authority councillors. The trend, however, is for the gap to increase. An analysis of the West Midlands Metropolitan County shows an initially slow rise in the number of appointees, increasing dramatically as FECs and GM schools became independent bodies and TECs were created. The trend was moderated somewhat by the reduction in size of the district health authorities in the 1990 reforms, although the subsequent creation of separate NHS trusts more than compensated for this. The numbers of councillors reduced by 104 in 1986 with the abolition of West Midlands County Council and has since remained static (Figure 1.3). Outside London and the six metropolitan counties, however, further reductions in the number of English, Welsh and Scottish councillors are taking place as a result of local government reform. This involves the creation of unitary authorities in place of the two-tier

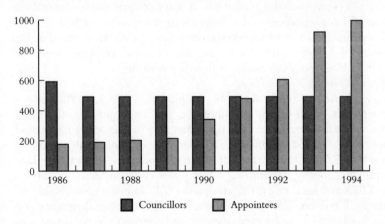

Figure 1.3 Councillors and members of local executive quangos in the West Midlands, 1986–94.
Source: Davis (1993).

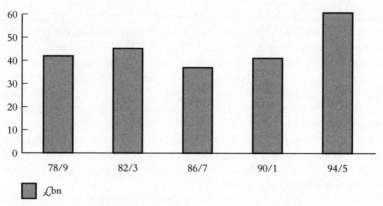

Figure 1.4   Expenditure by executive quangos at constant prices, 1978–9 to 1994–5.
Source: Hall and Weir (1996).

structure in Scotland, Wales and parts of England. Such changes will further increase the proportion of appointed quango members to elected councillors and consequently undermine local democratic government.

Appointed members are responsible for spending considerable sums of public money. Hall and Weir (1996) calculate that executive quangos currently spend in the order of £60 billion annually. At constant prices, this is an increase of 50 per cent on the figure in 1978–9 (Figure 1.4). Consequently, the expenditure and management of a considerable amount of public money is outside the direct control of elected politicians. Some of this arises from tax income, but there are also other sources. The introduction of the National Lottery in the UK in 1994 involved the formation of a set of quangos to control the distribution of that proportion of the proceeds allocated to public benefit – the 'good causes' fund. In its first two years of operation, £2.8 billion was allocated by the National Lottery Charities Board, the National Heritage Memorial Fund and the Millennium Commission together with the national Arts Council and Sports Council.

The appointed sector is also a big employer (Table 1.4). Almost one million people are employed by appointed bodies, the majority in the NHS. Employees' terms and conditions and pay scales may be nationally negotiated, for example if they are still classified as Civil Servants, or may be subject to local negotiation. NHS trusts and further education corporations, for example, have been introducing locally determined salary scales and conditions of service. Similarly, TECs and local enterprise companies (LECs) make considerable use of consultants hired on short-term contracts whilst keeping their core staff small. This flexibility in employment patterns and conditions is consistent with the notion of autonomy underlying quangos, particularly given the creation of many non-recognized bodies in the managerial and efficiency climate of the 1980s and early 1990s.

Table 1.4   Employment in the appointed sector

Type of body	Number of employees ('000s)
Executive NDPBs	107
NHS bodies	763
Further and higher education	63
TECs/LECs	2
GM schools	20
Total	955

Source: Cabinet Office (1996); Department of Health (1996); Department for Education and Employment (1997). TECs/LECs assume mean of 20 staff; GM schools assume mean of 20 staff.

The dimensions of the debate

Quangos come in various shapes and sizes and are defined in different ways according to the political advantage sought by the commentator. Even though the previous Conservative Government failed to recognize the growth of many local bodies in its figures, disowning them because ministers were not responsible for their appointment even if they had oversight of their performance, they still exist. And their existence is part of the dustbin category identified earlier – not elected government, not profit-making company, not public corporation and, to update the picture, not voluntary/charitable body. The problems of definition, however, should not impede an understanding of the significance of the appointed sector in the overall structure of British government. Whether the criteria is number of bodies and appointees, scope of policy interest or scale of expenditure, quasi-government is a major and well-established part of the British public service. It is the way governance and management are now undertaken.

The growth of the sector is associated with two other developments. One is the growth of market ideology in public services. The discussion of contracts, business plans, marketing and income targets provides a familiar milieu for board members, many of whom come from a business background, and encourages a presumption of commercial sensitivity that constrains public openness. The closed nature of quango boards is also a function of the Companies Acts framework within which some have been constituted, an issue discussed further in Chapter 6. The other development is the fragmentation arising from the emphasis on single-purpose bodies and the purchaser–provider split. This has led to the creation of multi-organizational partnerships drawing together quangos with statutory bodies, business, community and voluntary bodies. The result is yet another layer of governance removed from direct electoral control, with the resulting issues of accountability and democratic deficit.

The call for greater accountability of quangos, symbolized by the investigations of the Committee on Standards in Public Life, is the latest manifestation of a long-standing debate about the proper place of appointment in the

British system of government. Quasi–government is not a modern phenomena but reaches back to earlier times and to fundamental questions about good governance and the case for democracy. Why have government by appointment? What are the quangos' accountability and probity safeguards? To what extent is patronage exercised in appointment? What are the characteristics of the members of appointed bodies? How do they reach decisions and exercise their discretion? What evidence is there about their performance? How should they be reformed? These are the questions to be addressed in the following chapters.

2

Examining the democratic deficit

One of the central criticisms of quangos is that they suffer from a democratic deficit. The idea of the democratic deficit arose from the revelation that the requirements placed on these appointed bodies to satisfy public accountability are less stringent than those applying to their elected counterparts. The most visible manifestation of the democratic deficit is the absence of election. Quango members forego the process of selection as a candidate, arguing a set of manifesto promises and being judged at the ballot box – let alone the regular contact with constituents that mark the MP and councillor's daily routine. However, it is not just a matter of democratic process. There are numerous other elements of public accountability in which differences can be discerned, including public access to meetings, redress procedures and freedom of information. Together, these features limit the extent to which board members are required to give an account of their actions and on this basis can be held to account by the community (Davis and Stewart 1993).

Lower levels of public accountability in the appointed sector were largely tolerated until the 1980s. Prior to this, quangos were more limited in number and were predominantly NDPBs – extensions of central government departments with ministerially appointed boards. They also existed in an environment in which there was a significant degree of political consensus and public acceptability of the purposes for which quangos were created. Nationalized industry boards, new town development corporations and the post-1974 health authorities were there to deliver goals around which there was considerable public support – revitalized industries, better homes and environments and improved health services respectively. Although critics such as Holland and

Fallon (1978) challenged the growth of quangos, even in the early 1980s these bodies were still a relatively small part of a British governmental system dominated by large welfare bureaucracies governed by elected politicians. Since then, however, the rapid growth of the non-recognized quangos, the emergence of conviction politics on the part of the Thatcher Governments and a greater diversity in the political environment has stimulated a more fundamental examination of the appointed sector. Suddenly, the centralist conventions of the British state no longer seem to guarantee that ministers could or would ensure proper behaviour on the part of their appointees. Part of the difficulty was that a large proportion of quangos members were in the non-recognized bodies, were not appointed by the minister and therefore were largely outside the influence that would normally arise from such patronage. As important, however, was that the goals towards which these bodies were directed did not necessarily acquire the kind of public acceptance evident in the period of consensus politics. The FAS, NHS trusts and some UDCs, for example, were subject to considerable public disquiet. In this context the question of accountability has become significant.

This chapter argues that quangos suffer from a marked democratic deficit, but highlights its varying extent across different types of appointed body. Some have a high degree of conformance with the requirements placed on elected bodies while others exhibit minimal standards. The non-recognized bodies fall predominantly in the latter case. However, it is important to take a wider perspective on the democratic deficit. We move beyond a narrow comparison of elected and appointed bodies to investigate the overall regulatory environment within which quangos operate. Through an assessment of contractual relationships, the role of select committees and auditors, legal and quasi-legal redress and the impact of the media, the case for a more considered view of quango accountability is presented. The conclusion is that accountability should be seen in the context of the discretion available to quangos in making policy and delivering programmes and the constraints within which that freedom of action is exercised. Although the specific statutory requirements placed on quangos are deficient when compared with elected bodies, the wider regulatory environment compensates by limiting and scrutinizing their decisions and performance. Yet despite these counterbalancing forces, citizens lack rights in relation to quangos. Consequently, these bodies lack the transparency of governance that is expected in the elected sector.

Measuring the democratic deficit

Hall and Weir (1996) follow James Madison, the eighteenth-century North American democrat, in arguing that the electoral process on its own is not sufficient to ensure good and responsive government. *Auxiliary precautions* are also necessary. These should have the ability to ensure that the activities of government are transparent to the public and hence to reinforce democratic control and accountability. Auxiliary precautions become even more important where there is a democratic deficit. Hall and Weir identify ten auxiliary precautions which broadly apply in UK central and local elected government. They are:

1 required to publish annual reports;
2 required to publish annual accounts;
3 subject to full public audit by National Audit Office/Audit Office for Northern Ireland or Audit Commission/Accounts Commission (in Scotland);
4 under the jurisdiction of an ombudsman;
5 required to observe the *Code of Practice on Open Government*;
6 public right to inspect a register of members' interests;
7 public right to attend board or committee meetings;
8 public right to inspect agendas of meetings;
9 public right to see minutes of meetings;
10 required to hold public meetings.

There are some variations in the extent to which these conditions apply to central and local government, for example Cabinet is closed to public access although the equivalent forum in local authorities (the policy and resources committee) is not. Overall, however, they are found in all types of elected governmental body in the UK and their equivalents can be seen in most advanced democracies.

An assessment of appointed bodies against these criteria reveals some considerable shortfalls and variations between bodies (Table 2.1). NHS bodies score highly on the audit, ombudsman, members' register and open government criteria, but there are limited public rights of access to meetings and to inspect agendas. NDPBs are weaker than NHS bodies on audit and open government compliance. Less than half come under the jurisdiction of an ombudsman and only a few permit public access to meetings or the right to inspect agendas. There is little requirement to maintain or permit public access to a register of members' interests. Non-recognized quangos are the best performers on public rights to inspect agendas and minutes, but perhaps by way of compensation do not have a complementary right of access to meetings. There is limited application of the *Code of Practice on Open Government* and the ombudsman's jurisdiction does not extend to them. All are required to publish annual accounts, but less than half are subject to public audit.

The extent of variation between bodies within national NDPBs is apparent from Table 2.2. This lists twelve major NDPBs and evaluates them against the ten auxiliary precautions. While broadly meeting the criteria on audit, ombudsman and open government, these bodies are notably deficient in relation to public access. Hall and Weir argue that the national scale at which such bodies operate is no defence to these restrictions. They point out that their boards make highly political decisions of considerable public interest, and that an effective means of public scrutiny is essential. At present:

> The concerned citizen simply has no basis for finding out relevant information, no status in seeking it and no practicable chance of being able to

Table 2.1 Auxiliary precautions – an assessment of NDPBs, NHS bodies and non-recognized quangos

	Executive NDPBs		NHS bodies		Non-recognized quangos		Total	
	No.	%	No.	%	No.	%	No.	%
1 Required to publish annual reports	193	62	784	99	1428	31	2405	42
2 Required to publish annual accounts	228	74	784	99	4653	100	5665	99
3 Subject to full public audit	247	80	788	100	2066	44	3101	54
4 Under the jurisdiction of an ombudsman	130	42	788	100	0	0	918	16
5 Required to observe the Code of Practice on Open Government	194	63	788	100	213	5	1195	21
6 Public right to inspect a register of members' interests	35	11	762	97	3946	85	4743	82
7 Public right to attend board or committee meetings	19	6	148	19	0	0	167	3
8 Public right to inspect agendas of meetings	0	0	156	20	1879	40	2035	35
9 Public right to see minutes of meetings	0	0	9	1	1879	40	1888	33
10 Required to hold public meetings	9	4	507	64	103	2	619	11

Source: Hall and Weir (1996).

Table 2.2 Auxiliary precautions – the performance of major NDPBs*

NDPB	1	2	3	4	5	6	7	8	9	10
Arts Council	✓	✓	✓	✓	✓	✗	✗	✗	✗	✗
Audit Commission	✓	✓	✓	✗	✗	✗	✗	✗	✗	✗
Environment Agency	✓	✓	✓	✓	✓	✗	✗	✗	✗	✗
Funding Agency for Schools	✗	✓	✓	✗	✗	✗	✗	✗	✗	✗
Further Education Funding Council	✗	✓	✓	✗	✗	✗	✗	✗	✗	✗
Higher Education Funding Council	✗	✓	✓	✓	✓	✗	✗	✗	✗	✗
Housing Corporation	✓	✓	✓	✓	✓	✗	✗	✗	✗	✗
Human Fertilisation and Embryology Authority	✓	✓	✓	✓	✓	✗	✗	✗	✗	✗
Northern Ireland Housing Executive	✗	✓	✓	✗	✗	✗	✗	✗	✗	✗
Public Health Laboratory Services Board	✗	✓	✓	✗	✗	✗	✗	✗	✗	✗
Scottish Enterprise	✓	✓	✓	✗	✓	✓	✗	✗	✗	✗
Welsh Development Agency	✓	✓	✓	✗	✓	✗	✗	✗	✗	✗

*See the ten auxiliary precautions listed in Table 2.1.
✓ = found in agency; ✗ = not found in agency.
Source: Hall and Weir (1996).

mobilise people around her or his chosen issue. And that is exactly what most current UK quasi-governmental arrangements seem designed to ensure . . . A completely quangoid state would indeed be a polity where in every sphere of social life specialist élites would have the freedom to exploit the ignorance and rational inactivity of citizens.

(Hall and Weir 1996: 11–12)

There is, then, a strong case for the reform of quangos in order to strengthen auxiliary precautions and close the democratic deficit. Such reform could be about filling the audit, public access and governance gaps identified above or a more radical restructuring based on alternative forms for choosing, monitoring and removing boards. There are also wider questions about the nature of the British constitution and its reform which would affect the appointed sector. These issues are considered in detail in Chapter 8.

A similar approach has been used in our study of local appointed bodies in London (Skelcher and Stewart 1993). We constructed an accountability

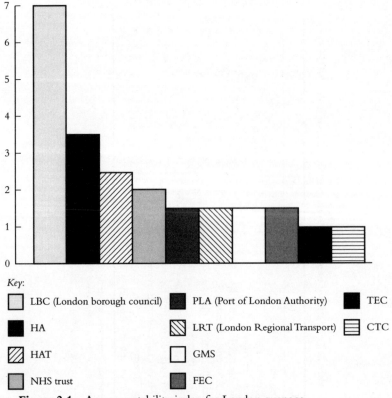

Key:

- ☐ LBC (London borough council)
- ■ HA
- ▨ HAT
- ◼ NHS trust
- ■ PLA (Port of London Authority)
- ◹ LRT (London Regional Transport)
- ☐ GMS
- ◼ FEC
- ■ TEC
- ☰ CTC

Figure 2.1   An accountability index for London quangos.
Source: Adapted from Skelcher and Stewart (1993).

index so that London quangos could be scored against the seven key accountability requirements of a London borough council, namely whether:

1 they are directly elected;
2 they come within the remit of one of the public service ombudsmen;
3 there is extensive statutory public access to policy and decision-making
   meetings;
4 there is extensive statutory public access to information;
5 members of the body are liable for surcharge in the event of expenditure
   ultra vires or through wilful misconduct;
6 members of the body have a statutory requirement to declare any interests
   which may conflict with their duties;
7 there is a nominated monitoring officer with a statutory duty to ensure
   probity and financial regularity.

The results of the accountability index illustrate the failure of central government to require local appointed bodies in London – and elsewhere – to meet
the standards it requires of elected local authorities (Figure 2.1). There is also
considerable variation in the standards applied to different types of quango.
HATs, for example, are similar to local authorities in two respects – that the
public have a right of access to meetings and that their administrative actions
are subject to scrutiny by the Commissioner for Local Administration. City
technology colleges, in comparison, are not required to admit the public to
their board meetings and neither do complaints of maladministration fall within
the remit of any ombudsman.

The regulatory environment of quangos

This analysis above illustrates the extent of the democratic deficit amongst
appointed bodies. Some fall a long way short of the standards expected of
elected bodies when, in the absence of a democratic process, it might be
expected that the accountability requirements would be greater. However it
should not be inferred from this limited compliance with the auxiliary precautions that quangos are able to exercise extensive discretion and autonomy free
from oversight and control. A comprehensive analysis of the democratic deficit
should consider factors beyond those listed by Weir and Hall or Stewart and
Skelcher. It should evaluate the broader regulatory environment within which
quangos operate. This regulatory regime provides points of oversight and
accountability, but more importantly places information and analysis about the
performance of quangos into the public domain. It also provides a number of
avenues through which the public can seek redress. Whether it is the work of
backbench Members of Parliament on the select committees of the House of
Commons, officials of the National Audit Office or ombudsmen, the media,
contractual relationships or the judicial process, all form important checks and
balances for quangos.

Contractual relationships

All quangos, to some extent at least, operate in a contractual environment through which their intended policies and activities and actual performance are subject to scrutiny by a central government department or some other body. These contractual relationships vary from one type of quango to another. Often the mechanisms for agreeing activities and monitoring performance are the corporate plan and annual report respectively, although the latter can sometimes be little more than a public relations document. The Housing Corporation illustrates the process. It, along with many other executive NDPBs, is required to submit an annual corporate plan to the Secretary of State. This enables government to oversee and steer the board's activities but also feeds its priorities and spending requests into the public expenditure planning process. Similarly, health authorities agree an annual corporate contract with the regional outposts of the NHS Executive. This sets the context for the annual contracts negotiated with NHS trusts and other providers. The BBC has a rather longer cycle of formal review and objective setting, its charter normally being subject to renewal every ten years. However, triennial decisions on the licence fee provide an important intermediate check (Barnett and Curry 1994).

Some of the more detailed contractual relationships occur in the education and employment training fields, covering further education colleges and TECs in particular. It is worth examining the contractual position of TECs since these bodies demonstrate a significant democratic deficit in terms of the criteria discussed in the previous section. TECs exist in a complex web of contractual and control relationships. Their major role is to manage the delivery of the Government's Youth Training (YT) and Training for Work (TFW) programmes. The Department for Education and Employment (DfEE) contracts with individual TECs to secure provision of these programmes. TECs then contract with providers such as further education colleges, voluntary bodies and independent training organizations to deliver particular courses and activities. Training courses often contribute to National Vocational Qualifications (NVQs) or other awards and thus providers will be accredited with the relevant awarding body. Training providers are also required to agree a training plan or contract with the individual trainee (Figure 2.2). Funding from the TEC, however, is dependent on trainee attendance or when certain outcomes are achieved. In the latter case the DfEE's Performance-Related Funding (PRF) system pays a TEC an additional amount if it achieves certain specified targets.

YT and TFW involve substantial amounts of public money going to a wide range of agencies, mediated through the TECs. Planned expenditure in 1995–6, for example, was £1.25 billion. Consequently there are a series of monitoring and audit procedures which run alongside the process of delivering training under these programmes. The DfEE requires TECs to explain their own financial control system and describe how they will assess and monitor the

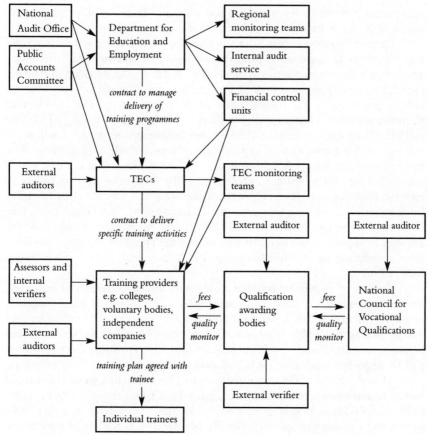

Figure 2.2 The delivery and monitoring of Youth Training and Training for Work programmes.
Source: Adapted from National Audit Office (1996).

system operated by each provider. TECs must visit each provider annually and undertake an appraisal of that agency's system which should conform to the DfEE's *Training Quality Assessment: Supplier Management* standards. DfEE regional monitoring teams, working from the government office for each region, then appraise the TECs' systems and audit claims made by them under YT and TFW. This involves following audit trails through TECs to individual providers. The DfEE's central Financial Control Unit in turn assesses the regional monitoring teams on a regular basis. DfEE's Internal Audit also undertake investigations, providing independent advice and recommendations to the Department's Accounting Officer. Elsewhere in government, the National Audit Office has undertaken studies of aspects of the YT and TFW system. Finally TECs, as private companies, will have their own auditors. Training providers, as well as being part of this system, are the subject of accreditation and monitoring procedures operated by the awarding bodies – who in turn are overseen by the National Council for Vocational Qualifications.

Despite this monitoring infrastructure, the new training system inherited and continues to experience problems of incorrect and uncertain (i.e. with questionable documentation) payments. This led the Comptroller and Auditor General to qualify the accounts of the Department of Employment (DE, the DfEE's predecessor) for several years in the early 1990s. The problem of incorrect payment is less serious now than it was. It reduced from £67 million in 1989–90 to £6.7 million in 1993–4, and is estimated to be £9.4 million in 1994–5 – 0.7 per cent of total expenditure (National Audit Office 1996). The latter figure includes £1.5 million associated with South London TEC, which was forced into receivership in December 1994. This arose from its failure to establish effective systems to enable the monitoring and substantiation of claims for payment on training programmes undertaken by contracted providers. Following warnings and intervention by DE, the worsening situation led the minister to appoint administrators to wind-up the company. Its responsibilities were distributed to two neighbouring TECs (National Audit Office 1995a; Jones 1996).

Contracts, therefore, provide a means by which government can regulate and monitor quangos and established some form of accountability. However, many of the documents and procedures involved tend to be private or at least not publicly advertised. For example, when the Environment Select Committee undertook an enquiry into the Housing Corporation it had to negotiate with that body's chairman to gain access to the corporate plan. This was because the document, in the Government's view, constituted advice to ministers – particularly in relation to the theoretically highly secret public expenditure planning process. Although such advice is rarely published, the Committee were eventually permitted a confidential viewing of the corporate plan. The Committee, however, did recognize the dilemmas involved in publication:

> The case for the Corporate Plan remaining secret is twofold. First, as advice to Ministers the Plan is classified alongside the Chancellor's Budget options and the Ministry of Defence's nuclear strategy. This is the justification used by those inside the process. From outside comes the second argument against publication: that such a step would produce bland statements and glossy photographs such as are contained in the Corporation's Annual Report, with the real issues continuing to be dealt with in unpublished papers the very existence of which might be unknown to the outside world.
>
> (Environment Committee 1993: para 56)

The closed world of quangos thus combines with the quasi-market environment of the 1990s public service to create an environment in which contracts and their review are perceived as matters of commercial and political sensitivity and not for public scrutiny.

Select committees

Select committees of the House of Commons provide an important opportunity for detailed and public investigation into the world of quangos – despite the problems faced by the Environment Committee in its scrutiny of the Housing Corporation. The Public Accounts Committee (PAC) performs a central role in reviewing the expenditure and management of funds voted by Parliament. In parallel are a series of departmental select committees which undertake investigations into the expenditure and activities of the particular ministry and its 'associated public bodies'. The latter are defined quite widely and include NDPBs, nationalized industries, police authorities and other bodies sponsored by the department. The select committees have a staff and other resources and the political weight to call ministers and other influential individuals to give evidence, although there have been some disputes over their power to call civil servants. By excluding ministers, parliamentary private secretaries and opposition frontbench spokespersons from membership, the select committee system has enabled backbenchers to develop a greater degree of specialization in a particular field of policy and thus to test and challenge the government of the day. Although their recommendations may be rejected by government, select committees nevertheless have considerable ability to put issues under the microscope and stimulate widespread public debate. The televised coverage of their hearings has added to this potential.

Select committees are responsible for determining their own topics of enquiry, but in making these decisions are influenced by a number of considerations. One concerns the balance of attention to be given to quangos rather than any other area of concern since their responsibilities spread widely across quangos, executive agencies, government departments and general matters of

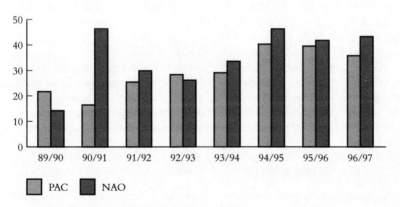

Figure 2.3   PAC and NAO reports on quangos as a proportion of total reports, Parliamentary sessions 1989–90 to 1996–7.
Source: Analysis of PAC and NAO reports.

government activity. Priorities need to be determined given the constraints of time and resources available and the particular interests of members. Party political processes, lobbying and the work of pressure groups may also influence the agenda setting process. Overall, however, the attention given by select committees to quangos is increasing (Figure 2.3).

The work programme may focus on a particular issue – for example, the PAC's study of value for money at grant-maintained schools in England (1995a). In other cases it will consider the overall performance of a group of quangos as in the case of the Employment Committee's (1996) analysis of the work of TECs or the Scottish Affairs Committee's (1994) study of enterprise agencies and LECs. Yet however well programmed and rational a select committee's annual work programme may be, the emergence of specific events of public interest can disrupt this and result in it launching a rapid investigation into the affairs of one particular quango. This occurred in the case of the Welsh Affairs Select Committee's (1997) report on the breakdown of relationships between doctors and management at Morriston Hospital (see Chapter 6) and the Public Accounts Committee (1995b) enquiry into the severance package for the Vice-Chancellor of the University of Huddersfield. The ability of select committees to mount such rapid enquiries and bring material about the performance of quangos into the public domain are one of the hallmarks of their success.

The select committees' contribution to evaluating and exposing the operation of quangos has parallels with their work on the more recently established executive agencies. In this latter field, Natzler and Silk (1995) make a number of important observations. In the first place, they point out that executive agencies were created to distance executive functions from detailed supervision by ministers or senior Civil Servants involved in the policy function. They were intended, in theory at least, to enable the service delivery function of government to be able to concentrate on its business and in the process to facilitate its ability to innovate, take risks and exercise devolved managerial responsibility. In this context, they argue, it could be counterproductive if detailed select committee investigations by Westminster reduced the relative autonomy that agencies had gained from Whitehall. This argument can be applied to quangos, since the rationale for their creation is broadly similar. Alternatively, it can be argued that select committees should take an interest precisely because executive agencies and quangos have been given greater discretion. Indeed, the capacity of select committees to review specific issues or general arrangements and to be independent of the government of the day in producing its recommendations produces an effective and public mechanism for supervision. Secondly, Natzler and Silk point to the danger of select committees having their agendas shaped by current government initiatives. This leads to the risk that they will be:

> tied up in scrutiny of what may prove to be transient administrative arrangements when they would be better occupied on other matters of greater political moment and impact.
>
> (Natzler and Silk 1995: 79)

This point relates back to the agenda setting process and the way in which the select committee's work programme is determined. A review of any select committee reveals that it deals both with the detailed and the strategic. However, the scale of the quango movement and its embeddedness in the British political system is such that it would be inappropriate to term it 'transient'.

This observation leads directly to the third and final point drawn from Natzler and Silk's analysis. It is that select committees have done relatively little to examine either executive agencies or quangos as an institutional feature of British government. They comment (1995: 77): 'It remains . . . broadly true that select committees have as yet undertaken little by way of detailed examination of . . . the merits of the establishment of agencies.' The same conclusion applies to quangos. It is here that the departmental basis of the select committee system creates an impediment, for there is no corporate forum through which Parliament can undertake a detailed investigation of an issue that cuts across all or most of their remits. Although Northern Ireland, Wales and Scotland have select committees that could perform this function in respect of quangos in their own regions, none have taken the opportunity so to do. The PAC is the closest the House of Commons comes to a corporate forum, yet its focus is on public expenditure and value for money. The more general questions of trends in organizational arrangements are outwith its remit. However the Public Accounts Committee (1994) was so concerned at the series of reports produced by itself and other select committees detailing the lack of probity and poor value for money in quangos that it published a report on these matters in 1994. This document – *The Proper Conduct of Public Business* – is the first evaluation of the performance of quangos in general undertaken by the House of Commons.

The auditors

Substantial amounts of public money are channelled through quangos and the audit process provides one means of monitoring and accounting for its use. It provides the hard quantifiable data from which the public, ministers, MPs and others can draw conclusions about the performance of appointed bodies and often informs the work of the PAC.

External public audit covers a number of areas, including:

- reporting on the accuracy of the organization's own financial statements;
- ensuring compliance with external and internal legislation, rules and procedures;
- evaluating whether the expenditure incurred is in accord with the purposes for which it was allocated;
- monitoring expenditure in terms of economy, efficiency and effectiveness;
- assessing procedures for decision making and corporate accountability.

The main bodies undertaking such public audit are the NAO and Northern Ireland Audit Office and the Audit Commission and its Scottish counterpart

Table 2.3 Responsibilities for financial and value-for-money audit in quangos and local authorities

Type of body	Responsibility for financial audit	Responsibility for value-for-money audit
Executive NDPBs	NAO or Secretary of State; the body itself in a few cases	NAO in almost all cases
NHS bodies	Audit or Accounts Commission; NAO	Audit or Accounts Commission; NAO
Further education	Institutions	NAO; funding councils; Scottish Office in Scotland
Higher education	Institutions	NAO; funding councils
GM schools	Institutions	NAO; FAS
Self-governing schools in Scotland	Institutions	NAO
Housing associations	Associations	Housing Corporation; Tai Cymru; Scottish Homes
TECs; LECs; careers service companies	Companies	DfEE; DTI; Welsh Office; Highlands and Islands Enterprise
Local authorities	Audit or Accounts Commission	Audit or Accounts Commission

Source: Adapted from *Spending Public Money* (1996).

the Accounts Commission, although work may also be contracted to account-ancy firms and consultants. Many but not all quangos come within the scope of these bodies. All NHS bodies' external audit is the responsibility of the Audit and Accounts Commissions. Approximately 50 per cent of NDPBs are within the NAO's remit (the responsibility in statute lies with its head, the Comp-troller and Auditor General), accounting for some 75 per cent of their grants (*Spending Public Money* 1996). Of the remaining 50 per cent, responsibility in most cases rests with the relevant secretary of state while the remainder appoint their own auditors. Large classes of local appointed bodies are responsible for their own financial audit, including housing associations and GM schools (Table 2.3). The significance of this partial coverage by government audit bodies is that it results in an incomplete picture of the probity and value-for-money performance of quangos.

The NAO emerged from the Exchequer and Audit Department, whose role had traditionally been concerned with certifying the accounts of govern-ment departments and related public bodies. The *National Audit Act* 1983 was shaped by the developing value-for-money environment and as a result the NAO was given a wider remit to undertake studies on economy, efficiency and effectiveness in addition to the conventional audit role (Bourne 1994).

Formally, the NAO is independent of government and in its work has maintained its position as Parliament's watchdog. Here its relationship with the PAC is crucial, and particularly the way in which the programmes of the two bodies are coordinated so that NAO reports can be considered in the context of PAC enquiries. The approach of the two bodies is complementary. NAO is able to develop an objective analysis of an issue and highlight probity and value-for-money considerations which the PAC is then able to discuss in depth with witnesses. In 1995, for example, the Limehouse Link – a major capital project undertaken by London Docklands Development Corporation – was the subject of investigation and reports by both bodies (NAO 1995b; Public Accounts Committee 1995c). Roberts and Pollitt see strengths in this relationship:

> Elected representatives, often left in the position of under-informed amateurs facing ministers backed by bureaucratic experts, were supported in their work by a statutorily independent body which commands considerable relevant expertise.
>
> (Roberts and Pollitt 1994: 546)

Despite the limitations on the NAO and PAC, this does provide an important basis for public accountability.

A considerable proportion of NAO reports are on quangos (Figure 2.3). As with the select committees, the NAO has a planned programme of studies but also responds to immediate issues, such as its investigation into the governance and management of overseas courses at the Swansea Institute of Higher Education (National Audit Office 1997b). Here, concerns about accredited courses provided in South-East Asia resulted in the college's governing body passing a vote of no confidence in the principal. The NAO investigation was stimulated in part by a complaint from Alan Williams, a local MP and member of the PAC (Hencke 1997). The NAO also monitors areas of concern over a period of time. A number of reports have been produced on the management of finance in GM schools, recommendations from which have been incorporated into guidance issued by the Funding Agency for Schools – the body with oversight for the GM sector and through whom finance for these schools is channelled.

The Audit Commission plays a similar role to the NAO in relation to local authorities and health authorities and trusts. It was created in 1983 with its predecessor, the District Audit Service, operating at an arm's length to it. Formally, it is a NDPB with a board of up to 20 members appointed by the Secretaries of State for the Environment, Health and Wales following consultation with interested organizations, including the Local Government Association and the Confederation of British Industry. Originally concerned with local authorities, its remit was expanded in 1990 to encompass the NHS. The Audit Commission undertakes a wide range of value-for-money studies and produces management papers on topics of current concern to its audience, drawing together and developing examples of good practice and promoting improvements in the governance of local authorities and health bodies. A recent example concerned the development of the non-executive directors' role on NHS bodies (Audit Commission 1995). Unlike the NAO, however, the Audit Commission lacks a political forum willing to collaborate in investigations or the promotion of recommendations. Instead it has to rely on its own publicity machine and formal and informal links with government, local authorities, NHS bodies and related professional associations.

Both the NAO and the Audit Commission are highly proactive in developing value-for-money studies relevant to quangos, and in highlighting the shortcomings that they identify. Such reports regularly obtain media coverage. However, their terms of reference constrain their ability to consider questions of policy. They are limited to a discussion of technical means rather than political ends. In this respect they, like the select committees, are unable to develop an analysis and critique of government's policy to increase the range and number of quangos. As Baines (1995: 110) comments, 'the NAO and PAC have always had to walk a tightrope in order to avoid commenting on the merits of government policy and both bodies must find that constraint inhibiting on occasion'. They can point to potential or actual problems with particular quangos, as the Audit Commission (1993) did when its annual report warned of the audit problems likely to arise in GM schools, but the overall policy is taken as given.

Means of redress: ombudsmen and the courts

Only some quangos are within the remit of an ombudsman, and it is NHS bodies that are most effectively covered. Here the ombudsman may investigate any complaints except those of a clinical nature which are examined by the professional bodies. The NHS ombudsman's remit was expanded in June 1995 to enable investigation of complaints brought by individuals unable to obtain information under the *Code of Practice on Openness in the NHS*. Individuals complaining to the ombudsman are first required to complain to the health body's nominated individual, then in writing to the chief executive. Between June 1995 and October 1996, 31 representations were made to the ombudsman under the *Code*, of which 21 were complaints. Some were referred back to the health body on the grounds that they could take further action to resolve the matter. Four were investigated, although one was subsequently deleted since the complainant decided to take legal action. The ombudsman's view was that NHS staff dealing with requests for information were not sufficiently aware of the *Code* nor were appropriate procedures widespread. He also decided to relax the grounds on which he would accept a complaint under the *Code*. Previously individuals had to show that denial appeared at first sight maladministrative or that they had suffered some hardship or injustice. In future, 'I shall . . . consider a failure to release information which, *prima facie*, may be disclosable under the *Code* as grounds for an investigation' (Health Service Commissioner 1996: 25). The onus, therefore, was placed more firmly on NHS bodies to clarify their grounds for non-disclosure.

The relationship between the NHS and Parliamentary ombudsmen and the Select Committee on the Ombudsman is a significant factor in giving weight to their findings, especially on high-profile cases and those raising general issues of governance and management. In March 1997 the Select Committee produced a very strongly worded rebuke to the North and Mid-Hampshire Health Authority, following an investigation by the NHS ombudsman. The Authority had decided to discharge 24 elderly dementia patients from a hospital they wished to close and relocated them in a private nursing home. They had avoided public awareness and debate by holding private meetings they described as 'informal' at which the decisions were made. The Select Committee concluded that this suggested 'some sleight of hand and an attempt to rush through a decision without the inconveniences of public scrutiny and possible controversy' (Select Committee on the Parliamentary Commissioner for Administration 1997: xvii). The Authority had also rejected an assessment by the patients' consultant which concluded that five of these individuals should not be moved. The Authority had sought a second opinion which found that the patients could be moved. Three of the patients died within 22 days of their discharge from hospital and transfer to the nursing home. The Authority's chairman, chief executive and director of primary and community care, under questioning by the Select Committee, each admitted that they had made mistakes but refused to resign. The Select Committee recommended that the Secretary of State for Health should review the suitability of the Authority's members – both executive and non-executive – to continue in positions of responsibility in the NHS.

The legal system provides the final means of redress for individuals and groups dissatisfied with the decisions of appointed bodies. Judicial review is the primary means, and rests on the complainant showing that administrative action was either illegal, irrational – in the sense that it defied logic or accepted moral standards – or procedurally improper (McEldowney 1993). Quangos are no exception to challenge by judicial review. Leeds UDC was taken to court by residents in Kirkstall Valley, following an investigation by the local government ombudsman, in a case concerning granting of outline planning permission. The issue revolved around two matters. First, whether board members should withdraw from a meeting having declared an interest and undertaken not to speak. Secondly, whether the chairman of the board stood to gain from aspects of the decision. The High Court found that, although the board's procedures on conflict of interest could have been stronger, no injustice was done. The case led to the Department of the Environment issuing revised guidance to UDCs (National Audit Office 1997a). However, the absence of a body of administrative law to regulate governmental activity limits the impact of the judicial review process and the courts to case-by-case judgements rather than ones which are informed by codified principles.

The media

Throughout the mid-1990s the media regarded quangos as the opportunity for a good story. Their investigative reporting and popularizing of studies under- taken by Members of Parliament, academics and others assisted in developing widespread public awareness of the issue. Much of that coverage was associated with the matters of 'sleaze' being revealed at that time (Dunleavy, Weir and Subrahmanyam 1995). Particular examples are *The Financial Times* survey of 40 top quangos (14 January 1993), *The Guardian*'s 'The quango explosion' (19 November 1993), BBC's 'Here and Now' programme (21 December 1994d) and the *Independent*'s 'The sleazy state: how the web of patronage works' (17 March 1994). Channel 4 commissioned several programmes on quangos and the Sunday papers also carried a number of substantial features.

This coverage brought various aspects of the issue into the public domain and also probed the attitudes and connections of individual 'quangocrats'. It revealed the complexities of the interconnections between quango members and other interests and illustrated the accountability vacuum in which they operated, albeit at the risk of oversimplifying some of the issues. However, it could be argued that the impact of such coverage and the issues on which it chose to focus, especially the affiliation of quango members to the Conserva- tive Party, helped to engender a public attitude that all appointed members were Tories who were only in post for political or personal advantage. The media's strategy of dealing with the broad issues by focusing on the particular clearly led in this direction. As a result, it underplayed the time and effort devoted by board members who saw themselves undertaking public service in the best interpretation of that term.

Conclusion

Quangos suffer from a democratic deficit. Most fundamentally their members are, with a few specific exceptions, not elected. Consequently, they lack the individual and structural accountability imposed by a competitive democratic process. There are no mechanisms by which citizens can directly hold ap- pointed members to account nor collectively express their opinions of the body's performance. Beyond the lack of an electoral process, it is a paradox that the auxiliary precautions applied to quangos and the rights of citizens in rela- tions to them are less – and in some cases considerably less – than is the case with central and local government. Where there is no electoral process, the expectation should be that auxiliary precautions would be more extensive and more strenuously implemented.

Although citizens' rights are important, they can only go so far in ensur- ing transparency and accountability of quangos. They help to overcome the democratic deficit, but other elements are important. The ability of select committees or auditors to conduct detailed and public investigations, for ex- ample, and to do so as events demand creates an important check on the activities of appointed bodies who are little troubled by freedom of information requirements, scrutiny by an ombudsman or public access to meetings. The contractual relationship offers a routine through which goals can be set and performance against them measured, although typically it is a mechanistic process focusing on a few measurable indicators (Walsh 1995). And the media provides a wild card in the game of scrutiny and accountability. Their news agenda prioritizes individual cases of failure or wrong-doing by quangos and their board members but will tend to move to another set of stories after a short time.

Overcoming the democratic deficit involves more than the auxiliary precautions. It is also to do with the wider regulatory and accountability environment within which quangos, and public bodies in general, operate. This context currently provides some checks and balances, but reform is also needed. These possibilities are discussed further in Chapter 8. But prior to this, a clearer understanding of the rationale for quangos is required. The next chapter considers the questions of why and how quangos developed and examines theories which may account for this particular form of public body.

3

Explaining the appointed state

The use of appointed individuals to oversee and deliver public services is not a new idea. Those with power have typically relied on the exercise of patronage to ensure that their policies are applied in practice. In the pre-democratic era, individuals of trust were awarded fiefdoms to govern on behalf of the monarch. Some remained loyal to their patron; others took an independent line. The same problems of discretion and control are apparent in contemporary quango appointments. Quangos remove the uncertainty created by election, yet appointees are not necessarily compliant to the wishes and intentions of government. The roots of quasi-government and the dynamics of its relationship with legitimated centres of democratic authority, therefore, can be traced back to the conventions and traditions of élitist British political culture and the reluctance with which democratic rights have been ceded to citizens.

This tension between government by appointment and government by election can be traced through developments in the twentieth century. Debates in the 1930s and 1940s about the proper governance structures for public enterprise and nationalized industry reveal an underlying tension between the desire to give managerial freedom and ensure democratic accountability. That the eventual outcome was in favour of the former explains much about the subsequent development of quangos, since it legitimized the weakening of ties between elected government and public bodies. The democratic deficit was the trade-off for the freedom to manage. A contemporary parallel is the removal of local government and community interests from health authorities in the 1990 NHS reforms and their replacement by a board of executive and non-executive directors modelled on that found in major public limited companies.

The first part of this chapter traces the history of this tension between democracy and enterprise and illustrates how the public corporation model formed the template for later developments. It also shows how, at various stages, board structures were created to incorporate or exclude particular interests. The second part of the chapter interprets the growth of quangos in terms of four areas of theory. Public choice theory, with its emphasis on utility-maximizing bureaucrats and board members, offers an appealing framework from which to understand the attractions of the quango form both for quangocrats and ministers. Managerialist and ideological control perspectives offer insights into the ways in which quangos enable value choices to be redefined in technical terms and in ways which fit the dominant political ethos. At a more abstract level, regulation theory may be used to locate the growth of quangos in terms of wider economic and social change.

Emerging models of quangos

The creation of UK quangos in the twentieth century has proceeded in three phases. The period up to the 1950s involved the development of the public corporation model and its application to enterprises and major cultural bodies in the state sector. The basic structure of the public corporation provides the basis for the two later phases. The first of these is associated with tripartite boards designed to incorporate key interests, particularly government, employers and unions. These developed in the 1960s and 1970s and were resurrected in the 1990s. The second is the business model of boards reflecting company structures, the model of the 1980s. Each model predominated in the particular phase, but such is the variety of organizational forms and relationships that individual quangos or types of quango may not fit the overall pattern. Nevertheless, the typology provides a means of examining the rationales underlying the purposes and structures of quangos.

The public corporation model

The main function of appointed bodies in the first half of the twentieth century was to manage public enterprise. The precursors were the Port of London Authority, Metropolitan Water Board and Mersey Docks and Harbour Board, all established around the turn of the century. These bodies were public corporations – organizations that managed commercial or semi-commercial activities on behalf of the state through an appointed board which had partial autonomy from government. Their structure and status marked a break with the earlier model in which a government or local authority department itself had direct managerial responsibility for commercial activities. The public corporation model continued to be utilized when, in the 1920s and 1930s, vehicles were needed for the enterprises arising from government-induced industrial rationalization and economic intervention (Table 3.1). This structure was adopted despite the contrary view taken by the Haldane Committee on the

Table 3.1   Selected public bodies incorporated 1900–39

Body	Date incorporated
Metropolitan Water Board	1902
Port of London Authority	1908
Forestry Commission	1919
Electricity Commissioners	1919
Central Electricity Board	1926
British Broadcasting Corporation	1926
Medical Research Council	1928
Coal Mines Reorganisation Commission	1931
Racecourse Betting Control Board	1933
London Passenger Transport Board	1933
British Overseas Airways Corporation	1939

Source: Robson (1962); Fry (1979).

Machinery of Government. Haldane's 1918 report was not supportive of the public corporation model on the grounds that it weakened ministerial accountability to Parliament, a theme familiar some eighty years later and one which lies at the heart of the debate about this type of appointed body.

The case for the public corporation was that it facilitated enterprise and good management by fulfilling the need for:

> a high degree of freedom, boldness and enterprise in the management of undertakings of an industrial or commercial character and the desire to escape from the caution and circumspection which is considered typical of government departments.
>
> (Robson 1962: 47)

The advocates of the public corporation looked to the private sector and saw the separation of ownership and control in joint stock companies. Owners invested in the company, day-to-day management was undertaken by professionals and the shareholders reaped the rewards of profit. In a similar vein the state would own the public enterprise, vesting control in an appointed board. This would overcome the problems of bureaucratic rigidity which observers argued constrained the performance of enterprises managed by government departments (Millward 1995). Further, it was intended to remove political interference and the impact of changing political priorities. In this way, boards were to become guardians of a public interest that was above party politics. The principle was enunciated by Hore-Belisha, a member of the 1934 National Government, who opposed too great a scrutiny of public corporations' day-to-day activities on the grounds that it would hamper 'their capacity to bring about the public good for which we look to them . . . [The board] has a single minded purpose and a sole duty of guarding the common interest' (cited in Fry 1979: 189). In a similar vein, the Board of Governors of the BBC, incorporated as a public corporation in 1926, were there to act as trustees of the public interest – a concept whose interpretation has since posed difficulties on numerous occasions (Burns 1977; Barnett and Curry 1994). This notion of the wider public good was one of the reasons that Conservatives in Parliament supported and indeed introduced public corporations both in the 1920s and 1950s.

The public corporation model, however, was not without some political dispute (Singleton 1995). Within the Labour movement the debate between Morrison and his supporters who advocated a managerialist model and others who stood for worker participation was part of a wider question – how should Clause Four of the Party's constitution be interpreted and applied? There was a commitment to nationalization, but not how to achieve – in the words of the Clause Four then applying – 'the best obtainable system of popular administration and control of each industry or service'. There were those on the Left who saw it as a means to enable worker participation in management and hence a basis for advancing the ideas of syndicalists and related socialist movements. Additionally, the Labour Party sought accountability of local public corporations such as the Port of London Authority to local authorities as well as to Parliament, countering the looser linkages advocated by Morrison and others. These disputes were eventually resolved in favour of the Morrisonian model of a managerialist public corporation having five main characteristics (Robson 1962):

1 Freedom from parliamentary inquiry into the management of the concern, as opposed to the policy guiding it.
2 'Disinterestedness', in the sense that the corporation serves the wider public interest rather than any sectional grouping – this is enhanced by an absence of shares or shareholders.
3 Members and chairs of the board are appointed by the minister for a fixed term, but may be removed at will.
4 Employees are not civil servants but come within the corporation's own arrangements for salaries and conditions of employment.
5 The finances of the corporation are not part of the national budget, although government may make funds available and control aspects of the corporation's expenditure (separation from the national budget only applies in the case of commercial enterprises).

The purpose, Morrison wrote in his 1933 tract *Socialisation and Transport*, was to create 'a combination of public ownership, public accountability, and business management for public ends' (cited in Robson 1962: 69).

The public corporation model was adopted as the template in the wave of nationalization following the election of a Labour government in 1945. It was also applied in non-commercial areas such as the cultural field, for example in the British Council and the Arts Council which were incorporated in 1940 and 1946, respectively. The principle of the public corporation can also be seen in the organizations that were created to develop new towns in the post-war period (Cullingworth 1979). The Reith Committee on new towns policy recommended that government-sponsored corporations financed by the Treasury would be preferable to development by private companies, housing associations or a local authority-controlled body. The thinking behind this conclusion had much to do with the political imperative to deliver the policy swiftly, given the severe housing crisis and limited managerial and financial capacity of local authorities. However, the creation of a new town was also seen as an opportunity to overcome social divisions by building a balanced community. In this context, it was thought that the wider public good was better served by a centralized governmental initiative than profit-seeking private enterprise or variable and uncertain local government capacity. 'After all,' Cherry (1988: 161) observed, this 'was the age of centralist planning: the State was the wise, beneficent steersman to a nobler future. New Towns would be civilised, attractive, agreeable places in which to live, with all the richness of community life which the new social order would bring.' However, in making appointments to each new town development corporation board, the minister normally consulted with the relevant local authorities. It is an interesting reflection on recent appointment practice that Morrison, who was Lord President in the Atlee government of 1945–51, discouraged the appointment of those who lost their seats in the 1950 general election (Cullingworth 1979). Members were predominantly from a local authority or business background and developed a strong commitment to the vision of their new community. Adjustments to board membership were sometimes necessary as the scheme progressed, bringing changes to the governance of the organization. In Redditch, for example, a number of retiring members were replaced by councillors

> with a declared political affiliation [which] altered not only the character of the Board but the nature of its discussion. There was a sharper edge to Board meetings and chief officers, unused to a political atmosphere, had to be prepared to argue papers at length.
>
> (Anstis 1985: 118)

The public corporation model has been particularly influential in subsequent thinking about mechanisms for the achievement and management of public purpose. Its central component is the arm's-length principle – the undertaking of governmental activity at one remove from the day-to-day processes of party politics. Robson (1962: 77) viewed this as 'the most important constitutional innovation . . . in Great Britain during the past fifty years'. In practice, however, the principle is more difficult to apply. The separation of ownership and policy from control and management is not clear-cut. Management and policy are interwoven and the same action or event can be viewed very differently depending on whether political or managerial spectacles are being worn. Fry (1979: 227) comments: 'the public corporations remained at one remove from the Government in theory, and when this was politically preferred. When it was not, the rules . . . could be swept aside.' This tension between quango boards and ministers has been apparent throughout the history of the appointed sector and is now replicated in the interactions between chief executives of executive agencies created under the Next Steps initiative and their ministers (Dudley 1994).

The tripartite model

The tripartite model provides a variant on the public corporation in terms both of its board structure and purpose. It is associated with the corporatist era of the 1970s in which government sought to build alliances with the peak groups of employers and labour as well as other interests relevant to a particular policy area. Members of these peak groups were integrated into the policy-making process and, in return, were expected to align their constituencies with the agreements so negotiated. Tripartite structures thus tend to be found in the economic and employment sectors of the economy, for example the regional economic planning councils of the 1960s and 1970s (Lindley 1982). The classic example, however, is the Manpower Services Commission (MSC) created by the Conservative Government's Employment and Training Act 1973. This oversaw the work of the Employment Service Agency in job placement and the Training Service Agency's responsibilities for employment-related skill development. These bodies had been 'hived-off' from their parent Department of Employment following the recommendations of the Fulton Committee that independent management of such activities would improve accountability and performance (Committee on the Civil Service 1968).

The MSC's board of ten consisted of a government-appointed chair, three members each from employers (nominated by the Confederation of British Industry) and labour (nominated by the Trades Union Congress), two from local government and one from the education profession. It thus brought together the key stakeholders concerned with these services. In other respects the MSC was similar to the non-commercial appointed bodies. Funding was provided by a grant-in-aid from the Treasury, its corporate plan required the Secretary of State's approval and ministers could also give directions of a general nature (Howells 1980). The tripartite basis of the MSC, however, came under some stress as governments changed and policy shifted from a collectivist emphasis on socially useful training programmes towards a narrower market-related perspective. In the period from 1979 to 1987 this ideological shift resulted in the trade unions becoming marginalized in the policy-making process, a change that was formalized when the MSC was replaced by the short-lived Training Commission in which employers significantly outnumbered trade union representatives. The process was completed by the abolition of the Training Commission and introduction of employer-led TECs (Marsh 1992).

Tripartite structures designed to incorporate key interests also formed the model for the district health authorities extant from 1982–90. These bodies had a chair appointed by the secretary of state, four members appointed by the relevant local authorities and the remaining eleven to thirteen members by the regional health authority. Five of these places were reserved – for a consultant, general practitioner, nurse, trade unionist and nominee of a nearby university's medical school. The reserved places were to be allocated to individuals after appropriate consultation. Despite containing relevant interests, the members of the board were not intended to represent a particular constituency. The board structure, in theory at least, incorporated key stakeholders who brought their own expertise and experience to bear on the decision-making process (Day and Klein 1987). In this sense it harks back to the alternative model of the public corporation, a collectivist rather than mangerialist body and one which is still found in some local appointed bodies – for example, city challenge boards and community health councils.

The business model

The business model for quangos emerged during the 1980s and 1990s. It has a number of variants, but essentially carries forward the Morrisonian idea of public managerialism in arm's-length bodies. Since the model is so significant in the current context, a brief outline is provided here and further detail included in Chapter 6.

One manifestation of the business model is the creation of companies to undertake public activity. This strategy is best exemplified in the TECs – employer-led bodies whose creation was directly stimulated by government request. They are in the relatively unusual position of operating within the Companies Acts yet being funded by and accountable to government. A second element of the business model is the predominant appointment of individuals with commercial experience to the board, a feature common across the quango sector in the past decade. Where ministers do not directly control board appointments, for example on further education corporations, they have specified requirements about the size and composition of the board to ensure sufficient business representation. This influx of business members has an impact both on the activities of the body and the culture and style with which it pursues its objectives. It reflects part of the new public management that has transformed institutions and their practices. The final component of the model is the importing of post-Cadbury private sector board structures into public organizations. The health authorities and NHS trusts are the prime examples of this development. Here, the board consists of a chair, five appointed non-executive directors and up to five executive directors who are the senior managers of the organization. This design, if not the exact balance of numbers, is familiar in major companies but transgresses the long-held public sector convention that policy making is the ultimate responsibility of elected or appointed members, and that managers are only there to advise (see Chapter 6).

The business and tripartite models thus owe their origins to the public corporation design, but represent variants developed in particular periods and for particular purposes. Within the notion of appointed arm's-length bodies, however, there is considerable variation and change. In addition, similar features may be suited to different purposes, for example company structures are used by business-led TECs but also by many of the city challenge partnership bodies created by local authorities, community organizations, business and the voluntary sector to deliver neighbourhood-based regeneration. There are now signs that the tripartite model for incorporating key stakeholders is making a return. The 1997 Labour Government has announced that the membership structure for NHS bodies, the Low Pay Commission and some other quangos will be designed to reflect a range of relevant interests.

Theorizing the emergence of quangos

The analysis of different models and motives for the creation of quangos can be strengthened by developing a more theoretically informed picture. Indeed, while much has been written about the problems of quangos, relatively little attention has been given to examining and theorizing their creation and recent growth. Yet the contemporary significance of quangos in the governance and delivery of public services, let alone the scale of their expenditure, marks a major shift in the organization of the British state. As such, the dynamics and rationale of this change merit attention. Four explanations are considered in this section. The starting point is public choice theory, whose object of analysis is the behaviour of individual utility-maximizing bureaucrats and politicians. Two meso-level approaches are then examined – managerial efficiency and ideological control. The fourth approach draws on regulation theory, a macro-level formulation of the processes of change in the economic, social, political and cultural spheres.

Public choice perspectives

Public choice theories have arisen from the study of political activity through the conceptual and methodological perspectives of economics. The extensive literature in this field has had a considerable impact on academic and practitioner debates about the growth of government and mechanisms by which it may be constrained, particularly in the prescriptions developed by the New Right in the UK and elsewhere. Central to the public choice school are two principles, one relating to human motivation and the other to social organization (Lane 1995). The underlying theory of human motivation is one in which rational actors are assumed to make instrumental decisions designed to maximize their own individual preferences. This perspective, transferred directly from micro-economics, clearly informs the work of Buchanan (1978) and other members of what has come to be known as the Virginia School of public choice theorists. Reservations about this perspective have been expressed on the basis that interests are inherently difficult to define theoretically and empirically, and that individuals may adopt suboptimal strategies on the basis of altruistic desires. Alongside the motivational assumption is a methodological individualism in which the activity of social entities such as governments and public organizations are treated as if they can be analysed from the behaviour of individual actors. The actions of organizations, therefore, can be reduced to the aggregate of the decisions made by the self-interested individuals within them.

Dunleavy (1991) distinguishes *institutional* public choice theory, with its concern to build an applied understanding of political processes, as a distinct subset of the whole field. He contrasts it with the more abstract and mathematical approaches used by others seeking to apply economic analysis to political activity. It is from this former field that public choice theory can be utilized to explain the development of quangos. Central to this is the notion of what Lowndes (1996) terms the 'manipulated institution', where utility-maximizing bureaucrats and politicians seek to advance their private, personal interests and as a result undermine a public interest in efficient governmental organizations. Two interpretations of this theme are Niskanen's (1971) model of budget-maximizing behaviour and that developed by Dunleavy (1991) around the idea of bureau-shaping activity. Budget-maximizing behaviour by public service bureaucrats arises from their desire to increase their status and material conditions. This theory reads across from the neoclassical view that managers in private firms are motivated to increase profits in order to secure the largest possible personal gain through performance-related bonus schemes. In the absence of a profit indicator in the public sector, it is assumed to be the size of the bureaucracy that will generate additional staff and layers of management and hence salary increases and other benefits for senior managers. This process of incremental budget growth is aided by the expenditure-consequent promises made by politicians at election time and their resulting budget-maximizing alliance with bureaucrats. The behaviour of politicians and bureaucrats thus combine to increase the size of and expenditure by public organizations. The budget-maximizing model, however, suffers from some unduly restrictive assumptions arising in part from its transposition from a private to public sector context. These include: its assumption of a hierarchically ordered line structure within the bureaucracy; its consequent failure to recognize the collective action problems that arise due to the existence of multiple interests and subgroups; its inability to explain variation between bureaux; and its treatment of systems of agencies as though they were a single body.

In response to these difficulties, Dunleavy proposed a bureau-shaping model of behaviour. He points out that the employment structure of public servants in the UK does not admit of a link between budget growth and personal financial reward and argues that in this context non-pecuniary factors motivate bureaucrats – in particular, 'higher-ranking bureaucrats place more emphasis upon non-pecuniary utilities: such as status, prestige, patronage and influence, and most especially the interest and importance of their work tasks' (Dunleavy 1991: 200). Rational officials, he suggests, want to work 'in small, élite, collegial bureaux close to political power centres. They do not want to head up heavily staffed, large budget but routine, conflictual and low-status agencies' (p. 202). Consequently, senior bureaucrats engage in behaviour which is intended to reshape their agency to be more in line with these utilities. One of the bureau-shaping strategies explored by Dunleavy is the 'hiving-off' by an agency of its routine and non-core functions to a quango. This aligns the agency more closely with the hypothesized preferences of bureaucrats, while at the same time preserving its programme budget – whose spending becomes the responsibility of the quango.

Both budget-maximizing and bureau-shaping models offer potential explanations for the growth of quangos. In the former case, the ability of ministers to direct spending to 'their' quangos on which sit 'their' appointees offers significant political advantage over its channelling through a large central department or a third party like a local authority. This is particularly the case with single-purpose bodies such as the UDCs and new town development corporations. Strong alliances can be built with bureaucrats in the quango and both they and the minister can be shown to have passed the test of political virility by securing specifically identifiable budget increases. Quangos also appear to resonate with the bureau-shaping model. There tends to be a good fit between the quango form and the utilities Dunleavy suggests are preferred by bureaucrats. The fit is particularly good at the local level where the organizing

Table 3.2 Analysis of the extent to which bureaucrats' value preferences are reflected in quangos

Bureau-shaping values asserted by Dunleavy (1991)	Extent to which values reflected in quangos
Staff functions	
● Individually innovative work	● High, especially in newly created quangos and those subject to changing procedures (e.g. purchaser/provider arrangements) or new policy initiatives (e.g. single regeneration budget)
● Longer time horizons	● Low, given widespread use of annual contracting cycles
● Broad scope of concerns	● Low, because of single service focus of many quangos
● Developmental rhythm	● High
● High level of managerial discretion	● High
● Low level of public visibility	● High
Collegial atmosphere	
● Small sized work unit	● High
● Restricted hierarchy and predominance of élite personnel	● High
● Cooperative work patterns	● Potentially, given single service focus of some quangos
Central location	
● Proximate to the political power centres	● Not necessarily
● Metropolitan	● Not necessarily
● Conferring high-status contacts	● Potentially, especially where linked into strategic partnerships across sector or involved in new policy developments

template for quangos gives high priority to managerialist values (Table 3.2). Although there are differences in the internal and external governance structure of quangos, considerable managerial isomorphism is apparent and hence will appeal to the 'let managers manage' ideology discussed below. Finally, the adoption of a dynamic into the analysis enables both budget-maximizing and bureau-shaping explanations to be accommodated. Dunleavy proposes that as bureau-shaping behaviour progresses, and the agency becomes more concerned with regulation and contract-management rather than service delivery, so the budget-maximizing constraint is relaxed and 'senior officials' utilities become progressively unlinked from dependence on a high absolute level of programme or bureau budget' (p. 203).

The search for managerial efficiency

Notions of efficient management have constantly informed the case for appointed bodies. This rationale can be found in the public corporations, the new town development corporations and the post-1990 NHS bodies. The creation of an appointed body at arm's length to government was argued to be beneficial for the execution of what was perceived as the technical task involved in, respectively, running successful industries, creating new centres of population and employment and providing healthcare. The theory was that managerial efficiency would follow from the structural characteristics of the organization – single focus, often small-scale, a hand-picked board – and, in particular, the relative insulation of that board from the immediate political pressures found in an elected environment. Similar justifications are found in other fields, for example the regional water authorities created in 1974 and privatized some 25 years later (Day and Klein 1987).

The idea that the general structural form of the quango provided an efficient solution to the management of public services was legitimized with the emergence and codification of the 'new public management' (NPM) during the latter part of the 1980s and early 1990s. The new public management – or perhaps more properly the new public *managements* – contains a bundle of prescriptions to do with the structural, cultural and leadership aspects of the public service. Discussion of these ideas vary from the populist and polemical, for example Osborne and Gaebler's *Reinventing Government* (1992) to works which have a stronger theoretical and evidential basis. Pollitt (1993), for example, highlights the impact of neo-Taylorist ideas about the application of scientific rationality on the pursuit of public service efficiency. These are reflected in the development of performance indicators, target-based management and other devices associated with the image of the organization as a machine (Morgan 1997). Such features can be seen, for example, in the operating agreements and contractual procedures to which TECs are subject. However NPM also contains a second important strand of prescription oriented towards the enhancement of performance. This arises from the 'excellence' school of Peters and Waterman (1982). This perspective stands in contrast to neo-Taylorism because of its emphasis on structural and cultural reform to promote decentralization, discretion and the empowerment of employees at all levels of the organization in pursuit of core goals and values. Newman and Clarke (1994: 16) argue that coexistence between these different and apparently contradictory models of management is possible because they are harmonized within a wider ideology of management: ' . . . the commitment to management as an overarching system of authority and the view of management as founded on an inalienable "right to manage".' These 'hard' and 'soft' dimensions of NPM resonate with the New Right political and economic agendas of the 1979–97 Conservative Governments. The consequence was a programme to reform public services in ways which initially sought to gain improvements in value for money and, latterly, customer satisfaction.

This programme can be related to the contemporary growth of quangos in two ways. The first is the emphasis on 'the right to manage'. This stresses the relative autonomy of managerial action from the political process, captured in Peters and Waterman's idea of 'simultaneous loose-tight properties' – a small set of clearly articulated core values (set by the political process) which managers use their discretion in delivering. Such decoupling of the guidance (political) and delivery (managerial) systems is well demonstrated in the field of quangos. Appointed boards are given briefs and allocated budgets through the political process of elected government, and are then floated-off to implement these intentions and make their own way in a largely independent managerial realm. In a sense this model reflects the traditional dichotomy between politics and administration, a dichotomy that rests on the notion that administration is somehow value-neutral. In the reality of public services, however, the decisions made by quangos have a considerable value component. They are essentially governmental, since they involve the differential allocation of scarce public resources. The second link between managerialism and quangos is the recent Conservative Government's ideological predisposition to assess the quality of public services largely in terms of the relationship between consumer and provider rather than, as Ranson and Stewart (1994) argue, the duality of customer *and* citizen. The introduction of quasi-market mechanisms and purchaser–provider separation, besides anticipating financial efficiency gains as a result of competition, also facilitates a potentially greater ability to deliver quality improvements because of the separation of previously confused roles (Walsh 1995). These managerial strategies are reflected in a number of local quangos. The restructuring of the employment training and further education quangos introduced greater involvement by one of the sets of customers for training – employers. Health service reforms, which created separate bodies for commissioning and provider roles in the new internal market and reduced representative involvement at board level, also emphasize the priority given to service delivery and patients. Ashburner and Cairncross (1993: 358), for example, observe that 'the declared purpose was to make them into more efficient strategic decision-making bodies operating in a more business-like way'.

It could be argued that in health and other fields, for example the disposal of nuclear waste and the safety of medicines, there are issues of such technical complexity that they are best resolved by panels of experts. Yet underlying these issues are significant value choices that in a liberal democracy should be debated and decided in the public arena. In the case of nuclear waste disposal, for example, the question of risk is not just a scientific assessment but also an emotional and political one. Taking an issue out of the political arena does not mean that the political implications go away. Despite this, however, quangos do provide a potential through which choices that could be dealt with in the processes of representative electoral democracy are transposed into managerial issues susceptible of technical assessment by boards of appointed individuals. Appearing to take the politics out of public service and collective issues can be a helpful device for a government wishing to distance itself from difficult decisions. The recent growth of quangos, therefore, can be associated with the acceptance of NPM by government, to the extent that it is congruent with its ideology towards public services. Yet elsewhere Teresa Payne and this author suggest that 'the *motive* – managerial efficiency – has been a more significant factor than the eventual *outcome*' (Payne and Skelcher 1997: 214). We point to the investigations of poor performance and inadequate financial controls as indicative of this problem. The question of the performance of quangos is considered further in Chapter 7.

The extension of ideological control

Quangos not only enable governments to remove areas of public policy from the direct political process but also provide ministers with the power to exercise patronage in the choice of board members. Thus they become a powerful instrument through which a government of a particular political disposition can extend and embed its ideological control over fields that are either politically salient or relatively difficult to control centrally. This is particularly significant in the case of functions which have been transferred from local authorities to local appointed bodies, including further education, employment training, some urban renewal activities, water (in 1974 in England and Wales), the careers service, housing in some localities and a number of primary and secondary schools. Such a shift of activities from the elected to appointed sectors has been stimulated by a number of factors to do with the relationship between central and local government. One stimulus has been the severe tensions demonstrated at particular moments since the late 1970s, especially in relation to Labour councils' opposition to expenditure reductions, rate capping, the 'poll tax' and various service-based legislation, for example the 'right-to-buy' provisions (Stewart and Stoker 1995a). Another is the relentless gain of council control in Scotland, Wales and England by Labour and Liberal Democrat parties in the late 1980s and early 1990s, including their success in traditionally safe Conservative seats. The by-passing of local government through the quangoization of their services is a means by which national governments can increase their capacity to realize political objectives in the face of opposition. Additionally, Shaw (1993: 182) argues that funding streams are designed to reward ideological compliance on the part of these new quangos: 'The creation of non-elected single purpose agencies has . . . allowed central government to maintain constraints on local authority spending while at the same time channelling increased resources through organisations more in tune with government policy.'

The pattern of appointments under recent Conservative governments supports this process. Although board members are not necessarily all committed Conservative Party supporters, there is a propensity to appoint people with business expertise who, consequently, are more likely to be in sympathy with that party's policies. There are some types of local quango where the minister has no say in the appointment process, for example further education colleges, but here the emphasis on business experience remains and thus a weakened but nevertheless consistent ideological imbalance may be expected. The effect, Payne and Skelcher (1997) conclude, is to produce an ideological concensus in quangos broadly supportive of government and hence a greater propensity to support and implement compatible policy initiatives than if the service had remained within the local authority's domain. The creation of quangos and the politically partial appointment of board members, therefore, produces the results desired by the centre regardless of local electoral opinion.

Regulationist explanation

The regulation school, as expressed in the work of Aglietta (1979), Lipietz (1987) and others, operates at a more abstract level than those theories discussed so far. Nevertheless, it provides a basis for conceptualizing changes in the form of the political and administrative institutions of the state in relation to wider economic processes. Regulation theory seeks, in Cochrane's (1991: 287) words, 'to explain the survival of capitalism despite the crises to which it is inherently prone'. Relative stability in the regime of accumulation – the macro-economic relations between investment, production and consumption – is achieved as a result of its interaction with a mode of regulation, i.e. a pattern of social and political institutions and cultural norms. The interaction between the institutional and cultural spheres and the pattern of economic activity facilitates the emergence of a particular mode of regulation. Chance plays a part in this interaction, since the mode of regulation may have arisen for purposes other than to facilitate the maintenance of a regime of accumulation.

The regulationists' work provides a methodology for examining and analysing the social order rather than one which seeks to depict the nature of a particular society. Consequently:

> the emphasis in regulation theory on change and periodisation holds out the promise of a theoretical account of urban politics which is historically embedded, and which can deal with qualitative shifts in the character of political processes and institutions.
>
> (Painter 1995: 281)

It is the application of a regulationist perspective to the interpretation of capitalism in Western liberal democracies during the twentieth century that has given rise to the notion that a process of transition from Fordist to post-Fordist modes of regulation is underway. From this perspective the Fordist characteristics of the labour process, such as the mass production of standardized products by large hierarchical organizations, are being replaced by the decentralized, flexible and niche post-Fordism. The impact of this apparent dynamic on the public sector – and particularly local government – has been explored by Hoggett (1987), Stoker and Mossberger (1995) and others in a mix of interpretative and critical papers. They particularly focus on changes in the labour process and the welfare state. These include contractorization, performance management, flexible work-forces and consumer orientation as well as the transition from the Keynesian welfare state to a Schumpterian workfare state emphasizing supply-side factors to stimulate structural competitiveness.

Particular types of quango can be seen in this light. City technology colleges, for example, reflect the emerging vocational emphasis in educational policy while the majority of TECs' activities are concerned with regulating the unemployed to the demands of employers. Both, therefore, are about the nature of the labour market. Urban development corporations, in contrast, are associated with opening up new economic opportunities and stimulating entrepreneurial activity. Besides the functions of quangos, their organizational form – small core staffs, decentralized control, disengagement from the political process, flexibility in employment conditions – all reflect the archetypal post-Fordist model. However, the application of regulation theory would not be complete without warning that it is subject to varying interpretations and considerable criticism. The validity of the Fordist model in a public service context has been challenged on the grounds that evidence suggests a more complex picture. Its facility as a theory of societal change is subject to the dangers of determinism and teleology. These and other limitations are compounded by differences in the theoretical starting points and use of terminology amongst writers. Nevertheless the work of the regulationists and their critics does offer an important wider context for considering the growth of quangos.

Phases in the emergence of quangos

The analysis of different models for appointed bodies illustrates the extent to which each can be related to a particular period in the twentieth-century political and economic history of the UK. Public corporations were largely about improving the efficient management of industries requiring restructuring and the injection of state finance. Tripartite models reflected the imperatives of incorporating key stakeholders into the governmental process. Business models arose from the predominance of employer interests. Yet across these run themes and ideas reflected in the theoretical literature.

Payne and Skelcher (1997) utilize these ideas to offer a framework for explaining the growth of *local* appointed bodies, since it is here that the majority

Table 3.3 Phases in the growth of local executive appointed bodies

Phase	Ideological dimension	Managerial dimension	Local quango type
Phase 1: 1960s–1970s	• Acceptance of pluralism in local public policy • Local authority *de facto* main local public service provider	• Administration of growing services and budgets • Professional dominance of services	• Health authorities comprising 'representative' boards with local authority rights of nomination • New Town Development Corporations ministerially appointed
Phase 2: 1980s	• Intolerance of pluralism in local public policy • Governmental action to support business interests • Desire to bypass Labour Party-controlled local authorities • Success to be manifest through physical development	• Party politics seen as an impediment to efficient and effective public management • Desire for efficient use of capital investment for urban regeneration • Desire to increase speed of decision-making	• UDCs, with investment and planning powers • Small board appointed by minister • Strong business representation • Local councillors may join board in individual capacity • Limited community representation
Phase 3: 1990s	• Pre-eminence of the market, even in relation to public services, applied through collective exit, contracting, etc. • Demonstrate that quality of non-privatized local public services can be improved • Need to legitimate Major Government in wake of Thatcher era, 'poll tax' débâcle, etc. • Undermining of citizenship in public services and replacement by notions of consumerism	• Contribution of private sector management expertise and techniques • Creation of quasi-markets to stimulate increases in efficiency and performance in local public services • Devolution of power to operational units and their decoupling from large bureaucratic structures • Ascendance of managerialism over professionalism at senior levels in organizations • Remote or indirect control of operational units through target setting and performance monitoring	• Use or emulation of company structures for local quangos, e.g. executive and non-executive board structures for NHS bodies, TECs as private governmental agencies, etc. • Introduction of self-appointing bodies regulated by contract or inspection, e.g. FE corporations, careers service companies • Removal of local authority nomination rights, e.g. to district health authorities, further education governing bodies, etc. • Limited incorporation of community and tenant representatives on City Challenge and HATs

Source: Adapted from Payne and Skelcher (1997).

of recent developments have taken place, following the regulationists in recognizing the changing nature of the regime of accumulation and a transition from Fordism. This dynamic produced severe pressures within the mode of regulation. As Painter (1995: 279) notes, 'the 1970s was the decade when the limits to Fordism began to become apparent, and the 1980s was when a series of (often conflicting) political strategies began to be adopted in attempts to resolve the problems'. One manifestation of these pressures was the heightened tension between central government's fiscal and deregulationist measures to stimulate and introduce flexibility into the economy and local government's desire to expand and develop services in a democratic context. We argue that the creation of local appointed bodies was part of a strategy to dismantle some of these pressure points by isolating the governance and management of public services from local democratic processes and hence developing a local state which was more aligned with emerging modes of regulation. Utilizing and extending the stages identified by Painter above, three broad phases of transition can be identified (Table 3.3). Each is associated with particular ideological and managerial attributes that can be traced through into the specifics of the organizational form of local executive appointed bodies created in that period.

Phase One is associated with the period of the post-war settlement. Although some local quangos existed prior to the 1960s and 1970s, this period can be taken as the benchmark against which later developments are compared. The economic buoyancy of the period combined with a broad ideological concensus enabled a tolerance of pluralism in local public policy and hence the lead role of the local authority in securing gains in the local welfare state. At a managerial level, services were growing as was the extent and influence of the new state professions. Pluralism was accommodated on quangos, for example through the incorporation of local political leaders on to new town development corporations. Phase Two, broadly the 1980s, marks an ideological regime intolerant of local pluralism and the emergence of collectivist and oppositional strategies by local authorities. A strong central government spearheads the process of economic, social and political restructuring. It is associated with the rise of public service managerialism cast in a private sector mould, and the application of this managerial approach to ideological ends. The form of local quango that resulted was one in which a small board of appointees, including significant business representation, was created to drive forward central policy objectives in relative isolation from local political processes. Phase Three is located in the period up to 1997. Here, the transition and experimentation undertaken in phase two is consolidated at the ideological level into the pre-eminence of the market with its consequent undermining of citizenship and emphasis on the consumer. The process of managerialization is formalized in the emergence of NPM, including the decoupling of operational units from direct political control as a result of internal bureaucratic reorganizations or contracting and hiving-off. The quangos created in this period either emulate company board structures or use appointment to incorporate local business interests. Questions of legitimacy raised as a result of Phase Two quangos are accommodated through limited involvement of community and tenant representatives on appointed bodies concerned with small area regeneration. Other quangos tend to relate to local political structures at a managerial rather than board level.

The analysis of the growth of quangos leads to the identification of clear themes: the tension between managerial discretion and democratic accountability; the changing structure of the board to accommodate political priorities and ideological dispositions; and the utilization of appointed bodies to restructure wider economic and political relationships. It is in this context that Chapters 4 and 5 examine the membership of quango boards and the question of patronage. For whatever the processes and structures that relate arm's-length appointed bodies to the political process at central or local level, the characteristics of board members and their obligations and ties to those who appointed them will be a key factor in shaping the policy and style of these organizations.

4

The members of quangos

The membership of appointed bodies has been a matter of public debate on numerous occasions during the last two decades. There have been accusations that members are not representative of their local community or the population at large and that they have been appointed as a result of party political patronage. These issues, however, are part of a wider debate about the nature of representative democracy in the British state and the extent to which those having political authority come from one section of society – being predominantly white, male, middle class and older. In a society increasingly aware of its variety and diversity, such imbalance challenges the legitimacy and competence of governmental institutions.

Until recently, there have been little hard data on the socio-economic and demographic characteristics of quango members and even less on their political affiliations. The problem has been compounded by the paucity of official information about the names of individuals who constitute these bodies, a situation described by Richards (1963) in his study of administrative boards and as valid almost four decades later as it was then. There is now a greater willingness on the part of government departments to publish lists of appointees, although the practice varies somewhat. The Department of Health and the Northern Ireland Office have commenced what they promise will be the annual practice of publishing full lists of the non-executive appointments they make. Some annual departmental reports only list the new appointments or re-appointments made in that year. Others presently do not publish any consolidated information, although this practice is likely to change as the recommendations of the Nolan Committee are implemented (see Chapter 8).

Researchers have only recently devoted their energies to understanding more about the attitudes and characteristics of appointees, but there is still less data available on the quango member than their counterparts in Parliament or the council chamber.

The first part of this chapter examines the age, sex, ethnic origin, educational qualifications and employment status of quango members. The analysis highlights the general unrepresentativeness of quango members compared with the population as a whole, but also illustrates considerable variability between different types of appointed body. The second part of the chapter then considers the motivation and appointment of members. It reveals the significance of informal recruitment and appointment methods, especially in the non-recognized sector. I conclude by reviewing the debate about board composition. The case that boards should broadly mirror the characteristics of the community it serves is assessed in the context of the alternative view that they should be composed of individuals having relevant technical or managerial experience. It is argued that where the latter expertise is necessary, it should be provided through the recruitment of appropriate managers or consultants. The essence of boards in the public service should be that they comprise a reasonable cross-section of the population.

Member characteristics

A student answering an examination question on the socio-economic profile of Members of Parliament and local authority councillors would have little new to say compared with a contemporary writing 20 or 30 years ago. Their answer would highlight the predominance of white, middle-class men who tend to be middle-aged or older. A snapshot of members of appointed bodies in the mid-1990s shows that, to the extent that data is available, they are broadly reflective of such elected politicians (Table 4.1). Members of quangos tend to be drawn from the professional and business classes, with women and ethnic minority groups under-represented in comparison with the population as a whole. These characteristics, through accident or design, are those of the British establishment.

The lack of statistical data on the socio-economic characteristics of members of national quangos is in contrast to the wealth of information now available about the membership of executive quangos at the local level. This has been generated by surveys undertaken by, *inter alia*, Shaw *et al.* (1996) on quangos in the North East of England, Kearns (1994) on housing association committee members, Graystone (1991a) on further education governing bodies and Ashburner and Cairncross (1993) on health authorities and NHS trusts, as well as that by Skelcher and Davis (1995) on eight types of local appointed body. These studies provide a detailed picture of the membership of local quangos and reveal important differences between the various types of body (Table 4.2). Such variation in membership characteristics can also be found between local authorities (Young and Rao 1994). Consequently, generalization about the members of either type of local governmental body should

Table 4.1 Socio–economic characteristics (in percentages) of public body members, local executive quango members, councillors, MPs and population

Characteristics	Members of public bodies in UK, excluding local NDPBs and NHS bodies	Local executive quango members in England	Local authority councillors	MPs	UK population
Male	70	74	75	91	49
Female	30	26	25	9	51
Age					
18–29	–[a]	0	6[b]	0	24
30–44	–	18	17[c]	54[d]	27
45–59	–	55	39	32	21
≥60	–	27	39	14	28
Employment status					
Employed	–	73	58	–	55
Unemployed	–	1	4	–	6
Other	–	26	38	–	39
Employment sector					
Public/voluntary	–	33	37	–	28
Private	–	67	63	–	72
Ethnic origin					
White	97	97	99	99	95
Black/Asian	3	3	1	1	5
(Base)	(35,595)	(1,501)	(1,612)	(651)	–

Source: Public bodies data from Cabinet Office (1996), using their definition ('non-departmental public bodies and nationalised industries') but excluding UDCs, HATs and NHS bodies which are included in the data on local executive quango members. Local executive quango data from Skelcher and Davis (1995). Councillor data from Young and Rao (1994), except for ethnic origin which is from Sohpal and Muir (1995). [a] Data not available; [b,c] figures for under 35 years and 35–44 years, respectively. MP data for 1992 intake from Butler and Kavanagh (1992). [d] Figures are for 30–49 years; 30–39 = 14% and 40–49 = 40%. Population data from 1991 Census.

Table 4.2 Socio–economic characteristics (in percentages) of members of local appointed bodies

Characteristics	City challenge boards	Urban development corporations	Housing action trusts	Further education college governing bodies	Training and enterprise councils	Career service companies	Health authorities	NHS trusts
Male	83	83[a]	64[a]	78	87	89	59[b]	60[b]
Female	17	17[a]	36[a]	22	13	11	41[b]	40[b]
Age								
<30	1	0	0	0	0	0	0	0
30–44	29	10	19	18	14	15	12	16
45–59	58	44	56	53	71	70	55	53
≥60	13	46	25	29	15	15	33	31
Ethnic origin								
White	95	100	87	98	94	98	94[b]	95[b]
Ethnic minority	5	0	13	2	6	2	6[b]	5[b]
Location								
Live in area	50	41	54	78	85	74	92	84
Work in area	78	56	42	78	97	85	71	73

Source: Skelcher and Davis (1995), except [a] Cabinet Office (1996). [b] Department of Health (1996). Due to updating, figures are not directly comparable with those in Table 4.1.

be undertaken with care. Neither local appointed bodies nor local authorities are homogeneous. The overall data hide variety, yet the pattern is clear. It is this pattern that will now be explored.

The age profile of quango members

The age profile of local appointed body members has a rather less even spread than that of councillors or the 18 years and over UK population, and is biased towards older age groups than the Parliament elected in 1992. Three in every four local board members are over 45 years of age, with over half in the 45 to 59 years age group. City Challenge directors have the youngest profile, but even here only 29 per cent of directors are aged under 45 years. UDCs have the oldest membership with nine out of ten respondents aged over 45 years. The bias towards older age groups can be explained largely with reference to the propensity to recruit through informal networks of contacts. Those who have become members of 'the great and the good' in a particular sector or locality and have built up a reputation or position that makes them attractive to boards with vacancies are likely at least to be middle-aged.

Structural factors in the employment sphere are significant in shaping the age profile of local quango members two ways. First, the predominance of business and professional people on quangos is facilitated by their greater ability than those in service or manual occupations to build flexibility into their working lives. Board membership also can be advantageous to such individuals and their organizations because it increases the information flow and network of contacts available to them and hence may lead to new business opportunities. The commercial world of professional and business activity thrives on social encounters and networks, and quangos provide yet another arena for this to occur. Secondly, retired people potentially have considerable time flexibility and therefore have always been in demand for appointed positions. However the Department of Health, in advising on the recruitment of non-executives for the new health authorities and trusts, recommended that only the 'recently retired' should be considered (Ashburner and Cairncross 1993). Further education college governors are not eligible for appointment or re-appointment if they have reached 70 years of age unless a majority of the existing governors wish it or they are appointed by the Secretary of State. There are, then, some indications of a retirement age or upper age limit for quango members.

Women on quango boards

Women are significantly under-represented on the boards of quangos, holding one-third of positions on public bodies but only one-quarter of local appointed board memberships. The proportion of women on public bodies has increased since 1988, with a slight dip in the early 1990s due to the reduction in the number of NHS appointments, many of which were held by women. However, by 1996, only 1 per cent more women had been appointed to public

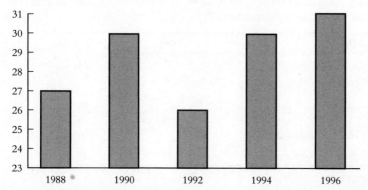

Figure 4.1 Women appointed to public bodies as a proportion of all appointments, 1988–96.
Source: Public Bodies, various years.

Table 4.3 Representation of women on types of public bodies in the UK, 1996

Type of public body	Number of appointments	Women appointed	
		No.	Percentage
Executive bodies	3,733	906	24
Advisory bodies	8,125	2,198	27
Tribunals	21,906	6,725	31
Board of Visitors	1,777	811	46
Nationalized industries	110	12	11
Public corporations	113	22	19
NHS bodies	4,292	1,665	39
Total number of appointments	40,056	12,339	31
Total number of ministerial appointments [a]	34,564	11,040	32

[a] Not all appointments are made by ministers or the sponsoring department.
Source: Cabinet Office (1996).

bodies than had been six years earlier (Figure 4.1). Data from *Public Bodies* suggests a rather stereotypical distribution of women's appointments across different types of public body (Table 4.3). Women are well represented in the more social and personal fields of the NHS and the Board of Visitors, whose role is in relation to the welfare of prisoners. Conversely, women comprise a very low proportion of members of the more commercially-oriented nationalized industry and public corporation boards. Separate figures are available for Wales, covering new appointments and re-appointments made by the Secretary of State in the six months to September 1995 (Table 4.4). This again

Table 4.4 Appointment of women to public bodies by Secretary of State for Wales, for six months to September 1995

Type of public body	No.	Percentage
Executive body	41	23
Advisory body	26	18
Tribunal	5	15
NHS bodies	138	38
Other	8	19
Appointments to bodies covering whole of UK	15	16
Total of ministerial appointments	233	27

Source: Welsh Office (1996).

Table 4.5 Representation of women on public bodies sponsored by the ten largest appointing departments, 1996

Department	Number of appointments	Women appointed	
		No.	Percentage
Scottish Office	3,871	1,671	43
Home Office	2,207	898	41
Department of Health	4,729	1,784	38
Northern Ireland Office	2,352	835	36
Department of Health and Social Security	8,215	2,903	35
Department of Trade and Industry	3,512	868	25
Department of the Environment	3,368	758	23
Lord Chancellor's Department	5,765	1,263	22
Welsh Office	1,132	250	22
Ministry of Agriculture, Fisheries and Food	1,549	140	9

Source: Cabinet Office (1996).

illustrates the difference between women's representation on NHS and other bodies.

An examination of the ten government departments having the largest number of appointed positions illustrates that the Scottish Office, with women occupying 43 per cent of appointed posts, reaches almost five times the level attained by the Ministry of Agriculture, Fisheries and Food (Table 4.5). This might reflect the degree of emphasis given to identifying and appointing suitably qualified women to these positions or an individual's personal interest and predisposition. The Government is a signatory to the 'Opportunity 2000' campaign to increase women's presence in senior positions and asked departments to set targets for its public appointments in the period up to September 2000. In January 1997, for example, the Home Office announced its aim that

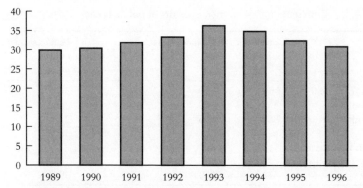

Figure 4.2   Proportion of women on Public Appointments Unit List, 1989–96.
Source: Cabinet Office, Privy Council and Parliament (1996).

women should fill 45 per cent of posts on the public bodies that it sponsors. The Ministry of Defence set a 10–15 per cent target and the Foreign Office 30 per cent (Norton-Taylor 1997). However, the proportion of women on the Public Appointments Unit list of potential appointees is almost the same now as it was in 1989 (Figure 4.2). No data are available on the lists held by individual departmental appointments units. It remains to be seen whether the trend towards advertising appointments will attract more women on to public bodies.

Women are also under-represented on quangos at the local level although again there are significant variations between types of body (Table 4.2). Local NHS boards have the highest proportion of women non-executives, following a decline in their level of representation on regional and district health authorities at the time of the 1990 reorganization. HATs are also noticeable, with women comprising over one-third of members. This may be due to their nomination by tenants' and residents' groups for the seats reserved for local people. A high proportion of women committee members is found on non-developing housing associations (i.e. housing associations that manage but do not build properties). Kearns' survey records a 50:50 split on these committees, somewhat different to the developing housing associations (which have both management and property development roles) where only 23 per cent of members are women (Kearns 1994). The reasons for this difference are unclear, but may be to do with the desire by developing associations to incorporate individuals with a property development background and who therefore are more likely to be men.

These overall figures do not reveal anything about the extent to which women are in positions of formal power on quango boards. In order to do this, the data on women chairs need to be examined (Table 4.6). This illustrates that, in proportion to their membership of each type of public body, women

Table 4.6   Representation of women as chairs of public bodies, 1996

NDPB	Chairs available	Women chairs		Percentage of women members
		No.	(%)	
Public bodies, of which:	3,955	990	25	31
executive bodies	338	49	15	24
advisory bodies	860	156	18	27
tribunals	2,195	626	29	31
nationalized industries and public corporations	26	0	0	18
NHS bodies	536	159	30	39

Source: Data calculated from Cabinet Office (1996). Excludes public bodies where the chair is vacant or is held by a Civil Servant or minister. Number of chairs exceeds number of bodies given in Table 4.4 because *Public Bodies* counts some classes of public body (e.g. industrial tribunals) as one regardless of the number of individual boards or tribunals there are in that class.

are under-represented as chairs. The under-representation is much less in tribunals than nationalized industries and public corporations, as would be expected from the analysis above. Care should be taken in interpreting the proportions in the latter class of public body due to the small numbers involved.

Research on particular types of quango reveals a number of trends in women's representation. The trend in the further education sector may be towards a reduction in the number of women on college governing bodies. Graystone points out that the governing bodies established under the Education Reform Act 1988 have tended to abolish or reduce the already small number of staff and student governors, and not to reappoint local education authority (LEA) nominated 'first' governors after their term of office has expired. He concludes that this will particularly affect women and black and ethnic minority representation, since they are often nominated to fill these reserved places. A further effect will be to reduce the proportion of women chairs, two-thirds of whom were LEA-nominated governors. He concludes (1991b: 151): 'Unless governing bodies and principal decide otherwise, governors will be mainly white, male and able-bodied, reflecting the business world but not the other communities [colleges] serve.'

On TECs and careers service boards – where directors are appointed either by the founding partners or the board itself – only a small proportion of directors are women. One factor influencing this was the Government's guidance that TECs should recruit its business directors from senior executives in the area's larger employers. Male dominance in the company boardroom is therefore translated into a largely male TEC board. Once again, this level of under-representation limits the perspectives and experience available to TEC boards in meeting the employment-related training needs of the whole community. Many careers service companies are partnerships with TECs and local chambers of commerce, their boards replicating those bodies' preponderance of men at senior levels.

Table 4.7   Ethnic minority representation on public bodies, by gender, 1992–6

Year	1992	1994	1996
Total number of appointments	41,011	42,876	40,056
Ethnic minority appointees	802	1,096	1,310
Ethnic minority appointees (%)	2.0%	2.6%	3.3%
Ethnic minority appointees who are women	158	327	428
Ethnic minority appointees who are women (%)	28%	30%	33%

Source: Cabinet Office (1996).

Racial equality and board composition

Just as women are under-represented on appointed bodies, so too are individuals from ethnic minority backgrounds. In 1996, 3.3 per cent of the members of public bodies were from ethnic minorities, a significant increase since 1992 when data were first published. Similarly, there has been an increase in ethnic minority appointees to public bodies who are women (Table 4.7). In January 1997 the Cabinet Office was reported as saying that the then Conservative Government was committed to bringing the proportion into line with that in the economically active population – approximately 5 per cent (Norton-Taylor 1997). Despite this trend to greater representation, there is considerable variation between departments. Table 4.8 shows the proportion of ethnic minority appointments by the ten departments having the largest number of appointed posts. The spatial distribution of the ethnic minority population accounts to some extent for the relatively low Scottish and Northern Ireland

Table 4.8   Ethnic minority appointees on public bodies sponsored by the ten largest appointing departments, 1996

Department	Total number of appointments	Ethnic minority appointees	
		No.	Percentage
Home Office	2,207	167	7.6
Department of Social Security	8,215	512	6.2
Department of Health	4,729	203	4.3
Department of Trade and Industry	3,512	129	3.7
Department of the Environment	3,368	105	3.1
Lord Chancellor's Department	5,765	87	1.5
Welsh Office	1,132	15	1.3
Scottish Office	3,871	8	0.2
Northern Ireland Office	2,352	7	0.3
Ministry of Agriculture, Fisheries and Food	1,549	<5	0

Source: Cabinet Office (1996).

figures, but that between other departments could again be to do with recruitment practice, the pool of potential appointees or personal predispositions. It is noticeable that the method of identifying a member for a quango position does not generally accord with the Equal Opportunities Commission's guidance on recruitment and selection – namely that posts should, with few well-specified exceptions, be advertized openly and that short-listing and selection should be on the basis of job-related criteria.

The survey of English local executive quangos undertaken by Davis and Skelcher leads us to estimate that, on average, only one board in every nine has an ethnic minority member (Table 4.2). Only 2 per cent of respondents identify as having Asian origins and 1 per cent as black, African or Afro-Caribbean. This compares with the population of England where 5 per cent are from ethnic minority backgrounds. Once again, there is wide variation across different types of local appointed body. The difference between HATs and UDCs is particularly noticeable since both are engaged in physical, social and economic regeneration of specific localities. We explain this difference in terms of the appointment process. Unlike UDCs, HATs have a number of board seats reserved for individuals nominated or elected by the local community who are appointed subject to the Secretary of State's agreement. UDCs, by contrast, are much more centrally controlled in terms of appointments.

Within the NHS, there has been a continuing debate about the under-representation of black and ethnic minority people amongst those appointed as chairs and non-executive members. Ashburner and Cairncross's 1991 survey identified that only 2 per cent of non-executives on the new health bodies were from ethnic minorities. Two years later, a joint study by the National Association of Heath Authorities and Trusts (NAHAT) and the King's Fund Centre found that all but two of the regional health authority, local health authority and NHS trust chairs were white, and that 45 (3 per cent) of the 1531 non-executive members on NHS boards were from black and ethnic minority communities (National Association of Health Authorities and Trusts/King's Fund Centre 1993). This research highlighted the barriers to greater racial equality on health bodies, including the reliance on informal recruitment methods by the predominantly white male membership, inappropriate or discriminatory selection criteria, lack of role models and the low profile of board membership within black and ethnic minority communities. It recommended a number of steps to overcome these constraints (Box 4.1). Shortly afterwards, the then government launched a programme to facilitate increased black and ethnic minority representation. Entitled *Ethnic minority staff in the NHS: a programme for action*, the primary focus was under-representation amongst NHS employees. However, one of the programme's goals was to increase the number of black and ethnic minority chairs and non-executive members of NHS authorities and trusts. Various measures were proposed, although the ability to appoint is clearly one of the key instruments available to ministers in achieving their goals.

NAHAT and the King's Fund Centre undertook a further study in May 1995 and found that the proportion of black and ethnic minority non-

---

Box 4.1   Strategies to increase Black and ethnic minority membership of NHS bodies

- Information campaign promoting non-executive membership of NHS local bodies and targeted at Black and ethnic minority communities, including networking with community leaders.
- Regular publicity to ensure Black and ethnic minority communities are aware of current NHS roles, bodies and activities.
- NHS bodies to advertise vacancies and sell the benefits of being a non-executive.
- Formal recruitment and selection process, including job descriptions for chairs and non-executives, commitment to training and clarity about time demands on members.
- Interview panels should include Black and ethnic minority members, and have provision for feedback to unsuccessful candidates.
- Mentoring scheme for new non-executive to 'shadow' an experienced board member.
- Corporate initiative on race in the NHS to be initiated by ministers.
- Monitoring data to be collected and published, and guidance to all NHS bodies on corporate standards for recruitment of non-executives.

Source: National Association of Health Authorities and Trusts/Kings Fund Centre (1993).

---

executives and chairs had increased to almost 5 per cent. This overall change concealed important local variations. In some NHS regions, membership was in proportion to that in the regional population (for example, the North West with 3.9 per cent and 3.8 per cent, respectively) while in others there was still considerable under-representation (for example, Anglia and Oxford with 1.7 per cent and 4.4 per cent, respectively). The Department of Health's own data indicate that 5.9 per cent of health authority and 5.0 per cent of NHS trust non-executives identify as black or minority ethnic (Department of Health 1996). Perhaps more significantly, the NAHAT/King's Fund survey found that there were only three black or ethnic minority chairs. Increased representation in ordinary non-executive positions, therefore, was not reflected in the key and powerful role of chair.

This manifestation of both change and continuity in the racial composition of NHS bodies reflects the earlier discussion about the representation of women on quango boards. The opportunity to make further advances in board membership for black and ethnic minority members on NHS bodies is made more difficult by the reduction in the number of places available, particularly because of Family Health Service Authority and health authority mergers. In this context, the second NAHAT/King's Fund Centre report recommended:

- Targeted activity to encourage more candidates from black and ethnic minority communities, especially for the position of chair.
- Standardized data collection and monitoring of board composition by NHS region.
- Health authorities and trusts should review their policies and practices for recruiting and selecting non-executive members.
- Gathering and disseminating good practice examples where NHS bodies have increased their appointment of black and ethnic minority non-executives.

Some TECs have also taken a particular interest in recruiting ethnic minority members to their board. The Skelcher and Davis survey and other work (e.g. Haughton *et al.* 1995b) suggest that the proportion of ethnic minority members on TEC boards is approximately equivalent to that in the UK population. This is important given the over-representation of individuals from ethnic minorities amongst the unemployed and long-term unemployed. Rolfe *et al.* (1996) report that a number of TECs have recruited board members specifically to give a lead on equal opportunity issues. However, although the proportion of ethnic minority members on TEC and some other boards are comparable to that in the UK population, it is also important to consider the numbers involved – because where a board has an ethnic minority member he or she is likely to be the only one. This creates the danger of isolating that individual, especially if they are also given responsibility for equal opportunities issues, and creating the unreasonable expectation that they will be knowledgeable about all ethnic minorities.

Educational qualifications of members

Quango members are a very highly educated group. Some 80 per cent of local appointed body members in England hold a degree or professional qualification. No systematic data are available for national and regional quango members, but the profiles that are available suggest their educational background is similar to that of their local counterparts. This level of formal education is significantly higher than that for councillors, and both are more highly qualified than the population as a whole (Table 4.9). Comparable data are not available for MPs, but 68 per cent of those who were elected in the 1992 general election had completed a university education.

Younger councillors are more likely to be better educated than middle-aged and older councillors (Young and Rao 1994), but this is not the case amongst the membership of local appointed bodies. Respondents aged 60 years and over are almost as likely to hold a degree or professional qualification as those in other age groups (Skelcher and Davis 1995). This is to be expected given the propensity for appointed members to be from professional and business backgrounds, hence having a greater degree of occupational uniformity

Table 4.9   Educational qualifications of members of local appointed bodies in England, Members of Parliament, local councillors and UK population

Highest qualification	Percentage local appointed body members	Percentage Members of Parliament	Percentage local councillors	Percentage of population
No formal qualification	4	–	18	28
O level or equivalent	7	–	18	32
A level or equivalent	7	–	10	12
Degree or professional qualification	82	68[a]	54	25
(Base)	(1,492)	(627)[b]	(1,610)	–

Source: Local quangos, Skelcher and Davis (1995); Members of Parliament, Butler and Kavanagh (1992); councillors, Young and Rao (1994); population, *Social Trends* (1995). [a] Percentage holding degree, since data on professional qualifications not available; [b] Data only available on 627 of the 651 MPs.

than is found amongst local councillors. In this sense the educational and employment background of members of local appointed bodies (and, by inference, quangos generally) is closer to MPs than councillors. Only 10 per cent of MPs were manual workers prior to election while 65 per cent are from professional or business backgrounds (Butler and Kavanagh 1992).

The predominance of business people

The *Financial Times* (1993) studied 40 of the largest spending quangos and concluded that 'today's top quango chairman is much more likely to be a businessman'. Two-thirds of the chairmen were senior figures in business and industry compared with one-third in 1978–9. Then, a greater proportion of chairs were held by individuals whose main occupation was serving on public bodies, by Labour peers and by others in non-business employment. Data on local appointed bodies reveal a predominance of individuals who are either employed in the private sector or self-employed. When compared with local councillors, local quango members are more likely to be in employment and conversely less likely to be retired (Table 4.1).

The drive to recruit business people to quango boards and other public service bodies became an explicit strategy of Conservative Governments in the mid-1980s. The Education (No. 2) Act 1986, for example, required school governing bodies to pay regard to members of the local business community. In the NHS, the appointment of individuals with business experience was designed to facilitate its reform in the post-1990 period (Table 4.10). Ashburner and Cairncross (1993: 358–9) comment that:

Table 4.10   NHS trust chairs by occupation

Occupation	No.	Percentage
Company director	152	42
Consultant	31	9
Education	28	8
Legal	27	7
Accountancy/finance	22	6
Manager	22	6
Housewife	18	5
Other	46	17
Total	361	100

Data include individuals currently in employment as well as the occupation of those who are retired. 'Other' includes, *inter alia*, local government officers, farmers, voluntary sector workers, architects and engineers.
Source: *Independent* (1994).

> Attracting business people [reflected] the ethos of the reforms which modelled the new authorities on the structure of private sector boards of directors . . . The declared purpose of the changes was to make them into more effective strategic decision-making bodies, operating in a more 'business-like' way.

Ministers at the Department of Health were particularly keen to identify committed and proactive individuals with commercial skills to chair the new NHS trusts operating in the internal market. A number of such high-profile appointments were made, with the intention that active business leadership could spearhead the transformation of health service efficiency and quality. Examples included Roy Lilley at Homewood Trust and John Spiers in Brighton. By the mid-1990s, however, the political agenda had changed to one of consolidation and a number of these early NHS trust chairs had either not had their contracts renewed or understood that it was time to step aside.

Some quangos, of course, have a board structure which mandates a certain level of business representation. TECs and the further education corporations are the prime examples. City Challenge boards are also expected to include business people. The Housing Corporation's *Performance Standards for Housing Associations* (1994: 11) follows earlier guidance in requiring associations to have 'a suitably skilled and representative committee', an injunction that has influenced board composition to the extent that the two biggest occupational groups involved are those from the housing and related professions and finance (Kearns 1994). Formally constituted representational structures tend only to be found in quangos not subject to ministerial appointment. In effect it was a way of safeguarding the then Conservative Governments' political strategy to use business people to commercialize public services and avoid the capture of these local institutions by forces who might wish to adopt a more democratic or community-oriented style of operation. However quangos themselves also see

Board member	Background
Sir Brian Pearse, Chairman	Former chief executive of Barclays Bank; chairman of Lucas Industries and of British Invisibles
Peter Cooke, Deputy Chairman	Former associate director, Bank of England; chairman, Price Waterhouse World Regulatory Advisory Practice; former member National Churches Housing Group
Anthony Mayer, Chief Executive	Former managing director at NM Rothschild Asset Management and Civil Servant
Robin Thompson	Farmer; deputy chairman of Rural Development Commission; chairman of South Shropshire Housing Association; president of Rural Community of Shropshire
Julia Unwin	Freelance consultant to voluntary and charitable sector; former director of Homeless Network and member of London and Quadrant Housing Trust
Lady Montgomery	Chairman of Manchester and District Housing Association; non-executive member of Manchester University Hospital Trust
David Kleeman	Managing director of financial services company; non-executive director of public and private companies including NHS Supplies Authority; former senior partner in firm of solicitors and chairman of New River Health Authority
Ken Griffin	Deputy chairman of Ugland International Holdings, a shipping firm; former deputy chair of British Ship Builders and advisor to Department of Trade and Industry; chairman of Network Housing Association and board member of North British Housing Association; member of Law Society's Disciplinary Tribunal
Roger Council	Welfare and benefits advisor; tenant and board member of Yorkshire Metropolitan Housing Association; chair of Sheffield Disability Housing Services; member of Disability Income Group executive and National Tenants Association committee; member of a number of other housing and disability groups and committees
Dr Peter Williams	Head of Research and External Affairs at the Council of Mortgage Lenders; formerly held academic posts and was deputy director of the Chartered Institute of Housing; previously was member of Tai Cymru (Housing for Wales) and chaired the Welsh Secretary's Housing Management Advisory Panel
George Cracknell, Chairman of Audit and Finance Committee	Formerly deputy managing director in Barclays bank; director of various finance and venture capital companies and chairman of quoted catering group; former treasurer of Chartered Institute of Banking
Sylvia Denman	Former academic lawyer, now independent advisor on anti-discrimination law and practice; chairman of Camden and Islington Health Authority; part-time Tribunal chairman; was member of Lord Chancellor's Advisory Committee on Legal Aid and Equal Opportunities Commission
Derek Waddington	Formerly director of housing with Birmingham City Council and advisor to Association of Metropolitan Authorities; member of Duke of Edinburgh's Inquiry into British Housing; past president of Chartered Institute of Housing and chairs its Good Practice Unit; management committee member of Waterloo Housing Association; non-executive director of Johnson Fry Housing Ltd

Source: Housing Corporation (1996).

advantages in securing business experience. Bush *et al.* (1992), for example, illustrate the way in which newly established grant-maintained schools identified the desired business backgrounds of their 'first' or 'foundation' governors from an analysis of the skills and qualities that would be most advantageous to them in their new, more autonomous status.

A typical quango board?

Despite the variety between national and local quangos boards, and between classes of body, the overall picture is that members are well educated, predominantly white and male and have considerable status in their own walk of life. They are less representative of the population than councillors and, to a smaller degree, MPs. The typical quango board probably does not exist, but the profile of the Housing Corporation gives an example (Table 4.11). The 13 members at the time of its 1995–6 annual report include three women, one black member and seven individuals with business backgrounds. The members of the Corporation as a whole have a considerable record in public service, particularly in terms of board memberships in the housing association and health sectors. There is also extensive board experience in the private sector.

Joining the board – motivation and recruitment

Influences on the prospective member

The public service ethos has, and continues to be, significant in motivating individuals to accept appointment to quangos. Board members on local appointed bodies stated that a desire to serve the community was one of the main factors in their decision to accept appointment. One UDC member commented that he joined the board:

> 'because I strongly support the aims this body has for my native city, and I feel that this role would give me a means of putting something back into my home community.'
>
> (Quoted in Skelcher and Davis 1995: 37)

In the case of more personal public services – for example, education and health – members talk about their own interests. A non-executive on a NHS trust thought the work of the body 'relates to the issues I'm interested in' (p. 37). Parents accept nomination to GM school governing bodies out of a desire to do the best for their children. Such self-interest can also take a more commercial turn. One City Challenge board included the managing director of a major employer who saw his role both as contributing to the regeneration of the area and supporting the growth of his company through the new opportunities for networking that would result. Ashburner and Cairncross's study (1993) found that in the new health bodies non-executives and chairs were most likely to accept appointment because it gave them the opportunity to

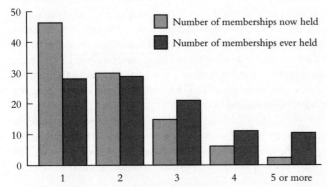

Figure 4.3 Multiple public appointments amongst members of local appointed bodies.
Source: Skelcher and Davis (1995).

exercise the skills and experience gained elsewhere. A similar conclusion was drawn by Thody (1994) in her analysis of business community representatives on school governing bodies.

There is also a wider perspective. Members of quangos are likely to be involved in public life in other ways – perhaps on another quango or the management committee of a voluntary organization. Just over half of all local appointed body members hold more than one concurrent public appointment. For only a quarter of current members is this their first local quango appointment (Figure 4.3). Peter Richards, in his classic study of patronage in British government, observes that appointments to public bodies 'are the result of, or an extension of, activities connected with various voluntary organisations concerned with politics, freemasonry, trade, employment or charity' and sees individuals being 'impelled' towards public service for the same altruistic or selfish reasons that they engage in other voluntary activity (Richards 1963: 254). They are the 'élite volunteers' identified by Ashburner and Cairncross who are 'motivated by a combination of altruism and a desire for personal development' (1993: 365). This has parallels with the analysis of the motivation of candidates for local council by Barron *et al.* (1989). They concluded that candidature is less a deliberate objective and more a process of cumulative drift where individuals who have been involved in other community activities are persuaded to stand for election. Game and Leach (1993) develop this analysis into a model of councillor recruitment, arguing that candidates for elected office have certain predispositions, including a politically active family background, acquired political skills and self-confidence. Their decision to seek election is precipitated by particular events, such as involvement in others' campaigns. There is a crucial difference between the elected and appointed sectors, however. Those invited or persuaded to join a quango would (in most cases) merely be deciding whether or not to accept appointment. Those wishing to become a councillor or MP must (normally) decide to subject themselves to a party selection process which, if they succeed, will enable them to become a candidate in an electoral contest. This will involve the procedures of hustings, canvassing, public presentations and challenge and media coverage. The stages involved in becoming an electoral candidate, therefore, can be seen as a test of the individual's commitment to the particular body in question and to the governmental process in a way that appointment cannot (Skelcher and Davis 1996).

Whether or not the individual is interested in appointment, there are other factors that will influence the decision. Remuneration, which is available from some quangos, can be of considerable benefit to the self-employed. One member, referring to discussions about his possible appointment, observed:

> 'When they said, "And you get paid" – Ah! I had a little computer in my head to work out what the rate per day was. The salary makes it much easier for me [because I am] self-employed.'
>
> (Quoted in Skelcher and Davis 1995: 27)

The membership of an appointed body by an individual employed in the public sector is normally regarded as part of their work activity. This is because they are seen – even if in an informal sense – as representing the organization's interests. Such a representational role is not necessarily one of advancing particular views and policies; rather, membership of the body provides a channel through which the member's own organization can become aware of developments and issues in which it may have an interest. The private sector, too, may decide that a manager's or director's time devoted to appointed body membership is legitimate, although this is tempered by the particular environment within which the individual works. A board member who is also a company chief executive commented:

> 'Overall I probably spend about three hours a week work time and one and a half hours private time . . . I've never had to justify the time but now the company's been taken over maybe I'll have to!'
>
> (Quoted in Skelcher and Davis 1995: 28)

Thody's (1994) study of business representatives on school governing bodies found that some companies encouraged their employees to become school governors as part of its corporate strategy for involvement in the local community. However, there have also been concerns about a few individual companies seeking to influence school policy through their governor-employees. Private sector board members do hold significant positions, being the chair in half of all local appointed bodies (Skelcher and Davis 1995).

The process of appointment

Informality, secrecy and personal contacts have been the hallmark of the appointment process to quangos. Around 10,000 appointments a year are made by ministers to 'recognized' public bodies (Weir and Hall 1994). In the best traditions of the British system of patronage, vacancies have been offered to individuals whose names emerge through soundings with interested parties or appear on the lists of 'the great and the good' compiled by departments of government or the Public Appointments Unit (PAU). The PAU receives 200–300 search requests annually. Given the number of appointments made each year, this suggests that departments also make considerable use of their own sources. *Questions of Procedure for Ministers*, the Cabinet Office guidance on ministerial practice, and the PAU's *Guide on Public Appointments Procedure* advise ministers to consult with either the Prime Minister or the Chief Whip's Office in cases involving major public bodies or those having 'political significance'.

Having reviewed this system as it existed in 1994, Weir and Hall (1994: 17) conclude that it constitutes 'a considerable degree of political patronage, almost entirely unconstrained by the legal order'. They highlight, in particular, that although ministers claim the system is blind to the political affiliation of appointees, in practice it is not. A bigger problem arises with the local quangos that do not come under the NDPB or NHS label – for example TECs, GM schools and further education colleges. These bodies appoint their own members (other than the parents and teachers on GM schools who are elected by their respective constituencies) and are therefore outside the departmental or Public Appointments Unit regime. Public criticism of these appointment systems and the investigations of the Nolan Committee led to some changes from the mid-1990s. Some further education colleges and TECs now have search committees to identify potential board members. Government departments are introducing public advertisements inviting applications for board memberships on the public bodies they sponsored and some housing associations have adopted the same approach (see Chapter 8). The PAU was transferred from the Cabinet Office to the new Commissioner for Public Appointments, Sir Leonard Peach, in December 1995. This implemented one of the recommendations of the Nolan Committee.

However, the system remains relatively opaque. Studies reveal that even where appointment is in the hands of the minister, the body to which the appointment is being made will tend to have significant influence. For example, the first chair of a new quango commented:

> 'I made it clear right from the beginning that I wanted to be able to make nominations [to the Secretary of State]. I wanted to see specific experience that would help [this body]. I also wanted balance across the political spectrum.'
>
> (Quoted in Skelcher and Davis 1995: 35)

In another case, the member had worked as a consultant with a group of managers in the organization. His name was mentioned to the chief executive when a vacancy on the board arose since he had specialist expertise in one area of the organization's work. The prospective member was invited to informal discussions with the chief executive and chair of the board. His name was put at

Table 4.12 Members of local appointed bodies: perceived sources of nomination

Respondents mentioning . . .	Percentage
Chair, chief executive or senior manager of the body	39
Secretary of state or regional health authority	18
Local authority or other local public body	17
Business organization	12
Voluntary or community organization	7
By personal application	7
(Base)	(1,305)

Source: Skelcher and Davis (1995).

the top of a short-list of candidates and passed to the relevant ministry. He subsequently received an invitation to join the board. This experience is not uncommon. Four in ten respondents in the survey of local appointed board members thought that the chair, non-executives or senior managers of the body were the source of their nomination (Table 4.12). It may be, of course, that existing members and their senior managers are best placed to identify the gaps on the board and locate appropriate and willing candidates. This can be particularly important where the board is structured to contain a variety of special interests. Personal knowledge of potential candidates can lead to a degree of sensitivity and subtlety in team-building that is not possible through remote appointment by a minister or an open advertisement for applicants. However, against this should be set the tendency for informal and word-of-mouth recruitment to produce an unbalanced board composition and hence to perpetuate the existing biases in characteristics noted above. One member involved in the selection process observed that 'names were tossed around and people said "We don't want him," or "We don't want her"' (quoted in Skelcher and Davis 1995: 35). Local contacts are also important in finding replacement governors for grant maintained schools:

> The process seems to follow the use of local networks to maintain the character of the original governing body and to secure effective gover-nors in the light of past experience. The head[teachers] and chairs of governors appear to have made nominations for consideration by the rest of the governing body.
>
> (Bush *et al.* 1992: 97)

Ferlie *et al.* (1996: 127) report a similar informal process in the health author-ities and trusts they studied, the main means of recruitment being word-of-mouth 'within which the use of local business connections rated highly'. Although reliance on the personal predispositions and connections of existing board members is one way of gaining new recruits, is not necessarily the best way of constituting and legitimating a governmental body responsible for spending public funds nor of making it accountable to the wider community.

Table 4.13 Recruitment methods preferred by members of local appointed bodies, percentage of members in rank order

	Members appointed by ministers					Members appointed by existing board or other nominees		
	Urban development corporation	Housing action trust	Health authority	NHS trust	City challenge	Further education corporation	Training and enterprise council	Careers service companies
	Local authority nomination (67%)	Local authority nomination (60%)	Open advertisement (70%)	Personal contacts (68%)	Local authority nomination (73%)	Personal contacts (79%)	Personal contacts (88%)	Business nomination (74%)
	Central government nomination (65%)	Election by users (51%)	Personal contacts (55%)	Open advertisement (54%)	Business nomination (70%)	Business nomination (71%)	Business nomination (64%)	Personal contacts (70%)
	Business nomination (46%)	Election by community (51%)	Voluntary sector nomination (41%)	Voluntary sector nomination (37%)	Voluntary sector nomination (70%)	Voluntary sector nomination (48%)	Voluntary sector nomination (44%)	Local authority nomination (65%)
	Personal contacts (42%)	Central government nomination (50%)	Local authority nomination (31%)	Business nomination (32%)	Election by community (65%)	Election by users (47%)	Local authority nomination (42%)	Voluntary sector nomination (41%)

Source: Unpublished data from Skelcher and Davis (1995). Respondents were able to select from a list of ten recruitment methods.

Quango members themselves vary in their preferred recruitment methods (Table 4.13). The lack of enthusiasm for central government nomination amongst UDC, HAT and health members is in marked contrast to their formal appointment by a minister. NHS trust members have a strong predisposition towards personal contacts, which is likely to reflect the way many of them were actually recruited, while health authority members strongly favour open advertisement – the system now being introduced. The mention of election by HAT members again reflects the process employed in order to identify tenant and community representatives whose names are forwarded to the minister for approval. There is also strong support for local authority nomination to HATs and UDCs. Members of these two bodies, it can be surmised, have a stronger sense of the channels that can be utilized to ensure relationships and accountabilities with the local community. Of those bodies not appointed by the minister, City Challenge members' preferences share many similarities with those of UDCs and HATs. Members on TECs, further education corporations and careers service companies have a strong predisposition towards personal contacts and business nomination, perhaps reflecting the background of many of the individuals on these boards.

Quango membership and representative democracy

There is a recurring debate about whether or not the members of bodies making governmental decisions should broadly mirror the characteristics of the population as a whole. The issue concerns the extent to which the age, ethnicity, gender and socio-economic composition of governmental bodies – the House of Commons, local authorities or appointed bodies – should reflect that of the community they serve. One view suggests that personal qualities and skills are more important and that these would be undermined in attempting to construct bodies which mirror the politically significant dimensions of a diverse community. This approach has considerable weight in the quango sector, notably through the emphasis on business appointment. It reflects one of the justifications for the appointed body – enabling particular expertise and experience to be brought to the task of government. From this perspective, government becomes a technical activity that is most efficiently and effectively undertaken by those with specialist qualifications. To do otherwise would be to risk suboptimizing. The alternative argument rests on the belief that a correspondence between the characteristics of a board and that of the wider community would enable governmental decisions more adequately to reflect the views of the population and hence respond to differing values and needs. In addition, some groups tend to be relatively more advantaged than others in gaining access to positions of power, for example individuals from black and ethnic minority communities. Use of the appointment process to create an adequate level of representation would ensure a just governmental process.

The position at the moment is that quango members do not reflect the socio-economic characteristics of the population as a whole. It could be argued that seeking to construct the membership of a public body so that it broadly mirrors the community it serves is impracticable in terms of ensuring that all possible types of individuals are included, and undesirable since ability and a willingness to undertake public duty should be the prime requirements for those holding public office. However, against this should be set the view that members' characteristics tend to shape the values and experiences brought to decision making. Governmental decisions are about determining priorities which affect different groups in different ways, and it is likely that outcomes will be more responsive to the needs and requirements of the community where the board is in some way able to encompass the broad composition of its locality. Wilson and Game explore this point in relation to the under-representation of women on local councils:

> Women are the main users of council services. They make an estimated three-quarters of all calls to council departments. They are the majority of tenants, the family members who make most use of swimming pools and libraries . . . They are likely to have distinctive priorities and agendas.
> (Wilson and Game 1994: 212)

The case, therefore, is that a breadth of experience supports appropriate and responsive decision making in a public service. A more representative board offers a wider set of experiences, values and knowledge from which to draw in making decisions. There are already some indications that quangos recognize this issue: local appointed board members identified 'narrow experience' as the most significant gap in their qualities (Skelcher and Davis 1995: 30). There are also new developments to open quangos to public influence, for example several health authorities have created 'citizens' juries' to help inform them when making significant policy decisions (see Chapter 8).

There is one group that does hold a sizeable proportion of seats on local quangos – members of the business community. The Conservative Government was keen to ensure that they infuse the local appointed sector, claiming that they brought their business and managerial skills to the public sector. They were seen as having an important role in transforming the public service into one which operated in a more competitive environment. However, the assumption that business experience has special value in governmental decisions can be challenged. Priority setting and resource allocation in relation to the needs of the community are inherently governmental rather than managerial activities. There is no requirement that MPs, ministers or local councillors should have special qualifications or experience. Where there is a case for special skills to be included, Stewart and Davis (1994) argue, then the appropriate place to seek them is in the appointment of managers or advisors. If, however, members of quangos are deemed to require specialist expertise then there remains the question of what the appropriate specialisms should be. The emphasis on business skills, for example, overlooks other skills that are important in the public service. These might include the capacity to understand the needs of diverse groups and to develop policies that reflect a wider public interest.

The legitimacy of a public body is also affected by the composition of its membership. For example, the legitimacy of some of the Ministry of Agriculture, Fisheries and Food's sponsored bodies have been challenged because industry members are primarily recruited from larger businesses and thus its decisions and recommendations may not be as responsive to the needs of small business as they might (see Chapter 6). Where a board's membership reflects the characteristics of the organizations or citizens it serves, it facilitates the notion of a pluralistic political system. In other words, the broader the membership of a board the more likely it is that a range of interests will be articulated. This question of legitimacy is particularly important since appointed bodies are relatively closed to public influence yet make decisions with significant impacts on their locality, clientele or the population at large.

However, a discussion of the articulation of interests raises the question of the status of board members. In other words, to what extent are they there to 'represent' – that is, act to advance the interests of – a group to whom they belong or with whom they are associated? Although they are formally required to be independent, it is hard for tenant members of HATs not to present the tenants' perspective. Arguably this is an important part of their role. It is also legitimized through some form of electoral or other open selection process prior to their name being submitted and formally approved by the Secretary of State. But is this also the role of business governors on grant-maintained school boards? Business benefits from the work of these bodies, albeit less directly than tenants do from the activities of the HAT. There is also a clear emphasis on vocationally relevant curriculum in schools. Yet the rationale seems to be that business people are there to contribute skills rather than represent the needs of their community. However, such individuals will have a view on the curriculum and its appropriateness for business which may be presented directly and openly or be expressed through the way in which agendas and debates are shaped. In this sense, they will 'represent' the views of their constituency. Yet formally, business people are appointed as individuals who happen to come from a particular occupational sector. And it is unique for an occupational qualification to be necessary to hold a public office (Thody 1994). But if some quangos are structured to incorporate particular constituencies, then this principle could be applied more widely. This device would ensure that alternative perspectives are aired and decisions reached through wider discussion and debate.

5

Patronage and appointment

The party political affiliation of quango members is the one issue on which speculation has been most rife and hard data the most lacking. In the mid-1990s it was frequently claimed that quangos, in the words of one newspaper headline, were 'packed with Tory placemen'. At the end of the 1970s, similar claims were made with regard to the activities of the then Labour Government. The ability of a government to exercise patronage through its covert and unaccountable appointment mechanisms provides an important source of influence. When that government's style is one of conviction politics – a strong commitment to certain policy lines, a belief in its correctness and a lack of willingness to bend to opposition – appointment provides a means of overcoming resistance by diffusing its supporters into a range of public institutions. In the case of the BBC, for example, O'Malley (1994) documents the way in which the Thatcher Governments of the 1980s grew increasingly critical of what they regarded as a bias against them and, during the Falklands conflict, an unwillingness to abandon impartiality for patriotism. Their appointments to the Board of Governors breached the convention of bipartisanship and were designed, along with deregulation of the broadcasting sector, to bring the BBC into line. The increasing significance of non-elected bodies in the British system of government accentuate the political leverage that can be exercised over policy and programmes through the exercise of patronage. The potential randomness of the electoral outcome is replaced by the relative certainty of appointment.

Patronage is neither a new phenomenon nor one that is constrained to the world of appointed government. In Britain, the allocation of posts and seeking of favour was central to the way the rather limited business of parliamentary government and local administration were undertaken prior to the Reform Act of 1832 and the Northcote–Trevelyan and local government reforms which took place in the second half of the nineteenth century. Such changes contributed to the process of excizing patronage from the allocation of public employment, the governance of local communities and the corrupt awarding of private benefits by public bodies. Other areas of patronage *de facto* have become legitimized. These include political appointments to Cabinet and other posts in government, the honours system and judicial appointments (Richards 1963). Although not without intermittent discussion and debate, such patronage has become institutionalized and is seldom questioned. Although this chapter concentrates on quasi-governmental appointments, it should be appreciated that patronage is formalized in other parts of the British system of government.

Yet, to what extent are appointments to quangos made on the basis of party political affiliation? Information is limited and partial. There are reasonable data on the health service and some national bodies, but little is known about the great mass of quango members' party linkages and predispositions. Consequently debate has proceeded on the basis of the occasional identification of a suspected Conservative supporter – or trades unionist prior to 1979 – and a popular perception that quangos provide a party politically-motivated sinecure for 'the great and the good' in their latter years. This chapter reviews the available data on party political affiliations of quango members and concludes that there are considerable difficulties in demonstrating empirically the extent to which *in general* such loyalties and linkages can be said to be related to their appointment. There are a number of high-profile cases, but generalization from these instances needs to be undertaken with care.

However, a conceptual analysis of patronage reveals a more complex picture than appointment purely on the basis of party political affiliation. The notion of the patronage regime is introduced. This provides a framework for understanding the extent to which the allocation of posts and favours is integrated into society and the various strategies that are employed both by patrons and clients. These strategies – patronism, patron–client and clientalism – reflect differences in the objectives and power-dependency relations of the parties involved. This understanding of different strategies within a patronage regime enables a more sophisticated assessment of the appointed state to be undertaken. It enables analysis to go beyond questions of whether appointments are made on the basis of 'jobs for the boys' and into a consideration of the subtleties of the politics and governance of the fragmented and non-elected state.

Patronage as responsive competence

The concept of patronage has two meanings that are seldom distinguished and often confused. One refers to the process by which those with political influence ensure that ideological or party supporters are allocated key positions in the governmental machine. It suggests a *purposive* private relationship of favour, involving personal or political gain and perhaps with a degree of corrupt or improper practice – 'the selective distribution of material benefits to individuals or small groups in exchange for political support' (Kristinsson 1996: 435). The other meaning concerns the *process* in which a post is allocated – by an individual on the basis of private recommendation rather than public competition (Finer 1952). This does not contain the value-loaded connotation with *motive* suggested by the idea of patronage, but clearly is open to subjective preferences becoming significant. In the employment field, for instance, recruitment and selection practices have sought to ensure equal opportunities by removing the process of patronage and replacing it with public advertising, person specifications and objective interview procedures. The failure to separate *motive patronage* from *process patronage* results in a lack of clarity in almost all the discussions about quango appointments. The confusion of the two meanings leads to an uncritical assumption that a patronage process will inevitably result in a partisan outcome. Process patronage may produce this result, and indeed is more likely to than an open appointments system, but it is not inevitable. Whether it does or not is one of the questions to be explored in this chapter. To aid clarity in the discussion, these two modes of patronage are prefixed where appropriate with the relevant adjective.

The placing of allies through motive patronage acts as a mechanism by which, in theory at least, the development and implementation of particular lines of policy can more effectively be sustained. It facilitates a network of political influence and commitment within government, and between government and other bodies, which reduces the uncertainty of relying on a merit or electoral system for the filling of posts. This is what Peters (1995) refers to as responsive competence. The political and governmental system of the USA provides a good example of this form of motive patronage in operation and, more importantly, of the way in which it is regulated and reconciled with the requirements of sound governance.

Patronage in the USA

Appointment operates throughout the US political and governmental system and is rooted in a widespread patronage politics that developed during the nineteenth century. In this 'spoils system', offices were distributed by the successful president, governor or mayor to those who had supported them in the past or whose support was sought in the future. Consequently, election results were more than just about the success of a particular candidate. They also determined who would occupy the many *sinecures* available, a process that Amenta and Skocpal (1989) regard as in effect a public employment programme. One feature was the appointment of politically sympathetic individuals to key positions in the bureaucracy, commissions and boards and the judiciary, a system that became thoroughly entrenched in the latter part of the nineteenth century.

A number of reforms to limit and regulate the patronage system were introduced during the twentieth century. These applied particularly to politically influenced appointments in the bureaucracy, rather than to boards and commissions – the US equivalent of British quangos. The movement in favour of what came to be known as 'progressive public administration' advocated recruitment of Civil Servants on the basis of neutral competence – their qualifications, experience and capacity to do the job required of them. Merit systems for appointment and promotion began to be introduced, paralleling the Northcote–Trevelyan reforms in the UK. The principle legislation was the Pendleton Act (the Civil Service Act) of 1883 which placed 10 per cent of Federal Civil Service posts under a merit system overseen by a Civil Service Commission. The merit system was extended and now covers some 85 per cent of such posts.

Although the 'make work' features of the spoils system identified by Amenta and Skocpal are not now so evident, the patronage system continues to play a role by providing:

a means of satisfying the demands of the party faithful, and at the same time assuring that an important part of the civil service is strongly motivated towards supporting the President, either out of personal loyalty and gratitude or because they believe passionately in his policies.

(Vile 1983: 209)

However the operation of such a motive patronage system produces a tension between the efficiency gains that should arise from neutral competence through a merit system and the policy benefits of responsive competence achieved by motive patronage. As Peters comments:

Merit recruitment . . . [implies] . . . bureaucrats as value-free administrators of programs who oversee public policies regardless of their intentions or impacts on society . . . Individuals selected by the spoils system were at least more disposed towards the programs of the political party in power.

(Peters 1995: 90)

The contemporary application of motive patronage in the USA, therefore, is closely related to the general problem of securing commitment to government policy. Responsive competence, it is argued, enhances the achievement of political objectives in a complex and fragmented political system built on a 'separation of institutions and sharing of power' (Hague et al. 1992: 316). The idea that motive patronage will enable responsive competence has echoes in the British context. Here, the problem is one of securing control and commitment in a fragmented or hollowed-out governmental system, where public bodies with executive functions have deliberately been created at arm's length to centres of elected political authority. Hoggett (1996) identifies simultaneous centralization and decentralization as one solution to this process, with central agencies controlling the policy framework and resources available to decentralized service delivery units. Alongside this managerial strategy, however, exists the political mechanism of motive patronage. This provides the potential to ensure that board-level decision makers are oriented to advance the specific features of a government's agenda. A precondition is that the members of quangos share political allegiance with the party of government.

The political affiliations of quango members

During the mid-1990s, there were countless press reports and small-scale research studies arguing that individuals with links to the Conservative Party were significant amongst the membership of quango boards at national and local level. *The Financial Times* (1993), in its examination of the individuals who chaired the 40 largest spending quangos, identified eight Conservative Party supporters but no one with known Labour or Liberal Democrat allegiances. These stories echoed those produced in 1977–8 when the then Labour Government was accused of similar party political patronage, including the 180 public appointments held by the 39 members of the TUC General Council (Weir and Hall 1994). The difference between the two periods, however, is that in 1978–9 there appeared to be a greater degree of bipartisanship: in 1978–9, the chairs of the 40 largest spending quangos included three known Conservatives and one Liberal as well as 12 Labour supporters.

Motive patronage has frequently been linked to financial benefit. The *Observer* (1994), for example, ran a story headlined 'Tory peers pile aboard the quango gravy train' which reported that a handful of Conservative peers were drawing salaries totalling more that £650,000 a year from their quango appointments. The inference was that ministers were using their position to provide gainful employment to friends and supporters and, in so doing, were ignoring the qualities of other individuals of a different political persuasion. These questions of motive patronage and financial benefit from quango appointments became associated with the wider concern about 'sleaze' and standards in public life.

A number of studies have sought to gather comprehensive data on the extent of quango members' party political affiliation. Of particular importance is the analysis of NHS and FAS members, work on quango members in Wales and the material collected by Peter Kilfoyle MP and Alan Milburn MP and analysed by the BBC. Following a review of this work, the adequacy of the underlying data is evaluated. Finally, the evidence on the attitudes of board members towards government policy is examined.

Funding Agency for Schools and NHS membership

The extent of Conservative Party influence on quangos was highlighted in the case of the FAS, a body central to the Conservative Government's policy of encouraging GM schools and reducing the power of local education authorities. 'Tories "pack" schools quango' was the headline to a report in *The Guardian* (1994) which noted that of the 12 members, two (including the chairman) were chairmen of companies that had made substantial donations to the Conservative Party in the previous year and another was the former leader of Conservative-controlled Wandsworth London Borough Council (an authority noted for its active pursuit of New Right policies). A fourth member was a prominent Conservative Party worker.

Table 5.1   NHS trust chairs having links with the Conservative Party, 1994

Nature of link	No.
Conservative councillors	22
Party workers/supporters	18
High-level links to companies that have donated to Party funds	9
Former Conservative MPs/Parliamentary candidates	8
Spouses of leading Conservative Party members	5
Total	62

Source: *Independent* (1994).

A few weeks later, The *Independent* (1994) produced an article headlined 'A quangocracy that bulges with Tories'. This included the results of a study of NHS trust chairmen (Table 5.1), drawing on evidence collected by Alan Milburn MP, which found that of the 185 individuals whose backgrounds could be examined in depth approximately one-third had 'clear links' with the Conservative Party. A further 29 NHS trust chairs are 'influential figures within the establishment, such as retired senior civil servants, high-ranking members of the armed services, and spouses of business figures' and thus are more likely to be Conservative than Labour supporters. In contrast, only seven chairs had links with the Labour Party or trade unions and just one with the Liberal Democrats.

This national picture of NHS appointments can be supplemented with a regional analysis based on studies undertaken in the North of England (Robinson and Shaw 1994) and the West Midlands (Davis 1993). Three of the nine health authority chairs in the West Midlands had Conservative Party connections and one had a Labour Party link. In the North of England, one of the eight chairmen was a Conservative councillor and none were identifiable as Labour Party supporters. A similar pattern was evident in the NHS trusts. In the North of England, it was possible to identify three chairs who were Conservative Party supporters but only one who was affiliated to the Labour Party. A separate study of NHS trust non-executives and chairs in the Northern and Yorkshire Regional Health Authority area identified 17 who had political links with the Conservative Party or were directors of companies that made donations to that party, compared with seven Labour and three Liberal Democrats (Labour Research Department/GMB 1994). In the West Midlands NHS region, 22 non-executives had Conservative Party links while only three had a clear affiliation with the Labour Party or trade union movement. In 1996, the NHS Trust Federation published the results of a survey which found that only 14 per cent of non-executives had a political connection. Of those who did, 10 per cent were with the Conservative Party and 4 per cent with other parties (*Health Service Journal* 1996). The survey's methodology was questioned by the Institute of Health Service Management and the Labour Party on the grounds that it merely asked NHS trust chairs to provide details of the 'known political connections' of board non-executives.

Table 5.2 Party political affiliations declared by appointees to NHS bodies, 1995–6

Appointee to . . .	No connection	Conservative	Labour	Liberal Democrat	Other parties
Health authorities	94	43	37	6	3
NHS trusts	323	40	8	6	2
Other NHS bodies	20	1	0	0	0
Total	437	84	45	12	5

Source: Calculated from Department of Health (1996).

The first official data on party political affiliations were published by the Department of Health (1996) in its national directory of the appointed members of NHS bodies. This lists the name of each member, their date of birth, sex, occupation and the postal town nearest to which they live. It also gives details of the political party in which each member is active, if any, for members appointed since July 1995. Retrospective details of political activity were not sought, and therefore the results understate the true picture. Members were asked to indicate whether they had any 'significant political activity', meaning:

> Activities that are a matter of public record such as office holding in, public speaking in support of, or candidature on behalf of any political party (or affiliated body) which fields candidates at local or general elections . . . or elections to the European Parliament.
>
> (DoH 1996: iv)

Twenty-five per cent of new appointees declared a political affiliation, twice as many being to the Conservative Party as to the Labour Party (Table 5.2). What is particularly noticeable, given the political significance of NHS trusts, is the much greater imbalance towards Conservative supporters than those affiliated to other parties. This may suggest that party networks were employed to identify potential members for these bodies.

A Welsh perspective on party affiliation

Party political patronage has been a particularly acute issue in Wales. Here, the Conservative Party's lack of success in parliamentary elections and local council control should be contrasted with their strength in the non-elected sphere prior to 1997. In 1994, David Hanson MP published the results of a survey of approximately one-third of the 1400 appointees to executive quangos in Wales. He found that of the 36 members whose political affiliation could be identified, 20 were Conservatives and 14 were Labour. Plaid Cymru and the Liberal Democrat supporters held one post each. His conclusion was that the pattern of appointments represented the face of the Conservative Party and their supporters rather than the people of Wales. Morgan and Roberts (1993) and Morgan and Osmond (1995) have also examined quangos in Wales and

Table 5.3   Examples of networks of Conservative Party influence on Welsh quangos in the mid-1990s

Individual	Quango positions	Known Conservative Party positions
David Rowe-Beddoe	Chairman, Welsh Development Agency; chairman, Development Board for Rural Wales	Member, Conservatives Abroad Strategy Committee for 1992 General Election; chairman, Monaco Branch of Conservatives Abroad Association
Michael Griffith	Vice-Lord Lieutenant of Clwyd; chairman, Countryside Commission for Wales; member, Higher Education Funding Council for Wales; chairman, Glan Clwyd District General Hospital NHS Trust	Has been active in Conservative Party
Sir Donald Walters	Former deputy chairman, Welsh Development Agency; chairman, Llandough Hospital NHS Trust; member, Development Board for Rural Wales; chairman of the Council of the University of Wales College, Cardiff	President, National Union of Conservative and Unionist Associations
Sir Geoffrey Inkin	Chairman, Cardiff Bay Development Corporation; chairman, Land Authority for Wales	Parliamentary candidate, Ebbw Vale, 1979; runner-up for nomination as parliamentary candidate for Cardiff North, 1983

Source: Morgan and Osmond (1995); *The Western Mail* (1993).

highlight a number of appointments of individuals with clear links to the Conservative Party. These include two parliamentary candidates who were defeated in the 1992 general election, both appointed to health authorities (one as its chair). The constituency secretary to the Welsh Office Health Minister was also appointed to a health authority, but resigned following the protest that ensued. However Morgan and colleagues point to a more significant feature of the Welsh quango scene, the way in which a few individuals with links to the Conservative Party hold key positions on several appointed bodies (Table 5.3). This interlocking network of influence is not unknown in other parts of the UK, nor is it confined to a period of Conservative government. It is the way in which a governing political party can exercise its power to ensure that its philosophy and policies are implemented.

Box 5.1   Factors indicating the likelihood of appointment to public body under pre-1997 Conservative Government

Individuals were more likely to be appointed if . . .

- They were a Conservative Party parliamentary candidate who failed to win a seat at the 1992 general election. Thirty-three quango appointments were given to unsuccessful Conservative candidates compared with three for unsuccessful Labour candidates.

(BBC 1994a)

- They were the spouse of a Conservative MP or peer. The spouses of 24 Conservative MPs and peers were members of quangos, but the BBC identified only one Labour MP's spouse holding an appointment.

(BBC 1994a)

- They were on the board of an FTSE 100 company which donates to the Conservative Party rather than one which does not. Nearly 150 quango appointments were held by directors from Conservative Party-supporting FTSE 100 companies compared with 50 positions held by directors of similar large companies that do not donate.

(BBC 1994b)

- They were a director of a company that donates to the Conservative Party rather than a senior trade unionist in a union that donates to the Labour Party. There were eight quango jobs held among the 282 executives of the top five trade unions compared with more than 300 appointments of directors from companies contributing to the Conservative Party.

(BBC 1994b)

The Kilfoyle/Milburn/BBC study

The most substantial attempt to gain an insight into the party political allegiances of quango members arose from the work of Peter Kilfoyle MP, Alan Milburn MP and the BBC Political Research Unit (BBC 1994d). Peter Kilfoyle and Alan Milburn asked more than 800 parliamentary questions in order to create a national register of quango members. This register, which covers 1500 bodies and contains some 25,000 entries, was analysed by the BBC Political Research Unit in order to identify party connections and multiple memberships. Their findings identify some of the differential party political linkages of appointees (Box 5.1). The BBC analysed quango memberships held by directors of individual companies that both donated and did not donate to the Conservative Party (Table 5.4). The number of cases considered is small and the extent to which they are representative of the wider population of companies is not ascertainable. However, when taken with the other data discussed

90 The appointed state

Table 5.4 The relationship between quango membership and company support for the Conservative Party, 1994

Contribute to Conservative Party	Do not contribute to Conservative Party
Hambros, the merchant bank The chairman of Hambros, Lord Hambros, is the Treasurer of the Conservative Party. Both he and the bank have donated to the Conservative Party in recent years. Lord Hambros and seven of the other sixteen board members also hold quango positions.	*The Co-op Bank* The bank does not contribute to the Conservative Party. No board members hold quango appointments.
Marks & Spencer Donates to the Conservative Party. Sir Derek Rayner, former managing director of Marks & Spencer, recruited by Margaret Thatcher in the early 1980s to lead campaign against waste in central government. Directors hold 12 quango appointments between them.	*The Body Shop* The company does not contribute to the Conservative Party. No board members hold quango appointments. Founder Anita Roddick, a successful businesswoman, has never been approached to be on a quango.
Kingfisher (Woolworth's parent company) The company contributes to the Conservative Party. The twelve directors hold five quango appointments between them.	*Iceland, Waitrose and Debenhams* These companies do not contribute to the Conservative Party. No directors hold quango appointments.

Source: BBC (1994b, c).

above it raises the question posed by Weir and Hall (1994) of whether the Conservative Government appointed business people who also happened to be Conservative Party supporters or Conservative Party supporters who also happened to be business people.

The attitudes of board members

While political party membership tells us something about the general ideological predisposition of quango members, it is important not to treat political parties as if they were unitary organizations all of whose members subscribed to a single agenda. British political parties contain numerous divisions and factions which can result in substantial differences of opinion. Consequently, board members' attitudes and beliefs towards government policy are more significant indicators of their propensity to demonstrate responsive competence than party political affiliation. In appointing boards to the first-wave NHS trusts, for example, an informal process was used to identify potential chairs and non-executives who had business expertise and were committed to the 1990 NHS reforms

(Ashburner and Cairncross 1993). This selection process is reflected in the finding that 87 per cent of chairs of NHS bodies and 73 per cent of non-executives thought that the internal market would make the NHS more efficient, compared with only half of board-level executive directors (Ferlie *et al.* 1996). The study also identified strong support for other elements of the then Government's policy towards the NHS. Such support within NHS boards, together with the successful shift to the NHS internal market, meant that by the mid-1990s, the agenda changed to one of consolidation and the need for ardent ideologically committed appointments was reduced. Consequently a number of the early high-profile chairs were not reappointed. One of these, Roy Lilley, commented:

> 'We [the first-wave] chairs were prepared to put our heads above the parapet and I think by and large we have delivered a very tricky political agenda in a very awkward environment. I am very sorry that the first wave trust chairs have largely evaporated. There is a feeling now that radicals need not apply.'
>
> (Quoted in Crail 1994: 13)

Just as it was necessary to anchor the membership of the first-wave NHS trusts firmly to government policy and ensure success, so too with other agencies, for example, the FAS.

Interpreting the evidence

These data illustrate that Conservative Party supporters or senior executives in companies that donate to the party were, prior to the 1997 general election, more likely to be offered appointments than Labour Party supporters or senior trade unionists. The available evidence from the pre-1979 Labour Government suggests that the converse applied then. Quangos, therefore, can be viewed as a sector over which the government of the day uses its power of appointment in order to gain advantage, extend its influence and achieve responsive competence. Appointment to boards is a politically contested space. This finding should not surprise any student of politics or government. However, a key change has taken place since 1979 – the growth in the number of non-recognized bodies whose boards typically appoint their own members. Like the self-perpetuating vestry boards of the nineteenth century, the existing members of a further education corporation (to take one example) may fill vacancies in a way that ensures a predominance of one party's supporters regardless of changes in government at national level. Ministers have no direct control over the membership of that body and thus the already obscure pattern and extent of motive patronage become further concealed. The problems created by such self-appointing and self-perpetuating bodies, so graphically exposed in Charles Dickens' novels, were one of the key reasons for local government reforms in the nineteenth century. The local non-recognized bodies of the 1990s are resurrecting that problem.

It is also important to consider the adequacy of the data on which the conclusions about motive patronage by ministers are based. The most difficult problem is identifying the political affiliations of the individual members of quangos. Typically, researchers have used two methods. One is to take the names of known party members or supporters and see whether these appear amongst the list of quango appointees. This was one of the methods used in the BBC study. The other approach is to piece together a biography from secondary sources such as *Who's Who* or its local variants, newspaper directories and other databases. This can be a rather difficult and unrewarding affair for a number of reasons. First, the individual may not be listed at all either because they do not have sufficient status or because they prefer not to be included. Secondly, there may be no way of confirming whether the 'Susan Jones' who is a member of a particular quango is the same person as the 'Susan Jones' listed in *Who's Who*. Thirdly, only significant party positions will tend to be included – for example, 'secretary of local Conservative association' but not 'Conservative voter and fund-raiser'. Even significant positions may be excluded by the individual on the grounds of privacy. Finally, only a small proportion of the adult population are members of a political party. Therefore researchers using secondary sources will only ever be able to identify the political allegiances of a very small proportion of quango members. For these reasons, as well as the practicalities of researching large numbers of names, attention has focused on the chairs of quangos. Individuals in these roles will devote more time to their duties than ordinary members, will have a closer relationship with the executive directors and will be more involved in policy development. Consequently, their impact on board decisions is likely to be greater. It remains to be seen whether the impact of the Nolan recommendations and the Commissioner for Public Appointments changes the picture as far as data on political affiliations of NDPB members is concerned. The publication of information on members of the non-recognized bodies is likely to remain problematic.

The mechanisms of patronage

The use of motive patronage to ensure responsive competence and ideological compatibility across the divides of the contemporary public service has considerable appeal. Although the data on political affiliations are partial, it appears to have considerable veracity when considered in terms of bodies having a high degree of political salience – for example, the first-wave NHS trusts. However, demonstrating that there is a tendency for the governing party's members and affiliates to be over-represented on quango boards or showing that certain quango members strongly support a particular ideology tells us nothing about whether this resolves the problems of responsive competence, compliance and regulation faced by the centre. In order to do this, it is necessary to investigate the institution of motive patronage itself and the various mechanisms through which it operates. This analysis is assisted by employing the concept of the patronage regime to describe a situation where motive patronage is institutionalized in a society. Exchange and resource dependency theory are then used to explore the individualized patron–client relationships that develop within such a regime. This forms the basis from which to develop more robust conceptualizations and explanations of the dynamics of patronage and to introduce the ideas of clientalism and patronism.

The patronage regime

Patronage can be considered a form of institution since it comprises 'a set of formal or informal rules which structure social action and are shared within a particular organisation or community' (Lowndes 1996: 193). Institutions are meso-level phenomena which form 'part of the broad social fabric but [are] also the medium through which day-to-day decisions and actions are taken' (p. 182). Motive patronage, therefore, is conceived as a logic of action in the wider society. It sets a constitutive framework which 'define(s) the nature of actors and their capacity for action' (Scott 1994: 61). Motive patronage as an institutional form may be more or less integrated into a society and hence susceptible of or resistant to other forces. Eisenstadt and Roniger (1984), for example, make a distinction between patronage as the dominant way in which a society operates and its manifestation as an 'addendum'. In the latter case it develops in the interstices of the dominant institutional form and may or may not be legitimated by it. Returning to the earlier discussion of the British system of government, for example, motive patronage in the second half of the twentieth century could be regarded as an addendum within certain distinct fields – Richards (1963) highlights Cabinet selection, honours and life peerages. Where motive patronage becomes institutionalized we can talk about a *patronage regime*. The nature of the patronage regime will affect the way individuals and groups operate, shaping 'the construction of trust, . . . the structuring of the flow of resources, . . . exchange and power relations and . . . [actors'] legitimacy in society' (Eisenstadt and Roniger 1984: 164). The evidence regarding quango members' selection and appointment, party political affiliation and attitudes to government policy suggests that motive patronage has become institutionalized and that this field can be regarded as a patronage regime.

The patronage regime can be conceived as offering a number of strategies in the relationship between patron and client. One is the patron–client relationship in which a negotiated pattern of mutual ties and obligations develops from the need to exchange resources. In the case of quangos, ministers and other appointers (the patrons) would provide benefits to board members (the clients) in return for their support. Patron–client relations are not the only form of relationship available within a patronage regime. Theoretically, there are other strategies by which appointers can seek to secure the commitment

Table 5.5   Strategies within a patronage regime

Strategic orientation	Patronism →	Patron–client ←	Clientalism
Characteristics	Patron (actual or potential) co-opts clientele	Provision of resources by patron against future normative obligations on client	Clientele co-opts patron and/or gains legitimization as patron's primary client
Elements of strategy	• Personalized and informal offering of a gift • Construction of member's task as managerial or technical and at arm's length from party politics resonates with individual's values	• Necessity of exchange • Asymmetrical distribution of resources creates power dependency relationship • Informal and individualized contract between patron and client	• Client seeks to be seen by patron as representative of wider constituency • Client conveys ability to deliver on patron's intentions
Motive	Maximize patron's utility	Long-term symbiotic relationship	Maximize client's utility

and compliance of quango members. Two possibilities can be identified – patronism and clientalism.

- *Patronism* involves a patron (or potential patron) seeking to gain advantage either by creating a clientele or by having an existing clientele transferred to them. Here the motive of the (potential) patron is to co-opt others into what is apparently an exchange relationship but where the distribution of benefits is significantly weighted towards themselves.
- The alternative is *clientalism*. This has two forms. The first is where actors seek to reposition themselves from being the potential to actual clients of a patron. In other words, actors desire to enter into a clientalist relationship in order to maximize their utilities within a patronage regime. The second form of clientalism is where actors become recognized and legitimated as the primary clients of a given patron. This notion adapts Peters' (1995) discussion of *clientela* relationships whereby an agency accords an interest group the status of representative of a sector or community (Table 5.5).

This strategic framework provides a richer understanding of the nature of motive patronage in relation to quangos than is possible from purely seeking to identify party political affiliations.

The patron–client model

Although motive patronage is institutionalized in society, it is manifest and maintained through individual relationships. These consist of essentially informal normative agreements arising from the need to exchange resources in a situation of differential power. The argument takes this form. An individual controls only a proportion of the resources they need to satisfy their needs. The required resources are controlled by another who, in turn, wishes to obtain some of the resources held by the first party. In order to satisfy both individuals' needs, an exchange of resources takes place. Typically, resources are differentially distributed. Consequently, one of the parties will be more dependent on the other and there will be a power imbalance (Blau 1964). It is in this context of asymmetrical resource dependency that a mode of patronage based on informal social obligations develops. This takes the form of a relationship between a powerful patron and a dependent client. The patron controls resources and dispenses these as favours to the client. In return, the client offers loyalty, or a more tangible resource such as money, or may undertake a particular service for the patron at some point in the future.

Patron–client relationships have been central to the governance of traditional and developing societies. They have also been identified in developed nations, for example 'city bosses' in the USA. Here, key political figures have maintained their electoral support in two ways. Firstly by acting as brokers to facilitate the resolution of particular problems faced by electors, and secondly through the allocation of jobs, contracts and other benefits to this clientele (Freedman 1994). This process bears some comparison with practices in England in the Hanoverian period prior to electoral reform in the mid-nineteenth century. Then, 'electoral patronage was an indispensable method for distributing office and allocating power' (O'Gorman 1989: 250). The election was the point at which the parliamentary candidate would provide or promise favours to the electors in return for their support. In all these settings, patron–client relations evince a number of common characteristics. In addition to the individualized nature of the exchange relationship, these include a reliance on informal and essentially interpersonal understandings and their unconditionality – in the sense that the normative obligation may not be reciprocated for some considerable time. It is this highly institutionalized structure of norms and mores surrounding the patron–client relationship that hold the key to its significance:

> Exchange in patron–client relations is constructed . . . in such a way as to combine access to crucial resources . . . with promised reciprocity, signs of good will, elements of force and respect, solidarity and interpersonal obligations.
>
> (Eisenstadt and Roniger 1984: 250)

Individual relationships, therefore, are structured by the norms and logics of the patronage regime in which they are set.

Securing commitment by quango boards: the patron–client model assessed

The central problem in applying the patron–client model to the case of quangos is the notion of resource exchange since, with the exception of the special cases considered below, membership of an appointed body does not give an individual significant access to scarce resources. Resources can be considered at three levels:

- *tangible resources* such as money and material goods;
- *relational resources* such as access to key individuals, networks and information; and
- *symbolic resources* such as status and recognition.

Taking the issue of tangible resources first, individuals appointed by a minister to an executive NDPB or NHS body are normally eligible for remuneration. The level depends on the particular body in question. For local quangos, this is typically around £5000 per annum for an ordinary member and £15,000 to £20,000 per annum for a chair, the latter based on two days work per week. At national level members will normally receive significantly more, depending on the body in question (Cabinet Office 1996). Such remuneration is relatively insignificant in the context that members, in the main, are already employed or self-employed and frequently are senior figures in business or professional occupations. This is reflected in their attitudes to the honorarium. In studies of NHS non-executives, for example, six in every seven said that it had not been a factor in their decision to accept appointment (Ashburner and Cairncross 1993). Payment is only important in the case of self-employed individuals whose income would otherwise suffer. These data suggest that individuals are not motivated to seek or accept appointment as a means of gaining tangible resources. Indeed the study of NHS members and that by Davis and Skelcher found that interest in the body's work, a wish to contribute skills and expertise and a sense of public duty were their main motivating factors.

The high proportion of business people on appointed bodies, a trend encouraged by recent Conservative Governments, does raise the question of whether membership enables them to gain access to relational resources – contacts inside government opening the door to commercially sensitive information, contracts, and the like. There have indeed been a number of cases where members' interests were not declared and questionable procedures have been followed in allocating contracts (Public Accounts Committee 1994; Shattock 1994). Future opportunities for board members to gain commercial advantage will be constrained following the imposition of mechanistic and procedurally-driven approaches to probity, corporate governance and self-regulation such as those arising in the context of the Nolan enquiries (Chapter 8). Nevertheless, membership of a quango does provide new opportunities for networking and this may be important in terms of shaping or identifying future business opportunities.

Finally, there is the question of symbolic resources – the recognition and status that may arise from membership of an appointed body. This will undoubtedly be important for some individuals. Yet members of appointed bodies frequently are involved in a number of other public duties. Ashburner and Cairncross (1993: 364–5) found that around half of all non-executives on health bodies were involved in voluntary work and thus categorize these appointees as "'élite volunteers" or "active citizens" . . . motivated by a combination of altruism and a desire for personal development' and for whose help the health service is in competition with other areas of public service and voluntary activity. The additional status is likely to be marginal given the existing commitments of these active citizens.

The evidence, therefore, does not support the view that board membership offers appointees significant access to scarce and desired resources. Given the characteristics of members, the benefits of appointment are limited and therefore it can be concluded that the extent of any exchange relationship with the appointer is marginal. This limited nexus for the exchange of resources undermines the second aspect of the patron–client model, namely its assumption of an asymmetrical power distribution in which the client is in the dependent position and consequently obligated to accede to the patron's demands and requests. Indeed, it could be argued that if there is resource dependency it is the patron who is reliant on the client since the growth of government by appointment has created some difficulties in recruiting sufficient qualified individuals and ensuring their regular attendance when other pressing duties call. Such issues of scale create difficulties in terms of the third element of the patron–client model, since it is not feasible in general for appointees and appointer to have a personal relationship around which are woven ties of normative obligation. There are, for example, more than 4000 appointments to NHS bodies. It is certainly the case that chairmen of key national and – to a lesser extent – local quangos work in close relationship with their sponsoring minister, but it would be hard to see this as a patron–client relationship. The analysis, therefore, broadly reflects the conclusion reached by Doig in his review some twenty years ago that 'public bodies are not *in general* fertile grounds for . . . petty fiddling and political favouritism' (Doig 1977: 90; emphasis added). The evidence does not suggest that pure patron–client relations are evident. However, there are alternative formulations which have stronger empirical support.

The strategy of patronism

The strategy of patronism provides a variant on the standard patron–client model. It contains two main strands. The first involves the construction of the invitation to accept appointment as a 'gift'. Indeed, even the language of government reflects this – appointments to public bodies are formally described as being 'in the gift of the Minister'. The second is the apparent depoliticizing of the quango's purpose and work.

The gift constitutes a social mode of exchange, in contrast to the market-oriented exchange examined in the patron–client model. It is a special form of exchange because:

> seemingly, it is non–utilitarian and disinterested. At the same time, it is highly structured and based on relatively elaborated and specific rules of reciprocity.
>
> (Eisenstadt and Roniger 1984: 33–4)

Gifts help reinforce conditions of trust and solidarity and facilitate broad obligations for interaction within a social group. Through the gift of an appointment, therefore, the patron invites the individual into a social group which apparently is not hierarchically ordered but, rather, collegial. The patron does not dominate the clientele but is *primes inter pares* – 'first amongst equals'. Rather than the patron and clientele having separate interests which can only be met through asymmetrical exchange, patronism encourages a sense of integration, unity and singularity of purpose. Board members typically remember the receipt of the invitation to serve – the gift – with surprise, pride and pleasure. The sense of having been noticed and being asked to contribute places them immediately in a conducive position *vis-à-vis* the appointer. Two of the interviews conducted by Skelcher and Davis (1995) reveal this:

> 'I was brought up in [the area] and have a love for the region and if my peers felt my property and financial experience could help I was delighted to become involved.'
>
> (Member, urban development corporation)

> 'I was flattered to be asked . . . everything about the organisation felt good. And the services of the organisation relate to the issues I'm interested in.'
>
> (Non-executive, NHS trust)

A similar picture emerges from Barnett and Curry's research into the appointment of Marmaduke ('Duke') Hussey to the chairmanship of the BBC Board of Governors. They report Hussey describing the story in the following terms:

> 'I was quietly sitting at home one night, and the telephone rang. Someone said "Is that you, Dukie?" and I said "Yes". "It's Douglas Hurd here." "Oh," I said, "How nice," or words to that effect. I'd known Douglas for quite a long time, but we were acquaintances not close friends. He said "Are you busy? Are you alone?" I said "I'm quite alone, my wife is out at the opera" and he said, "Well, I've rather an odd request to ask you: would you like to be Chairman of the Governors of the BBC?" I replied, "You must be mad," to which he responded "I don't think you understand. I am the Home Secretary and I'm offering you this job on behalf of the Prime Minister." '

Barnett and Curry continue in their own words:

Hussey was given 24 hours to decide, and endured a sleepless night wondering what he would be taking on. He was under no illusions . . . but the approach was flattering and the allure too great to resist. The next day he phoned Hurd and said: 'Alright Douglas. I think we've made a ghastly mistake, but if it's really what you want me to do, I'll do it.'

(Barnett and Curry 1994: 39)

The offer of the gift of appointment invites a positive response by the recipient and is reciprocated through altruism and a willingness to defer to the judgement of the patron – at least with regard to their choice of individual. The informality and personalization of the approach encourages a bond between the individuals and facilitates the creation of a sense of shared enterprise. This is not to say that the appointee and the patron will continue to have a marriage made in heaven. Differences of view may appear, and the patron – if they are a minister – could well be replaced in a government reshuffle or election. However, the starting point of the relationship is one in which the patron has first-mover advantage and is able to co-opt the appointee towards his or her agenda.

The second element of patronism – the depoliticizing of the body's work – is also important in facilitating a unity of interest between appointer and appointee. The structuring of the quango's business in terms of technical rather than political rationalities casts the appointee in the role of functionary administering the delivery of services. The dialogue, therefore, may be conducted in the language of technical problem-solving rather than political and ideological value choices. In the health service, for example, the reforms of 1990 were designed to emulate a business model. Small boards of executive and non-executive members replaced the larger corporatist bodies that included health, local authority and other interests:

The object was to create bodies significantly different from their predecessors. The language signified changes . . . – from authorities to boards, from managers to executives, and from members to non-executives – signifying the intended shift of culture and values.

(Ferlie *et al.* 1996: 127)

Weir (1996: 28) draws a parallel in his discussion of the Housing Corporation's grant allocation role, commenting that 'quasi-governments inherently make policy issues technical'. The paraphernalia of the new public management – service specification, contracts, performance measurement, priority setting – reinforce the technical overlay on what in reality are some deeply political questions. Yet it is into this environment that appointed members are introduced, and while they may ponder the deeper issues these have no part of their day-to-day role as board members. Like the independent regulatory commissions in the USA and nationalized industries in Britain, quangos have been designed – in theory if not in practice – to be autonomous from the current of day-to-day party politics. Their arm's-length structure gives them the necessary

Table 5.6 Members of local appointed bodies – perceptions of party political independence

Perception	Mean level of agreement or disagreement*	
	Chairs	Other non-executive members
In general, non–executive directors see themselves as being independent of any political party	2.6	2.2
Greater political debate would benefit the work of this body	–2.2	–1.6

Range: +3, strongly disagree; –3, strongly disagree.
Source: Skelcher and Davis (1995).

distance – or so their proponents would argue. This perspective is conducive to board members since they tend to have a strong self–identification as being independent of and not wishing to engage in party politics. Research on members of local appointed bodies reveals a high level of agreement with the view that they are politically independent together with a lack of willingness to see this situation change (Table 5.6). Indeed, when members of local appointed bodies who were not also councillors were asked whether any factor had discouraged them from standing for electoral office, the most common response – given by half of all respondents – was a dislike of politics (Skelcher and Davis 1995). They perceive their position as one that transcends party politics and in this sense bring a flavour of the non–party, independent councillors formerly widespread in British local government. As one NHS non–executive commented (quoted in Skelcher and Davis 1995): 'I represent a standpoint – patients' rights.'

The strategy of patronism, therefore, operates at two levels. In the first place, the process of offering the gift is undertaken in a personal and informal way that conveys a sense of the patron valuing the recipient and inviting them into a collaborative relationship. Secondly, the substance of the gift resonates with the recipient's values – it is altruistic public service but involving technical/managerial questions apparently distanced from the messy and uncomfortable world of party politics. These combine to place the patron in a position of relative advantage, at least until the appointee either feels that they have reciprocated the obligations created by their acceptance of the gift or determines to take an independent line.

The strategy of clientalism

Clientalism provides the counterpoint to patronism. It involves an individual or group seeking to co-opt a patron and to be legitimized as that patron's primary client. Although there is a convention that quango members are appointed as individuals rather than to represent particular interests or organizations, a number of these bodies have boards structured to incorporate certain constituencies. Housing action trusts have a proportion of seats reserved for tenants and residents of the locality affected by the body's operation, while a number of quangos sponsored by the Ministry of Agriculture, Fisheries and Food have categories of member representing the interests of growers, employees, manufacturers and others.

Although the board structure is segmented, appointed members are expected to adopt a corporate perspective and not merely advance the particular interests of their constituency. Further education college governors, for example, are warned that they should 'not speak or vote at meetings as if delegated by the group they represent' and neither should they be 'bound by mandates' (Further Education Funding Council 1994: para 8.10). Despite this, the inclusion of certain organized interests will inevitably give 'their' members a particular perspective on issues and decisions before the board. They are legitimized by virtue of becoming part of the constitutional structure of the board. By implication, other voices are excluded. A consequence is to enable these represented interests to gain the possibility of moving into a clientalist relationship with the government department to which the quango is allied. In some cases, the recurring pattern of appointments produces de facto a representation of particular interests and the exclusion of others. Hall and Weir (1995) have interpreted the composition of the Horticultural Development Council in this light (see Chapter 6). They argue that the organizations with whom ministers consult in order to identify appointees from the industry tend to be dominated by large growers and individuals already networked with the department. Consequently the needs of smaller growers are less well represented on the Council. The picture, therefore, is of a policy community becoming formalized in the organizational structures operating in the appointed sector. Similarly Marsh's (1992) work on youth employment policy illustrates how the creation of the MSC, despite its tripartite board consisting of business, trade union, local authority and educational representatives, put the peak bodies from which they were nominated in a privileged position compared with voluntary organizations, youth bodies, individual trade unions and others.

The clientalist relationship can develop between the quango and other bodies, as developments in the urban regeneration field illustrate. Here the reduction in local authority expenditure has stimulated a climate in which these bodies develop a strategy of clientalism in relation to centrally funded quangos such as UDCs. In such a situation, Coulson (1993: 32) argues, 'the UDC becomes the patron, with the resources. The local authority is the client with the ability to develop and implement projects, if finance is available.' Similarly the creation of contractually-based public funding of the voluntary sector has stimulated these bodies to move into a clientalist relationship with local authorities, a process motivated by the economic imperatives of exchange. Yet the process of developing such a patron–client relationship in a situation where resources are asymmetrically distributed is couched in the dialogue of partnership and mutuality with its inferences of equity (Lowndes and Skelcher 1998).

Unlike patronism, clientalism is a direct function of limited and unequally distributed resources. The ability of the putative client to convey a 'can do' message to the patron, and to be able to realise this promise in practice, will place them in a position of relative advantage against their competitors. Being legitimized as the representative of a wider group will strengthen their position. Consequently patrons may fail to perceive that self-interest rather than loyalty is the motivating factor in their client's behaviour.

Conclusion

This chapter has explored the place of motive patronage in the British political system. It identified patronage as a purposive activity designed to secure responsive competence by quango members through the appointment of individuals who shared a political allegiance to the government of the day. The place of such political placement is significant in the governmental systems of the USA and Britain since in both nations motive patronage is one solution to the problem of securing control and commitment by government centrally over a fragmented and hollowed-out environment of public organizations. There is, of course, an alternative solution which is increasingly utilized. This is the explicit performance-based contractual relationship between the centre and the quango (Ferlie et al. 1996) (see Chapter 1). However, these procedural systems still involve questions of discretion and interpretation by the agents in the relationship. The appointment of ideological and party political supporters to board positions provides one strategy through which ministers can retain a degree of confidence that their policy objectives will be implemented.

But to what extent are members of quangos affiliated with the government of the day and support its policies? The evidence indicates that, at least until the 1997 general election, individuals associated with the Conservative Party were more likely to be appointed to quangos than those affiliated with other political parties. A number of key posts were held by significant Conservative supporters. Independently of party affiliation, research amongst NHS body chairs and non-executives reveals a strong level of support for the 1990 reforms. However, showing ideological affiliation does not reveal the mechanisms by which motive patronage secures responsive competence. The concept of a patronage regime – the institutionalization of the norms and structures of motive patronage – enables a richer form of analysis to be conducted around the strategies of patronism, patron–client relations and clientalism. The strategy of patronism, through which ties of social obligation are built around the gift of appointment, has a particular value in understanding how the problem of responsive competence is managed in the appointed sector.

6

The governance of quangos

Appointed government has grown, in part, because of the reform of the public service. Removing activities from the realm of party political debate and electoral contest and placing them in fora from which the public are normally excluded appears to offer the prospect of quicker, more efficient and technically sound decision making. The appointment of non-executives with business expertise reinforces this image. However, just as the private sector's governance has been exposed to scrutiny, so too has the public sector's. Issues originating in the appointed sector have had a major contribution to the process of re-examining the standards of conduct and ethical stance found in public institutions. It has led to a concern with corporate governance:

> the procedures associated with the decision-making, performance and control of organizations, with providing structures to give overall direction to the organization and to satisfy reasonable expectations of accountability to those outside it.
>
> (Hodges *et al.* 1996: 7)

One of the constraints to strengthening corporate governance in the appointed sector is that the work of quango members is shrouded in mystery. Little is known about their activity during and outside board meetings, their interaction with officials, stakeholders and other interests, the dynamics of the chair–chief executive relationship or processes by which decisions are reached. In contrast, there is a substantial literature on their counterparts in elected government. Copious studies have documented the working lives of MPs and councillors, and have observed and interpreted their roles, relationships and power. In many respects the published material on quango boards and their members is similar to that which is available on private sector boards and their directors – evaluative and prescriptive but lacking a solid base of empirical research (Pettigrew and McNulty 1995).

This chapter examines the governance of appointed bodies, focusing in particular on the processes and structures of direction and decision making. Initially, board members' patterns of activity are reviewed. This involves an exploration of their three main roles – the personal contribution of an independent view and expertise, the internal governance of the organization and the external relationship with users and stakeholders. Then the operation of the board is considered, including cultures of decision making, the role of the chair, questions of conflict and dissent and board linkages to special interests. The third part of the chapter discusses the relationship between non-executives and senior managers, with a particular examination of the NHS boards in which, unusually for the British public service, executive and non-executive members share the authority for decision making. Finally, the involvement of the public in the decision processes of quangos is considered.

Board members: patterns of activity

Job descriptions for non-executive members of quango boards are still rare. Guidance is published on the characteristics and qualities of persons deemed suitable for selection, but little detail is provided about the role they are expected to fulfil once appointed. Such statements as are made tend to place emphasis on the independence of non-executives with respect to outside interests. They are there to be concerned with the corporate body as a whole rather than to 'represent' the views of a particular group, even if their seat is specifically reserved for individuals from a given sector, e.g. non-private sector directors on TEC boards (Box 6.1). This can pose some role tensions for individual board members. A staff governor on a further education corporation commented:

> 'Very recently the governing body approved a code of procedures . . . and ethics . . . For instance: "Board members undertake to subordinate sectional concerns in the interests of the college as a whole." This effectively prevents me from representing the interests of staff [who elected me] and has also created difficulties when I have attempted to publicise my perception of events at [staff] meetings.'
>
> (Finch 1994: 14)

In the absence of a role specification, an understanding of the activities of board members will relate to their structural position in the organization. The role of the strategic apex in any sector can be defined as managing the organization in relation to its environment. In the public sector, this involves questions about the policies to be pursued and services to be delivered in the context of demands, issues and expectations in society and relationships with other

---

Box 6.1   The member's individual contribution – examples of guidance

From *Guide for Members of Governing Bodies of Universities and Colleges in England and Wales*:

> Members nominated by particular constituencies should not act as if delegated by the group they represent. No member may be bound, when speaking or voting, by mandates given to him or her by others except when acting . . . as a proxy for another member.
>
> (Committee of University Chairmen 1995, para 4.14)

From *Guide for College Governors*:

> Governors nominated by particular groups should not speak or vote at meetings as if delegated by the group they represent . . . no governor may be bound by mandates given to him or her by others. Each governor must take a view on each matter coming before him or her on the merits of the issue in hand. The strength of the governing body will depend on the quality and variety of individual contributions made to its discussions by each governor.
>
> (Further Education Funding Council 1994: para 8.10)

---

agencies. The board, therefore, will be undertaking internal as well as external activities. In addition, however, non-executives are appointed to contribute their skills and knowledge. This provides three role categories: the personal role; the internal role; and the external role.

Making a contribution: the personal role

The case for appointing non-executive directors to private sector boards emphasizes their potential ability to take an informed yet independent view of the company and to contribute their ideas and experience to the board's discussions. Cannon, for example, comments that:

> [non-executive] directors stand back to provide an independent view of the firm . . . [and those] with particular expertise or knowledge will often be expected to contribute this to the firm's operations.
>
> (Cannon 1994: 144)

Similar themes pervade the world of quangos. In this respect, the non-executive board member is there as an informed lay-person able to bring views, insights and experience to bear on particular public policy decisions. Unlike the MP or councillor, they do not have an explicit political agenda to realize or a manifesto against which their performance may be judged. To the extent that

Table 6.1 Members of local appointed bodies – involvement in board activity by position on board

How involved do you feel in the following activities?	Mean level of involvement*	
	Chairs	Other non-executives
1 Personal role		
Contributing skills and knowledge	2.7	2.4
2 Internal role		
(a) Strategy Development		
Influencing strategy	2.7	2.0
Setting board agenda	2.7	1.1
(b) Performance monitoring		
Monitoring performance	2.6	2.1
Determining standards of conduct	2.3	1.6
(c) Understanding the organization		
Contact with managers	2.6	2.0
Contact with other staff	2.1	1.5
3 External role		
(a) Contact with users	1.8	1.4
(b) Discussions with community	1.7	1.1
(c) Discussions with other agencies	1.8	1.2
(Base)	(194)	(1270)

*Minimum = 0; maximum = 3.
Source: Skelcher and Davis (1995).

they are assessed, it is likely to be in terms of their personal contribution to the debate and acceptability to key stakeholders.

Evidence of the extent to which board members do contribute their skills and experience is sparse. Skelcher and Davis asked non-executive members of local appointed bodies to score the extent to which they believed they brought their expertise to bear. Members overall returned a high score, while chairs reported making a greater contribution than ordinary non-executives (Table 6.1). It is likely that this result overstates the reality due to the methodological problems inherent in self-reporting as a research technique. However, the relative newness of many of the bodies at the time of the research together with the specific appointment of business people to introduce change suggest that levels of contribution are still likely to be high. Chumrow's (1995) observations on the way in which tenant members of one HAT board contribute their particular experience and understanding support this view. Such evidence should not automatically lead to the conclusion that all members are able to contribute their skills and experience, nor that they can do so in all situations. There are a number of structural features which act as constraints. Emmerich and Peck (1992) identify one when discussing how the private sector domination of TEC boards can result in the marginalization of any voluntary sector members. The culture of board decision making will also affect members' ability to perform their personal role. The Warwick study of NHS bodies notes a tendency to 'over-cohesion and groupthink' (Ferlie *et al.* 1995: 382). This may be compounded by the chair being significantly more involved in the board's business than the non-executives, together with the considerable organizational support available to that post-holder. A chair who leads the board and a board that operates by consensus and cohesion is likely to result in non-executives' contributing considerably less of their own skill and experience than might otherwise be the case.

Strategy, performance and understanding: the internal role

The internal role of the non-executive has three components – contributing to corporate strategy, performance monitoring and understanding the organization. Table 6.1 scores the involvement of non-executive members in local appointed bodies against each of these.

Contributing to organizational strategy
The first role involves contributing to organizational strategy, a standard function of boards in public and private sectors and part of the rational management model often prescribed for them. Chairs report a considerable role in strategy development, to a much greater extent than ordinary non-executives. This is not unexpected, as Briggs' (1979) study of the BBC's Board of Governors and its chairmen shows. What is particularly noticeable, however, is the limited involvement of ordinary members in setting the board's agenda and hence influencing the items which arise for discussion and decision. Control of the organization's formal and informal agenda is a source of considerable structural power which chairs may exercise, sometimes in collaboration with the executive (Pfeffer 1981). The Warwick study of health bodies, for example, reported on the 'filtering' of agendas:

> Agendas are discussed and decided before Authority meetings among the executive team and/or between the chair and the [chief executive]. Some items . . . never come to the authority at all. In other instances, the executives reach a consensus before the full authority meeting and thus discussion is largely between the non-executives and the lead executive member in the form of a question and answer session.
>
> (Cairncross and Ashburner 1992: 23)

The contrast between chair and ordinary non-executive member involvement is reflective of their different responsibilities and the extent to which they are involved in the organization's activities. The mean time commitment of chairs of local appointed bodies is 46 hours per week, compared with 26 hours for ordinary members and almost one-third of respondents thought that they were spending more time on their duties than they expected (Skelcher and Davis 1995). The amount of time that board members are willing and able to devote to their duties will shape their ability to contribute to strategy development and the other roles. One UDC member commented:

> 'You tend to roll up once a month to board meetings. I always read the papers and try to work out ahead of time what's happening. I will occasionally ring an officer. But I have not been willing to make the step and devote a lot of time and energy . . . I'm not willing to spend eight or ten hours a week to get into the organisation and learn all the issues.'
>
> (Quoted in Skelcher and Davis 1995)

A TEC director noted the problem of competing demands for what can be seen as a marginal commitment:

> 'Board members all have major responsibilities running their own companies, so at any meeting probably eight or nine of the sixteen directors will be there. And maybe three or four of these will be at the next meeting. This is a damaging condition for any organisation because you can't get the continuity of decision-making that ideally you'd want.'
>
> (Quoted in Skelcher and Davis 1995)

This problem is also revealed in a study of TEC boards (Vaughn 1993). In 50 per cent of cases studied, between one-half and one-quarter of directors were absent from the last formal meeting. It is likely that TECs face this particular problem because their board members are required to be selected from individuals holding senior positions in other organizations and who therefore have considerable demands on their time. In the NHS significant absenteeism rates were identified as a problem during the 1980s but this seems to have been resolved since the 1990 reforms (Ashburner *et al.* 1993) which introduced smaller boards and clarified roles within the internal market.

Although members report varying degrees of involvement in strategy development, other research suggests that this may not be a large part of their total role. It will tend to be occasional and spasmodic, and primarily concerned with commenting on, and responding to, strategy proposals developed by officers or executive members. For example, TEC directors have tended to focus on concrete operational issues and the steering of initiatives originating with staff or outside the organization rather than the development of an overall strategy (Crowley-Bainton 1993; Haughton *et al.* 1995b) while NHS non-executives were:

> probing, questioning proposals coming to them from the executives, and even sending them back for reconsideration. They are not however involved in an early stage in the formulation of strategic options.
>
> (Ferlie *et al.* 1995: 388)

This conforms to the pattern discerned in studies of private sector boards. Here, directors appear to spend rather less time on matters of grand strategy than the

classic model of board roles and functions would suggest (Mintzberg 1983).
Pettigrew and McNulty conclude that:

> [non-executive directors] find it much easier to say no – to prevent
> things from happening, to express negative influence, than to initiate and
> determine positive influence.
>
> (Pettigrew and McNulty 1995: 861)

Monitoring managerial and organizational performance

The second element of the internal role is the monitoring of managerial and
organizational performance, part of what Mintzberg (1983) terms the 'control
role' of the board. One aspect of this role is a concern with standards of
corporate governance and the conduct of the chief executive and senior managers (Cannon 1994). In theory, it is here that the independence of non-
executives from executive directors is important, enabling a degree of impartiality in the assessment of performance and behaviour against aspirations and
ethical standards. Chairs and non-executives both reported considerable involvement in performance monitoring (Box 6.1). This is supported by
Levačić's (1995: 36) work on school governing bodies, where she found that
the most common model was the 'advisory governing body . . . [which]
provided a forum in which the professionals report back to laity and are
responsive to their views'.

Performance monitoring tends to take place in a passive mode. Peck's
(1995) observational study of a NHS trust at work found that 84 per cent of
meeting time was taken up with receiving and approving reports from executive
directors while only 5 per cent was behaviour described as 'challenging'. This is
not to say that there is an absence of debate and discussion, but that the non-
executives on the board are structurally and culturally constrained to operate in a
reactive mode. This is hardly a good basis from which to undertake performance
monitoring, a role which requires a degree of initiating and investigative behaviour. The tendency to responsiveness is not confined to the boards of
quangos. Studies of private sector boards of directors reveal similar modes of
operation. Mintzberg suggests that it arises from a coincidence of interest between the executive élite and non-executives. This negotiated order, in which
the non-executives implicitly agree not to look too closely at the performance of
the executives, functions to ensure the smooth running of the business:

> Too many decisions deferred to the board raises questions about the
> ability of top management to run the organisation. And too many deci-
> sions overturned by the board raises questions about its confidence in the
> top management. And so *board approval of management decisions and perfor-*
> *mance under normal circumstances tends to be a foregone conclusion.*
>
> (Mintzberg 1983: 78, emphasis in original)

This commonality of interest will be strengthened by the social ties of loyalty
and cohesion that develop in the small group that the board comprises. The

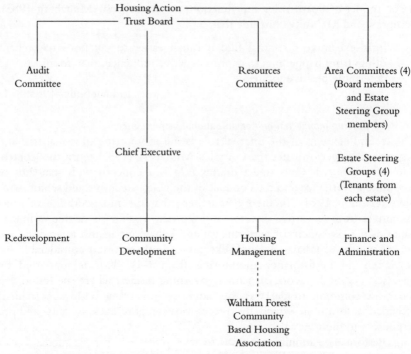

Figure 6.1   Board structures in the appointed sector: the example of Waltham Forest HAT.
Source: Adapted from National Audit Office (1997c).

exception to this general rule is where a block of board seats is reserved for users who are able to organize and operate as a coherent subgroup, as in the case of HATs. This incorporates into the board a clearly articulated set of external interests who have the potential to bring a degree of detachment to the process of performance assessment.

Understanding the organization
The third internal role for the non-executive is to gain an understanding of what is really happening in the organization. Pettigrew and McNulty (1995: 860) comment on the need for non-executives 'to be able to roam beyond the boardroom if they are to have the relationships, informal information and perspective to influence events in and around the boardroom'. Chairs reported strong and ordinary non-executives moderate to strong levels of contact with managers and – to a lesser extent – other staff (Table 6.1). A considerable amount of this contact will be at board meetings, the main focus for members' contact with the organization. However, boards may also have subcommittees, working parties or members' seminars at which contact with employees – and possibly users – will occur (Figure 6.1). The small size of some quangos offers

members the prospect of relatively easy contact with staff at senior and middle levels in the organization. Operation within a clearly defined local patch also helps. In some GM schools, for example, there is frequent informal contact between governors and staff, although this can also result in the former becoming too involved in day-to-day management (Bush *et al.* 1992).

Relating to stakeholders: the external role

The external role of non-executives concerns the relationship with stakeholders outside the organization where, in comparison with their internal contacts, both chairs and ordinary non-executives have more limited involvement (Table 6.1). One aspect of the external role is contact with users or citizens, a role more commonly seen as part of the elected politician's responsibility. There are some important variations between different types of appointed body. Seventy-two per cent of HAT members report having some or a great deal of contact with users and 69 per cent with the community more generally. This is because their agency has a specific task related to the needs of a geographically well-defined and often well-organized group – public housing tenants – who are also members of the board itself. Tenants are also, in the main, the local community. In contrast only 34 per cent of further education governors report some or a great deal of contact with users and 20 per cent with the community (Skelcher and Davis 1995). This reflects the changing composition of governing bodies and an absence of forums which bring together the college governors with students, other service users and the wider community. Prior to the incorporation of colleges in 1993, some of these external linkages were undertaken by local education authority governors acting as the representatives of the community. The NHS reforms also removed local authority nominees from district health authorities, although this erosion of community linkages was intended to be moderated through the nomination by the regional health authority of two 'community directors' on each Trust board. Ferlie *et al.* (1995) found that the individuals appointed to this position experienced a lack of understanding as to the nature of their role. A particular problem is that 'community directors' lack any legitimacy or formal context within the locality and thus no clear basis from which to offer a 'community' view – if such a thing is possible. This role ambiguity is noted also amongst GM school governors even though some of those have been elected by parents.

Attention, therefore, is directed towards the absence of mechanisms through which appointed governmental bodies and the community interrelate, a problem solved in elected government by direct election of members on a locality basis and the operation of political parties to channel and negotiate particular concerns and demands. Members of local appointed bodies, however, do not themselves want more contact outside the organization. Only one in eight of the non-executives desired greater involvement with users (Skelcher and Davis 1995). This suggests an important difference between appointed and elected members. Contact with individuals and groups outside Parliament and the local authority is the life-blood of most MPs and councillors. It provides the data and understanding necessary to contribute to the governmental process, as well as being essential to their problem-solving and cause-promotion roles. They are in the organization and also part of the community. Appointed members *qua* appointed members, however, are only in the organization – with the few exceptions where there are community-nominated directors on the board. Emmerich and Peck's (1992: 90) observation that TECs are neither 'born of, (n)or integrated into, their local communities . . . but imposed from outside, from above' can be generalized to most other quangos and has repercussions in terms of non-executives' perceptions and behaviour in their external role. This is not to argue that quango members as individuals are insulated from the community. They are active citizens engaged in other fora – societies, associations and so on. However, unlike the MP or councillor, they are essentially private individuals. Their role is invisible to the wider community and they are not the focus of the processes of influence to which their elected colleagues are subject.

The second component of the external role reflects the interagency environment within which quangos and other public and private bodies operate. Questions of resource dependency and alliance building are important factors in the selection of non-executives for private sector boards of directors. Mintzberg (1983) notes how board appointments are a means to secure the co-option of key external interests and gain access to networks. This feature is identified in the study by Haughton *et al.* of TEC relationships with their external stakeholders. They argue that although board members are not chosen in any formal sense to be representatives of a particular group, their selection from a class of organization is associated with an 'implicit or even explicit assumption that they can reflect the concerns of [that] sector' (Haughton *et al.* 1995a: 25). As a result 'they were expected to provide a ready channel of communication to the wider community' (p. 25).

Such incorporation of external sectors onto the board is one explanation for the low level of member contact with agencies and stakeholders revealed in Table 6.1. The other is that such interaction is undertaken primarily by officials rather than non-executives. Managers meet and liaise with their opposite numbers on other bodies, involving board members only when necessary. Indeed, in the case of TECs external stakeholders saw the chief executive and other managers – and not the board members – as the first point of contact on strategic and operational matters (Haughton *et al.* 1995b). Advisory groups of stakeholders at sub-board level are also important in this process. TEC subgroups typically cover industry sectors, particular client groups or other issues. Thomas (1994) estimates that in the case of one London TEC between 20 and 30 local authority officers are involved at this level. There are also regular liaison arrangements between about two-thirds of local authorities in England and Wales and their TECs. Thomas found that authorities in general were satisfied with these arrangements, but thought that they were rather limited in scope. Similar consultation and liaison activities have been undertaken by TECs with organizations representing business and the voluntary sector. Such arrangements, of varying degrees of formality, are found in other types of quango and reflect the fragmented institutional environment within which they operate. This is much more the domain of the officer, however, with non-executives being drawn in only at key points.

Boardroom behaviour

The boardroom is the focus of the appointed members' world. Lacking the party political and constituency arenas of the elected politician, the boardroom becomes the principal forum in which the appointee's role is played out. Non-executives bring with them expectations, preconceptions and experiences. Board members may have backgrounds in the private, public or voluntary and community sectors, and hence contrasting ideas about the processes by which decisions should be reached and the values that should be brought to bear. They will have different levels of expertise which may or may not overlap with those of senior managers. Some will be more committed than others to the agency or a particular policy. These individual variables are brought into play in the context of a small group with its own particular dynamics, structures and culture.

Cultures of decision making

The culture of decision making on appointed bodies is strongly influenced by members' perception of themselves as being non-party political. Despite the exercise of party patronage by governments, appointees have a clear and strong perception of themselves as independent of political structures and loyalties (Table 5.6, see page 100). They see their position as one which transcends party politics. Consequently, and in contrast to elected government, appointed bodies exhibit a consensual style of decision making where caucusing and voting are largely absent. The predominant norms are 'politeness, consensus and conformity' which in turn constrain challenge to the chair (Ferlie *et al.* 1995: 386).

The achievement of these norms at full board level is relatively easy. The board is a small group, typically comprising between ten and twenty members, and is the main point at which members meet *qua* members. Unlike elected bodies, there is no substructure of party political meetings in which to carry on the business of the body. Neither is there an institutionalized opposition or adversarial form to meetings. Consequently, members tend to arrive at each meeting afresh, facing an agenda shaped by the chair and executives. This makes the expression of dissent problematic. Board meetings – like full council meetings and the House of Commons – are often the points at which decisions and agreements are ratified rather than policy developed. One trust non-executive illustrated this by comparing the influence he was able to exercise at the formal two-monthly board meeting with that at the single topic seminar held in the intervening period:

'I think the board meetings are about as boring as any committee meetings. There are about 17 items on the agenda and the expectation is that
you go through pretty quickly – you know, "If you've got any problems
talk to so and so later" . . . [But] the seminars are where I've really been
able to make a contribution. They provide a greater opportunity for
debate and influence than board meetings.'

(Quoted in Skelcher and Davis 1995)

The seminars enable detailed discussion of single issues – hospital closure, local
pay arrangements, quality monitoring, and so on – unconstrained by the conventions of the formal board meeting. This is not to suggest that contrary views
do not emerge at board meetings. There may be real policy differences between members. The characteristics of the members will also be significant. A
TEC director observed that the business background of members contributed
to some lively meetings:

'There is spirited debate at board meetings – but obviously not as much as
if we contrived a leadership and opposition. But as with any group –
especially of people used to running their own businesses – disagreement
emerges.'

(Quoted in Skelcher and Davis 1995)

Overall, however, the appointed bodies are ones where the culture of decision
making tends towards a more concensual and accommodating style than is
possible in elected bodies in the UK. Where disagreements do emerge, they are
more likely to be on matters of personal values than party line. The absence of
political structures enables members to take an independent line. The cost is
that they come without the briefing and background available to elected politicians as a result of party mechanisms and the lobbying to which they are subject
due to their public status.

The model of the independent, non-party political quango should not
lead to the conclusion that it is *apolitical*. Executive quangos make governmental decisions – they allocate public resources and make decisions about the
incidence of costs and benefits. These are essentially political choices since they
rest on judgements about values which affect the wider community. As the
membership structure of quangos has changed so the ways in which these
decisions are made and the values considered relevant have become contested.
Briggs (1979: 20) observes this in his examination of the changing composition
of the BBC Board of Governors, commenting that they 'cannot escape the
influences of their own background, education and occupation. They bring to
broadcasting their own conception of society and the "national interest" '. The
desire to incorporate onto quangos business and, in some cases, user and
community interests affects the value base of these bodies. Some public bodies
sponsored by the Department of Transport and the Ministry of Agriculture,
Fisheries and Food are specifically designed to introduce the consumer
perspective through the appointments mechanism. Likewise, City Challenge

Table 6.2   Decision-making styles in various sectors

Organization	Typical decision-making style
Voluntary sector	Consultation with volunteers, staff and users
Local authorities	Party political group and committees; relatively open to public influence; multiple decision criteria
Local appointed bodies	Closed to public; members independent of political party and community mechanisms
Business sector	Closed to public; focus on organizational survival and growth; emphasis on speed of decision making using small number of criteria
Community organization	Open to influence; factions emerge and reform
Central government	Ministerially driven; relatively closed to public view

Source: Skelcher *et al.* (1996).

boards bring together individuals from the private, public and community sectors. These members bring their own preconceptions about the culture and processes of decision making – about the 'right' way to make a decision and about the values that should come into play (Table 6.2).

Significant tensions can be generated as public sector and private sector cultures come into contact. Some have reached national prominence through resignations of chairmen and board members of national quangos, NHS trusts and further education colleges and investigations by the National Audit Office, Audit Commission and Public Accounts Committee. Crowley-Bainton's study of TEC directors, who are all senior managers in significant businesses, highlights the particular adjustments they need to make:

> For most TEC directors, the role of non-executive is a novel one. They are used to playing an executive role in their own organisations and many are not experts in training or local economic development.
>
> (Crowley-Bainton 1993: 7)

A further education corporation governing body chairman, referring specifically to the period immediately following incorporation, illustrated the problems facing the new 'independent' governors recruited from the private sector:

> 'What was decision making like? Initially diabolical! It was almost impossible to get a decision out because they [the new governors] had all been brought up in the "one page of A4 and five minutes to make a decision" school. They hadn't the experience of making decisions when there's 18 of them in a room and they can't dictate the answer.'
>
> (Quoted in Skelcher and Davis 1995)

Other appointees from the private sector have highlighted what one termed 'difficulty with the concepts', in particular that the board is managing public assets with which it is not free to do as it pleases.

Community and voluntary sector board members find that they have to work in a bureaucratic environment which may be unfamiliar to them and places them at a disadvantage in relation to other board members and managers. This is particularly significant in urban regeneration quangos, for example HATs and City Challenge, where the body has a time-limited brief to deliver benefits to a specific locality. Such community directors can find themselves bearing the weight of residents' high expectations about what the board can deliver. Their accessibility to the public is considerably greater than other non-executives because they live locally and are normally elected by residents or voluntary organizations. Consequently they are subject to rather different stresses and strains:

> 'I don't care if I'm elected again because there's a lot of hard work – meeting after meeting [*said with resigned air*] and sometimes you think "Is it worth it?" The flak is unbelievable. And you think "What the hell is it all about?" And even after City Challenge goes we're going to get it – because we're living here!'
>
> (Quoted in Skelcher and Davis 1995)

This again creates an imbalance on the board, most members not having to live with the human effects of the decisions they make or be directly accountable to their neighbours and community for their actions. This directness of the accountability in such boards leads to what Hickson *et al.* (1986) term *sporadic* decision processes – a protracted sequence of events with intermittent delays, negotiations and obstacles in which:

> [participants] enter a twisting trail that will not end for a year or two or even longer. As they make their way along it they will come up against all sorts of obstacles that delay direct movement towards a conclusion . . . They will be drawn into bursts of activity in corridors and offices, in between the delays, when . . . answers to questions are demanded.
>
> (Hickson *et al.* 1986: 118)

The nature of such sporadic processes can cause considerable frustration to board members who arrive with a commitment to immediate and tangible benefits for the community. The management of these tensions is one that requires accommodation by the rest of the board and its managers as much as by the community.

Chairing the board

The role of the chair is particularly important in the operation of quangos. Chairs devote more time to the organization than other non-executive board members and may be remunerated accordingly. A deputy chair may also be appointed. The chair will have the administrative resources to support them in their role and, unlike the other non-executives, will be involved in the day-to-day business of the organization. Critically, the chairman will normally form a close link with the chief executive. One member of a NDPB commented:

> 'The chief executive and the chairman are close. The chief executive will be briefing the chairman all the time. The chairman is the one who will be handling the major issues – seeing the Minister, putting pressure on the Treasury, fixing things with the [central] government department.'
>
> (Quoted in Skelcher and Davis 1995)

This is a pivotal relationship for the organization and can develop into a strong partnership as both individuals – in their different ways – exercise leadership in the organization. Organizational policy may be formulated in the discussions between chair and chief executive and subsequently presented to the board. Consequently the non-executives are more likely to be in the flow rather than the vanguard of policy development. The power of the chairman/chief executive pairing can result in other board members feeling excluded or marginalized. Their backbench Parliamentary and local council colleagues at least have meetings of the party group in which to discuss some proposals prior to decision, although in this setting too the exercise of power involves the element of surprise and the absence or partial nature of consultation. Board members do not have the same opportunities for prior discussion – except where special members' seminars are held. The chair–chief executive partnership, therefore, is one of the factors that contributes to what Pettigrew and McNulty (1995: 857) term a *minimalist* board culture in which 'a set of conditions have been deliberately created to minimise the impact of part-time board members on the direction of the [organization]'.

Some chairs are appointed to initiate change. Marmaduke Hussey, appointed chairman of the BBC Board of Governors in 1986, started his period of office at a time of tension in the Corporation's relationships with the then Conservative Government. His remit was to change the style and philosophy of BBC management to bring it into line with the enterprise culture (O'Malley 1994). This led to a number of personnel changes at senior levels, including the appointment of John Birt as Director General. Under the banner of 'Producer Choice', Birt introducing elements of the new public management into the BBC including devolved budgets, cost-centre management and contracting out. Sir Christopher Benson was appointed as the first chair of the FAS because of his experience in chairing other high-profile and politically contentious bodies, notably the London Docklands Development Corporation. Similarly, the chairs of the first wave of NHS trusts were carefully selected enthusiasts for the reforms introduced by the Government. The chief executive may or may not be supportive of the policy or the chairman's line, but will have no doubts about the choices open to them. Equally, the chairman will know that the relationship with the chief executive is an important one, unless other partnerships with senior executives can be developed. The situation here is analogous to that of the incoming minister or local authority leader having goals that require compliance on the part of the bureaucracy.

Conflict and dissent

Unlike competitive politics with its open and institutionalized opposition (both within and between parties), conflict and dissent on quango boards rarely surfaces or enters the public realm. The maldistribution of information and other key resources between the chair and executives, on the one hand, and ordinary non-executives, on the other, together with the forces of small group cohesion and groupthink, ameliorate the recognition and open expression of tensions. Ferlie *et al.* (1995: 387), referring to the health boards they studied, comment that some exhibited a culture 'that was so homogeneous and punitive of dissent that an individual had to be extremely brave to launch a challenge'. On occasions, however, significant policy differences emerge and sometimes these reach the public arena. The BBC Board of Governors has, on recent occasions, divided over changes planned for the Corporation, including re-scheduling of popular programmes such as 'Woman's Hour'. At Stratford Grant-Maintained School, Newham, differences of view within the governing body about school policies and the extent to which governors could intervene in management resulted in a series of public disputes and legal actions. These difficulties were only resolved after the Secretary of State appointed two additional governors, the chair resigned and parent governor elections altered the balance of power on the body.

In other situations, the board finds itself in conflict with outside bodies, including those regulating or funding its activities. Here, resignation on a point of principle is the member's final sanction. One example comes from the Arts Council. In the early 1990s, the Arts Council went through a difficult period in its relationship with the Department of National Heritage (DNH), its sponsor and the source of its funding. DNH appointed consultants to report on the role and operation of the Arts Council, required cuts in its administrative and overall expenditure and gave a cool official reception to the Council's arts strategy. This coincided with a funding crisis for the four London orchestras and the Arts Council's proposal that in future it would fund only two of these. In June 1993, Lord Rix resigned from the Arts Council. He argued that the arm's-length principle, under which the government left the Arts Council to formulate its own policies and spending priorities, had been undermined. There were further resignations from the Arts Council's music advisory panel, again on the issue of government interference in policy and funding (Taylor 1995). More recently, the chair of another DNH-sponsored body – English Heritage – threatened to resign in protest at cuts in government funding. On the same day, the Heritage Secretary invited him to extend his term of office for at least a further three years (*The Guardian* 1996). These tensions and resignations are a function, in part, of a changing relationship between government and the quangos directly under its control – bodies established as quasi-independent agencies to undertake particular tasks but then faced with reduced funding. The resignations, however, also illustrate the commitment that board members can develop to the policies of their institution and the extent to which they are prepared to act as principled individuals rather than government place-men.

Member linkages with special interest groups

Principles of probity and good governance in the public service cause weight to be placed on transparency of decision making. While well established (if occasionally overlooked) in Parliament and local government, the Committee on Standards in Public Life discovered that this principle has not been applied universally within the quango sector. A recent study of the membership of ten national executive quangos raises questions about the dual loyalties of business members of quango (Hall and Weir 1995). Two of the cases considered were the FAS and the Horticultural Development Council.

The first members of the FAS, responsible for funding and regulating GM schools, were appointed in February 1994. There were several interconnections between individual members and other bodies having an interest in GM schools. The chairman of the Agency was also chairman of Sun Alliance, a major insurance company that underwrites Grant-Maintained Schools Mutual – a not-for-profit insurance scheme for the GM sector. The chairman of this

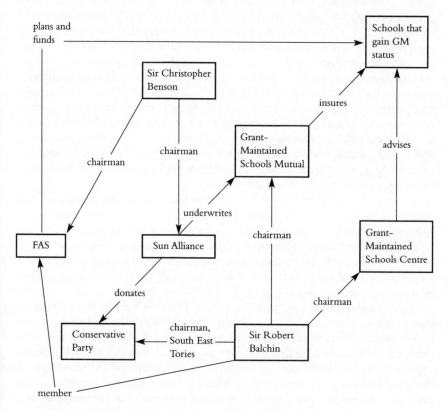

Figure 6.2 Business connections of FAS members.
Source: Adapted from *Independent* (1994).

insurance scheme was, in turn, chairman of the Grant-Maintained Schools Centre which promotes and advises on opting out. He was also a member of the FAS. There were other linkages involving the Conservative Party (Figure 6.2). There is no suggestion that the individuals involved will gain personally from this interlinkage of governmental and business activities. Rather, the example raises questions about the nature of the relationship between governmental agencies who have a responsibility for funding and planning the GM sector and other bodies with a commercial interest in the growth of the sector. There is an intermeshing of public and private interests which limits the transparency of decision criteria and, potentially, the ability of FAS to act against commercial benefit. In this sense, the composition of the body seems to constrain the principle of independence that underpins much of the case for quangos.

The case of the Horticultural Development Council also illustrates the relationship between appointed members' backgrounds and interests and those of the body's clientele. This Council is responsible for financing research programmes and is funded from a compulsory levy on growers having an annual turnover of £25,000 or more. Hall and Weir's analysis of the eleven grower-members of the Council (there is also provision for representation by employees and a marketing specialist) suggests that the interests of larger growers predominate and that mechanisms to enable small growers to influence the Council are relatively ineffective. Many of the large grower members are also current or past members of Horticultural Trade Association committees, a body to which – according to an Electoral Reform Ballot Services poll – only a small minority of growers belong. Hall and Weir conclude that this pattern of representation arises because government will tend to appoint figures who are active in the industry and who, by their membership of the trade association, will be networked with the relevant ministry. The effect of such an appointment strategy is to create an unbalanced body and one which has been 'captured' by a particular section of the industry.

A number of propositions can be developed about the impact of such dual loyalties. One is to say that it makes no difference and that members of appointed bodies leave their 'outside' interests outside the boardroom. In other words, members act as independent decision makers in a governmental role even if this adversely affects the organizations with whom they are related. A second view would suggest that these linkages shape the values and perceptions of members, influencing the way in which they interpret information and weigh the judgements they come to make. They are part of the experience they bring to the board, along with their educational, class and occupational background. The influence on decisions is subtle but nevertheless real. The third proposition is that the influence is more direct and that the use of appointees as a channel for the organization to communicate externally, as discussed above, is reciprocated by outside interests gaining favoured access to the body. Members with linkages to special interests thus become part of a stable policy community which, over time, develops shared views about issues and strategies in the sector (Rhodes and Marsh 1992).

Table 6.3 Comparison of the resources available to chairs, non-executives and executives in quangos

Resource	Chair	Non-executives	Executives
Time	Significant part-time; full-time in larger quangos	Part-time	Full-time
Tenure	Subject to renewal	Subject to renewal	Permanent, although renewable fixed term contracts now more common
Support	Normally has own office and secretarial/ administrative support	Little	Resources of their department
Background	More likely to have business background; may have some experience on other public bodies	More likely to have business background; may have some experience on other public bodies	In public service; may have professional or technical specialism in their area of responsibility

Relationships with managers

Quango chairs and non-executives, along with their Parliamentary and local authority counterparts, rely heavily on the organization's managers for advice, information and the implementation of decisions. The relative resources available to members and managers can lead to a position in which board members do little more than agreeing the executives' recommendations (Table 6.3). This concept of the 'dictatorship of the official' (Newton 1976) is one familiar to the world of elected government. In recent years it has been investigated by the Committee on Standards in Public Life, the Public Service Committee (formerly the Treasury and Civil Service Committee) and the Widdicombe Committee on the Conduct of Local Authority Business amongst others. It is also found in discussions about the pre-1990 health authorities, which were sometimes castigated as devices for 'rubber stamping' proposals driven by the powerful professional interests in the NHS. Haywood and Ranade (1985), for example, identified a strong propensity amongst health authority members to be loyal to staff. These members, who they termed 'patriarchs', demonstrated particular allegiance to senior managers – the group of staff with whom they had most contact and on whom they were most reliant for intelligence about the organization, its services and its performance.

The survey of local appointed bodies reveals that ordinary non-executives thought they had a significant influence on decisions, but overall were neutral on the question of whether a lot of the board's work concerned 'rubber stamping' the executives' recommendations. Chairs, as might be expected from the discussion above, took a much stronger view of their influence

Table 6.4   Members' attitudes to board decision making, by position on the board

Attitude	Mean level of agreement or disagreement*	
	Chairs	Other non-executive members
Non-executive directors (governors) have a major influence on decisions	2.1	1.5
A lot of the board's work is rubber-stamping managers' recommendations	−0.7	0.1
(Base)	(195)	(1267)

Range: +3, strongly agree; −3, strong agree.
Source: Skelcher and Davis (1995).

and disagreed – although not to any great extent – that they were 'rubber-stamping' (Table 6.4). There was, however, considerable variation between non-executives from different local boards. For example, two in every three TEC and City Challenge members felt that they were 'rubber-stamping' executives' recommendations. The structural context for these agencies provides one explanation. TECs and City Challenge operate within relatively rigid and bureaucratic frameworks set down by central government. A large part of the TEC's role is to be the delivery agent for central government-funded training activities, in pursuit of which they must abide by the Operating Agreement and other policies and procedures imposed by the DfEE. City Challenge has a similar set of constraints imposed by its action plan, specified output targets and Treasury-imposed spending profile. In these settings, managers will be presenting recommendations to the board over which the agency has little choice. Ferlie *et al.* (1996: 157) present an alternative explanation based on the negotiated relationship between executive and non-executive members of the board. Their survey reveals that the executive members generally agreed with the statement that 'they would not put proposals forward if they thought that the non-executives would find them unacceptable'. This suggests that executives see the non-executives as a group whose approval they need to gain in order for strategic decisions to be made, perhaps reinforcing the norms of collegiality discussed earlier.

It is important, however, to recognize that the board meeting is just the concluding stage of a longer process of policy development and decision making. Member seminars, informal discussions and the support of the chair are all strategies through which the executive are able to exercise their power to shape the agenda and predisposition of non-executives. And at the board meeting in NHS bodies there is a lack of distinction between the executive and non-executive classes of member. As one health non-executive observed:

'Besides the Chairman and the five non-executive and five executive members there are normally three or four other senior managers there.

We all sit round a big table. I have not felt any real distinction between them. We all seem to play an equal role.'
(Quoted in Skelcher and Davis 1995)

The participants in the formal decision process at board level therefore extend beyond the members of the authority – the eleven nominated individuals. In numerical terms, local NHS board meetings tend to be dominated by executives.

The post-1990 NHS bodies, and some other quangos to a lesser extent, demonstrate a distinctly different approach to decision making than has been the norm in the public sector. They breech the formal distinction between policy and administration that has been a long-standing convention within the British public service. This convention, which holds that policy is the preserve of politicians and administration of officials, has been maintained as the cornerstone of practice, despite the empirical difficulties of drawing a clear dividing line between these two concepts. Considerable effort has been devoted by government and Parliament to clarifying and codifying this relationship, including reports by the Treasury and Civil Service Select Committee, its successor the Public Service Select Committee, the Widdicombe Committee on the Conduct of Local Authority Business and memoranda and guidance from the Head of the Civil Service. All have concluded that the separation of political and official roles should be maintained in central and local government.

The design of the current NHS bodies unifies political and official roles at board level. The non-executives on these boards are 'members' in the familiar public service mould but the executives are a hybrid. They are paid officials who are also full members of the board. This produces some complexities in the accountability relationship: the Secretary of State appoints the chair and non-executives who themselves appoint the executives. It is unclear who takes responsibility in a position of policy failure or poor decision making. The comings and goings from NHS boards provide no clear answer, although the indications are that it is the chair and non-executives who are likely to bear most of the responsibility. They, anyway, have less to lose than the salaried executives. One recent illustration comes from the case of Morriston Hospital NHS Trust in south Wales. In 1996–7 the Trust faced a £3 million deficit. Plans for fifteen redundancies, including those of two consultants, were announced. Eight of the redundancies were in the geriatrics department, which was shortly to be closed and transferred to a neighbouring hospital. Consultants at Morriston passed a vote of no confidence in the Trust's chair and chief executive and called for their resignation. Under pressure from the Welsh Office and local health authority, the Trust board withdrew the redundancies pending further talks but also expressed their support for the chair and chief executive. Eleven of the Trust's clinical directors subsequently gave notice that they would not undertake administrative duties. The chair of the board and four of the five non-executives then resigned. Shortly afterwards, the chief executive took annual leave and subsequently left the Trust. In a move designed to restore the support of medical professionals at the hospital, the Welsh

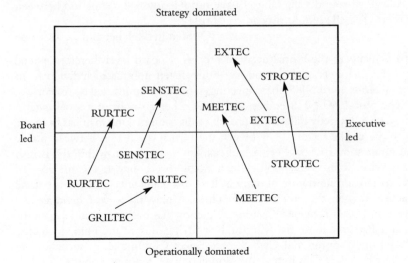

Figure 6.3   Shifts in leadership and focus on TEC boards.
Note: The acronyms are labels referring to anonymized organizations.
Source: Adapted from Haughton *et al.* (1995b).

Office appointed a clinician and former professor at the Welsh School of Medicine as the new chair of the Trust (Welsh Affairs Committee 1997). This case suggests that, despite executives and non-executives having a formal equality as board members, *de facto* the traditional model survives and that non-executives are more likely to be the ones held accountable.

The relationship between non-executives and executives is not static. External events and changes of personnel can shift the pattern of interaction and balance of power. Haughton and colleagues' (1995b) work on TECs provide a perspective on this issue. They identify four models of leadership evident on TEC boards:

- *Executive-driven*: Domination of the board by powerful and professionally competent chief executives. Their ability to take the TEC forward in positive ways secured this style of leadership.
- *Chair and chief executive-driven*: An influential chief executive matched by a strong and respected chair who was able to operate as a power broker and consensus-builder.
- *Balanced board–executive model*: Careful selection of directors to ensure the team is able to work together and that the potential for tension is minimized.
- *Board-driven*: Chair and board members able to devote time to steering the TEC, with a fairly weak executive.

Questions of leadership are then considered in terms of the extent to which the board is concerned with operational or strategic issues. Haughton *et al.* map shifts in leadership and strategic intent (Figure 6.3) and conclude that there is a process of convergence occurring. Although TECs have started from quite different points, there is a tendency for them to develop a strategic orientation and balanced board–executive style of leadership (Haughton *et al.* 1995b).

Public involvement

Public involvement in quangos, as with other public bodies, varies considerably. It is affected amongst other things by the nature of the issue, the stance of the board itself and the legal or regulatory framework determining the public's right to information. The latter differs from body to body, but even within one class of quango there can be considerable differences in the approach to public involvement (Painter *et al.* 1994). In addition there are highly vocal individuals and groups associated with some quangos, for example the BBC, the Arts Council and the Countryside Commission. In the case of the BBC, listeners have campaigned on numerous issues to do with scheduling and programme content. Sometimes their actions have no effect on the decision, but there are also notable victories – as in the retention by Radio 4 of its long-wave transmissions. Some local quangos, for instance HATs and City Challenge, have a much more direct and visible impact on their local communities and sponsor structures specifically to involve local people and specific sets of interests. These can include decision making and resource allocation devolved to community forums or area committees consisting of representatives from residents and tenants associations, voluntary organizations and other local groups. John Chumrow – who chairs Waltham Forest HAT – comments on the way in which they moved 'quickly to ensure the full participation by their tenants groups in all aspects of their operation' (1995: 264). Tenants are involved in project steering groups, recruitment panels and contractor selection boards, and may form up to 25 per cent of the Trust's staff (Figure 6.4). Other quangos are largely hidden from public view, relating instead to a specialist set of interests – for example, the Dental Rates Study Group or the Home Grown Cereals Authority. Besides the limited nature of public access to information in British government generally and quangos in particular, Weir and Hall (1994) point to the absence of procedural standards for consultation with the public and justification of decisions. They draw a comparison with practice in the United States where regulatory and executive agencies are legally required to advertise notice of proposals and permit time for public comment.

Members of local appointed bodies overall were disinclined to regard greater public involvement as beneficial, although attitudes vary across the sector (Table 6.5). There is already considerable public involvement in HATs, yet members show a desire for more. There is a marked contrast between members of the HATs and City Challenge boards and those on the UDCs which pre-dated them. This reflects the very different bases on which these urban regeneration bodies were constituted and consequently their relative willingness to accommodate a plurality of views. However, some UDCs have

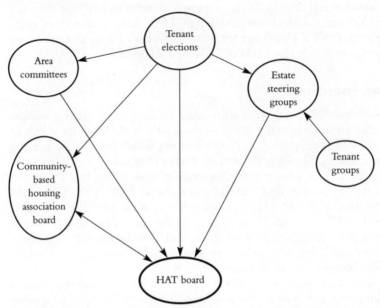

Figure 6.4   Mechanisms of tenant involvement in Waltham Forest HAT.
Source: National Audit Office (1997c).

developed more of a community orientation, following the disquiet about the activities of London Docklands Development Corporation in the early period of its life. Tyne and Wear UDC established a series of local monitoring panels following tensions with communities in and neighbouring its designated area. The power of the panels is dependent on the UDC board's willingness to take notice of their recommendations and requests. However, they have successfully kept community interests on the UDC's agenda and are beginning to secure some real gains (Robinson *et al.* 1993). Health authority non-executives' high level of interest in greater public involvement probably relates to their changed role and, more specifically, the problems of legitimacy involved in rationing scarce resources. Decisions about expensive treatments for individuals or complex moral and legal choices involved in rationing place board members at the heart of a highly political debate yet with no real channels to the community's opinions. It is this context that health authorities have begun to experiment with citizens' juries and other devices (see Chapter 8).

Often the public's view is mediated by local authorities. The relationship between local authorities and the quangos affecting their area can be close or distant, supportive or hostile. In the case of UDCs, for example, the initially difficult relationship between the London Docklands Development Corporation and the borough councils within whose area it operates has not always been replicated in later phases of UDC creation. A variety of linkages have been built, including high levels of councillor membership of the board, joint

Table 6.5   Board members' attitude to public involvement, by local appointed body

Greater public involvement in the board's work would be beneficial . . .	Percentage members agreeing strongly or to some extent
Health authority	70
Housing action trust	68
City Challenge	57
Training and enterprise council	57
Careers service company	39
NHS trust	37
Further education corporation	36
Urban development corporation	30
(Base)	(1462)

Source: Skelcher and Davis (1995).

committees and partnership programmes (Greer and Hoggett 1995). Strategies for mutual benefit have taken the place of initial hostilities. A similar pattern is apparent in TEC–local authority relations. Some local authorities had in fact been instrumental in bringing together the key partners who would eventually constitute the TEC board. This provided a solid basis for developing effective working relationships in the future, countering the disadvantage of only one or two directors being from local government.

The corporate governance of appointed bodies

The governance of the appointed sector is a dynamic process. Until recently, it was of little concern – the debates of the late 1970s and mid-1990s revolved fundamentally around questions to do with the place of quangos in the British public service and the relative opacity of these institutions to public scrutiny. Now there is a plethora of guidance, codes and regulations which are explored in more detail in Chapter 8. These are part of the structural context shaping quangos' governance (Table 6.6). They sit alongside other features. The legal and contractual instruments of the body, which may or may not be well defined, determine its scope for action. Public visibility, especially to key stakeholders, will have some influence on the body's style of operation and decisions.

It is individuals operating within an organizational setting who interpret and mediate these structural influences. The way in which board members perceive their role and the time, expertise and experience at their disposal will shape the behaviour of the body. The relationships between groups within the agency, and between it and other organizations, are also significant. There can be strong linkages with others leading to a stable policy community with consequent constraints on the board's autonomy. The distribution and exercise of power, both formally by post-holders like the chair and chief executive and

Table 6.6   Factors influencing the corporate governance of boards of appointed bodies

Individual factors	Organizational factors	Structural factors
Role perceptions of board members	Culture of decision making	Legal or contractual mandate of board
Members' balance of priorities – time, interest, other demands	Role of chair	Prescriptions or guidance on governance
Members' commitment to the agency	Treatment of conflict and dissent	Visibility to key stakeholders
Expertise, attributes and qualities of members	Members' linkages with constituency or outside interests	Specificity/measurability of targets
	Relationships between non-executives and executives	
	Level of public/group involvement	

informally through the decision culture, has a bearing on the organizational agenda, choices considered and actions agreed.

Research to date has concentrated principally on the governance of different classes of local appointed bodies. What this illustrates is that there is considerable variety within the sector as a whole. Some of this is attributable to the task and form of the particular type of local appointed body, but as important are the priorities of managers and members and the way they interpret the purpose of their organization. Variety is especially noticeable in the area of public involvement, with newer and community-based quangos engaging in significant exercises of engagement with residents and local interests. The incorporation of a plurality of interests onto the board together with changing philosophies of public management have helped shape their approach, especially when compared with bodies undertaking the same task but established in an earlier period. This variety is reflected in the organizations' cultures of decision making. Underlying the governance of appointed bodies, however, is the question of power – 'perhaps the essential governance question concerns the nature of power, its ownership, exercise and limitations' (Starkey 1995: 838). This power is exercised within the agency but ultimately in the decisions and actions that affect the wider community – decisions and actions taken, in theory, on the public's behalf. It is because of the tension between the private and public worlds of power that pressure for the reform of quangos' governance has arisen.

7

Evaluating quango performance

The widespread growth of quangos in the British system of government are closely associated with the debate about the performance of public agencies and services. This debate has maintained itself, despite changes of government, since the Fulton Report of the mid-1960s and in that time has generated a variety of organizational prescriptions for improving the performance of the public service. The Fulton Committee investigated the operation of the Whitehall machine and produced a strongly argued case for its reform. It proposed the adoption of modern management approaches in order to increase the capacity of government to respond to the scale of the demands placed on it (Gray and Jenkins 1985). Fulton, together with contemporaneous debates about the planning and control of public expenditure, helped shape the political and managerial climate towards a concern with measuring performance. This trend continued throughout the 1980s. The Financial Management Initiative (FMI) and other innovations by the Thatcher and Major Governments were intended to see that public programmes delivered both results and value for money. When combined with the decentralist and managerialist agenda of the new public management, the organizational forms of quangos appear to offer particular advantages over more traditional Whitehall and local authority structures for the management and delivery of public services. The model of a small appointed board free from the complexities of party politics and able to concentrate its energy on the management of a relatively narrow range of tasks contrasts with the bureaucratic and political Leviathan found – until recently – in central and local government. Although it can be hypothesized that quangos present an advantageous organizational form in terms of programme performance, establishing the evidence is a rather more complex task.

Performance assessment is bedevilled by conceptual and methodological problems (Carter *et al.* 1992). Conceptually, it requires the ability to isolate the various factors that influence organizational or policy performance and to model the causal relationships between them so that a change in one (the independent variable) can be hypothesized to have particular effects on others (the dependent variables). Because we are examining socio-political systems in which organizations and individuals have a degree of volition, the causal relationships are seldom unilinear. Further difficulties arise due to the significant degree of organizational fragmentation in the system within which quangos are embedded. The creation of new types of organization and the distribution of political, financial and other resources between them mandates the emergence of collaborative arrangements in order to achieve complementary goals. In their training role, for example, TECs effectively operate as managing agents for programmes delivered by a range of other bodies including further education colleges, chambers of commerce and private organizations. Evaluating the performance of TECs by implication also requires an evaluation of the

Table 7.1   Performance assessment – comparison of case study quangos

Parameter	UDC	TEC	GM school
Status	Non–departmental public body	Company limited by guarantee	Trust
Non–executive board members	Appointed by Secretary of State	Self-appointing/ appointed by members of company; two-thirds are senior business figures	Elected parent governors; elected teacher governors; 'first'/'foundation' governors including at least two parents and a representative of the business community
Timescale	Limited life	Permanent provided retains financial viability	Permanent provided retains financial viability
Tasks	Primarily physical regeneration	Delivery of human services, principally by contracting out; regulatory role regarding contractors	Delivery of human services in-house
Focus of assessment	Leverage of private sector funding; interpretation of task	Outputs and outcomes; administrative efficiency	Examination performance; school effectiveness

performance of these other service delivery bodies and the relationship be-tween the two. Such an interactive environment produces a complex evalua-tive task and raises questions about the availability and adequacy of data on outputs and outcomes.

Finally, there are questions about performance indicators themselves (Flynn 1986). Many aspects of performance are difficult to measure objectively, and surrogates may need to be used. This is the case with examination results which, as we discuss below, go only some way towards measuring educational attainment since they are influenced as much by the background of pupils as the quality of teaching. Where financial performance data are used, it is suscep-tible of widely differing organizational practices in expenditure coding and record keeping. Despite all these reservations and complexities, however, per-formance indicators are now a major part of the business of public management in all sectors, including quangos, and there is an increasing availability of evidence.

This chapter considers the performance of quangos in terms of their efficiency and effectiveness. In common with other parts of the public service the research evidence is patchy. There are considerable data on some types of quango and nothing on others. Additionally, the available evidence tends to be concentrated on local quangos. The analysis, therefore, is constructed around some well-researched quangos, namely UDCs, TECs and GM schools. These three types of body have structural differences that broadly reflect variations within the whole class of executive quangos (Table 7.1). Particular aspects of performance are emphasized in discussing each of these quangos.

The UDCs: levering private resources for physical regeneration

The impact of leverage planning

UDCs were created in three waves from 1981 and, despite some variation in emphasis, their underlying purpose has been to engage in market-led, property-based physical regeneration. The core activity of UDCs has been land acquisition, preparation and sale for development and it is to this end that the majority of their expenditure is directed. Nevin (1993) illustrates this in rela-tion to the Black Country Development Corporation (BCDC), commenting:

> The development process has been front loaded with public expenditure, as the BCDC assembles land packages for reclamation and disposal . . . The scale of the operation to assemble a marketable land portfolio has been huge . . . [with] 839 interested parties on 534 separate plots.
> (Nevin 1993: 109)

The technical task of land acquisition, however, was associated with the parallel process of 'leverage planning' (Brindley et al. 1996). UDCs were premised on the theory that investment by the private sector was constrained by the high

Table 7.2   Selected UDCs' losses on land deals

UDC	Expenditure on land transactions (£m)	Receipts from land transactions (£m)	Value of land at 31 March 1992 (£m)	Net loss (£m)
Black Country	68.0	3.7	38.8	25.5
Bristol	24.4	0	11.5	12.9
Central Manchester	12.3	0	4.0	8.3
Leeds	17.5	1.8	12.3	3.4
Trafford Park	41.6	9.3	22.3	10.0
Tyne and Wear	42.4	5.8	30.3	6.3

Source: *Independent*, 13 July 1992. Cited in Imrie and Thomas (1993).

costs involved in releasing the development potential of derelict and inaccessible urban land. Rather than being borne by the private sector these costs were collectivized and met through the public purse. Consequently public expenditure would release – or 'lever' – private investment wishing to take advantage of the improved development opportunities. The analysis of UDC corporate plans by Robson *et al.* (1994) indicates a predicted leverage ratio of 5 : 1. An earlier analysis of the eight second- and third-wave UDCs suggested a range of 1.8 : 1 by Bristol to 6.1 : 1 by Sheffield (National Audit Office 1993). At the start of the 1990s, however, the changing property market resulted in a significantly different outlook. Land prices slumped, property investment slowed and the UDCs were left with substantial land holdings that they were unable to sell or could only dispose of at a loss. This reduced the revenue stream to UDCs, causing difficulties over the short to medium term in relation to their ability to fund existing liabilities and capital schemes to which they were committed (Table 7.2).

An evaluation in terms of UDCs' own criteria would conclude that they had been successful at land acquisition, but that the development process had been constrained by factors outside their control. The 1992 collapse of property developers Olympia and York, who had previously persuaded a number of major financial institutions that they could survive the recession and complete the London Docklands Development Corporation's (LDDC) prestigious Canary Wharf scheme, is a case in point. LDDC needed this prestigious major development in order to symbolize its achievements and act as a magnet to further private investment. The developers had a high tolerance of risk and were able to compile an apparently solid group of investors. But the impact of the recession was too strong and the alliance disintegrated (Fainstein 1994). The Olympia and York collapse, together with substantial public investment in the Jubilee Line extension, led Brindley *et al.* (1996) to conclude that in Docklands, at least, the promise of leverage to pay for much of the essential infrastructure was lost:

> The 'leverage ratio' will turn out to be little better than 1 : 1. It is notable that the government has continued to increase spending in Docklands

while it has been cutting expenditure in almost every other sector. This suggests that there has been a political commitment to the 'success' of Docklands which has outweighed its real benefits.

(Brindley *et al.* 1996: 203)

Docklands, of course, is unique amongst UDCs by virtue of the scale of investment involved and its symbolically important location in the heart of the capital city. Other UDCs were not so severely affected and, as Parkinson (1996) notes, are achieving considerable physical regeneration in their localities. In terms of leverage, the Department of Environment (1996) claims that the private sector has invested £3 for every £1 spent by the public sector. More generally, however, this example illustrates the point that UDCs are designed to be instruments of government policy and that their performance directly affects a government's standing. When they experience difficulties, in this case caused by the market environment with which they were intended to have a symbiotic and benign relationship, and particularly when this affects flagship projects in the capital city, government is drawn to support them.

An alternative strategy: community regeneration

The conclusion that UDCs were broadly successful but constrained by wider economic forces is contested. The Employment Committee (1989) and others (for example, Docklands Consultative Committee 1990) argued that the basic strategy of physical regeneration was misplaced and that UDCs should adopt a more balanced approach in which social development and employment creation also play an important part. This was a call to which UDCs, to varying extents, responded. Brownhill (1993), for example, identifies three phases in the LDDC strategy. The first (1981–5) was largely concerned with land assembly and property development; the second (1985–9) amended this approach and developed a number of social and community programmes; the third (1989–93) involved responding to the property collapse and a range of associated issues but also commenced a strategy to develop social housing. There is a fourth phase (1993–8) which involves developing an exit strategy as the UDC prepares to conclude its 17-year association with Docklands and its communities.

Other UDCs were able to learn from the Docklands experience and give greater weight to social and employment programmes, including community services and vocational training. The proportion of expenditure spent on support to the local community by the eight second- and third-round UDCs up to 1993, however, was between 0.3 and 2.3 per cent (National Audit Office 1993). The approach adopted by each UDC varies depending on the way in which the board interpret their statutory brief and the circumstances of the designated area. Robinson *et al.* (1993) illustrate the differences between the relatively extensive funding and structures established by Tyne and Wear Development Corporation to stimulate and support community development compared with the more limited approach then employed by Teesside Development Corporation. They also review the employment generation effects claimed by the two UDCs and conclude that they should 'be regarded with caution, and viewed in relation to important caveats about displacement effects, local relocation and the effects of multiple assistance' (Robinson et al. 1993: 31). Here Robinson et al. draw attention to a wider problem affecting all initiatives designed to stimulate employment in a particular locality – that the employment growth arising in the designated area may be at the expense of job losses in the wider metropolis, region or nation. Green-field retail parks, for example, have a detrimental affect on shops and therefore employment in neighbouring urban centres. Effectively employment is being transferred from one location to another. The same is true of footloose business which decides to relocate in the designated area and hence take advantage of the benefits and incentives that are offered. Finally, UDCs are normally located in areas subject to other forms of selective government assistance to business, and hence it is seldom possible to disentangle the impact of the UDC from these other factors. There is genuinely new employment growth created in UDC areas, but the figures quoted by UDCs and government are gross and do not take account of losses to other areas due to such movements. The causal complexities involved in accounting for job creation are widely recognized, but given the importance of employment as a public indicator of UDC performance the presentation of such data inevitably becomes enmeshed in a political process.

From this perspective, therefore, UDCs have continued to give priority to a property-based development strategy. This has undoubtedly achieved significant improvements in their designated areas – Robinson et al., for example, comment on the unlikely success of the marina developments in the two North East UDCs. They go on to conclude that 'in relation to the DoE's performance indicators . . . they have done well and have deserved Ministerial plaudits' but '[they] will not generate a great deal of (net) employment and their contribution to reducing unemployment, especially in the inner urban areas, will be small' (ibid.: 1993: 58–9). Parkinson (1996: 9) shares this view, commenting that 'despite their physical and in some cases innovative social and community achievements . . . UDCs are now seen as the classic 1980s regeneration initiative . . . government-imposed, property-oriented and dominated by the private sector'.

This analysis raises the question of whether the alternative community-oriented regeneration strategy could have been adopted by UDCs and, if so, whether it would have been more successful. Ignoring the counterfactual problem this introduces, in other words that we can only speculate on whether it would or would not have been more successful, it highlights the structural constraints on UDCs. The resource context, board composition, political expectation and performance criteria were all aligned towards an interpretation of task in terms of physical regeneration. Robinson et al. and others are correct to argue that the UDCs' brief was expressed in a way that provided considerable discretion in its interpretation. However, as with many other quangos, UDCs need to be seen as an organizational expression of a particular government policy. They were effective in achieving that policy to the extent that wider market forces permitted. What this performance assessment suggests, perhaps, is that it was the policy that was inappropriate. And if that is the case, UDCs might not be the appropriate organizational form to deliver a community-based regeneration policy. Hence the emergence of multi-organizational partnership arrangements in the City Challenge and single regeneration budget initiatives (Skelcher *et al.* 1996).

The TECs: delivering cost-effective positive outcomes

The placing of public money into private hands was a recurring theme during the Thatcher and Major Governments of the 1980s and 1990s. It is exemplified in debates about the level of profits made by first investors in privatized corporations and the contracting-out of public service provision to commercial enterprises. The same theme is apparent in the reform of the UK training system towards the end of the 1980s with the creation of TECs in England and Wales and LECs in Scotland. (In Northern Ireland, responsibility continues to rest with government agencies.) The responsibilities of TECs and LECs differ slightly, but essentially they are responsible for the delivery of training and enterprise services to their local communities, under contract from central government. These responsibilities are exercised principally through sub-contracts with individual providers (see Chapter 2). TECs and LECs are unique institutions in the British system of government – 'a puzzle in constitutional taxonomy' (Guy and Howells 1994: 22) – since they are private not-for-profit companies, limited by guarantee, who are funded by the taxpayer to deliver public services. The business stance of TECs and LECs is reinforced through their board structure, where two-thirds of directors must be either the chairman, chief executive or equivalent from the private sector. They therefore represent a radically different means of delivering government training programmes and policies than the tripartite (state, employer, union) area manpower boards which operated as local arms of the Manpower Services Commission (MSC), latterly the Training Agency (Bennett *et al.* 1994). This assessment of TEC performance concentrates on two issues: first, the outcomes of their activities in terms of training, employment and enterprise, and second, TECs' cost-efficiency in terms of their administrative overheads and population base.

Achieving outcomes

The government's funding of the TFW and YT programmes are heavily weighted towards performance, principally defined as attracting trainees on to courses and the subsequent achievement of a 'successful outcome' – a situation in which the individual either obtains a job, becomes successfully self-employed, enters full-time training or education or has completed a recognized

Table 7.3   Inter-TEC performance indicators, 1996

Indicator	Definition
YT cost per weighted NVQ (£)	Calculated by multiplying qualification outcomes by multipliers defined in the TEC contract.
YT NVQs per 100 leavers	Includes all NVQs obtained by the TEC, whether or not they are funded by DfEE. Includes trainees who left one course only to move to another, and therefore understates performance.
TFW cost per weighted outcome (£)	Calculated by multiplying qualification outcomes, differentiated by the four categories to which trainees belong, by multipliers defined in the TEC contract.
TFW jobs per 100 leavers	Where an individual has been in either (a) employment for 15 hours or more a week for at least 7 consecutive days within 13 weeks of leaving TFW, or (b) unsupported self-employment for 15 hours or more per week for the 13 weeks since leaving TFW.
TFW NVQs per 100 leavers	Includes all NVQs obtained by the TEC, whether or not they are funded by DfEE. Includes trainees who left one course only to move to another, and therefore understates performance.
Large organization IIP recognition	Calculated by expressing the TEC's recognitions as a percentage of a March 1996 target, based on a linear progress from its March 1995 achievement to its share of the national target for December 1996.
YT guarantee	TEC performance in meeting the Government's guarantee of a suitable training place for 16- and 17-year-olds not in full-time education, measured 13 weeks after the trainee has left the course.
YT weighted NVQs per 100 leavers	Weighted version of YT NVQs per 100 leavers (see above)
IIP large organization commitment	Large organizations (with 200 employees or more) that have committed themselves to Investors in People and have developed an action plan to achieve recognition. Includes organizations subsequently achieving recognition.

Source: Labour Market Trends.

course or units towards one. This emphasis on outputs and outcomes is reflected in the inter-TEC performance data that has been published annually since September 1993. The first tables clustered TECs into quartiles on each of seven criteria, reflecting both unit cost and outcomes. Unlike the comparative statistics published on local authorities and health authorities and trusts, the first year data did not contain figures for individual TECs. Subsequently, the annual performance tables have identified individual TECs although as with any comparative statistics their interpretation needs care. The indicators have also been refined and for 1996 nine sets of comparative data are available (Table 7.3). The performance indicators do not contain information on management costs, and thus still differ from health bodies and local authorities in this respect. Additional data are available from the DfEE's follow-up surveys with individuals six months after having undertaken YT and TFW programmes. The results are published monthly in *Labour Market Trends*.

These data provide a basis for the comparative assessment of performance between TECs. There are, of course, inevitable limitations and qualifications that must be made. Some of the data relies on returns from employers and former trainees, and evidence to the Employment Committee (1996) suggested that its quality was sometimes less than satisfactory. NVQ figures include trainees who may have left one course only to join another, but who effectively count as non-completers and therefore understate TEC performance. And the imperatives of performance funding may lead the raw data to be categorized in a more favourable light than is deserved. The raw data, however, tells the reader little. YT cost per weighted NVQ ranges from £1542 to £2562, but the question of why this occurs remains. Is it due to problems of data collection or the relative efficiency of the organizations? Similarly TFW jobs per 100 leavers vary from 26 to 74. Local conditions certainly have an effect, but what else might account for these differences in performance?

Such performance data are useful for identifying questions to be answered, and in the process enabling an evaluative interpretation to be made. Unfortunately such reviews, if they have been undertaken by DfEE or the TECs, generally remain unpublished. One that has been reported is the DfEE's own assessment of the effectiveness of TECs in achieving jobs and qualifications for disadvantaged groups (Rolfe *et al.* 1996). As with the earlier study by Boddy (1995), this principally discusses the issues involved in attracting such trainees, appropriate forms of programmes that might be delivered and questions of organizational structure and process. When they turn to the performance of TECs, however, Rolfe and colleagues (1996) have relatively little success in interpreting the data. They calculate the gaps in job outcome performance between ethnic minority and white trainees and disabled and non-disabled trainees, and discover that this varies markedly from year to year within and between individual TECs (Table 7.4). In the light of this statistical analysis and their interviews with individual TECs they are forced to conclude that:

138 The appointed state

Table 7.4 Job outcome performance gap for ethnic minority/white and disabled/non-disabled trainees in six TECs, 1993–4 and 1994–5

	Job outcome performance gap between ethnic minority and white trainees		Job outcome performance gap between disabled and non-disabled trainees	
TECs	1993–4	1994–5	1993–4	1994–5
A	6	5	10	1
B	0	8	5	3
C	2	9	12	4
D	2	18	1	12
E	−6	−6	3	11
F	4	11	10	6

Source: Rolfe et al. (1996).

It was not possible to identify 'good' and 'bad' performing TECs . . . using the performance gap as a criterion for comparison. It is not therefore possible to link particular practices to 'good' or 'bad' TECs and draw conclusions on their effectiveness in this way.

(Rolfe et al. 1996: 11)

The TEC performance indicators raise the more fundamental problem of whether they do actually measure the performance of TECs. There are two points to consider here. The first was raised by Robert Bennett in his evidence to the Employment Committee. He argued that since TECs contract-out their responsibilities for providing TFW and YT courses, the output-related indicators are actually measuring the performance of the providers – the further education colleges, voluntary organizations and private training concerns. TECs operate as contract managers and thus measures of their performance should employ indicators related to this function – hence the concern with administrative costs discussed later. The second point involves the relationship between the changes in output and the wider economic climate in the UK. The Employment Committee (1996: para 122) compared these data series and concluded that:

the total number of positive outcomes achieved by TECs does broadly reflect the general trends in job creation and employment . . . The success of TECs, in short, is closely related to broader developments in the economy as a whole.

Broadly speaking, as vacancies and employment rise and fall, so too do positive outcomes. Consequently TEC performance appears to be strongly influenced by wider changes in the economy and labour market.

Value for money in administration

If the existing indicators are better seen as measures of provider activity, then how can the performance of TECs be assessed? One approach is to adopt the

Table 7.5   Administration costs of TECs, 1992–3 to 1994–5

Costs	1992–3	1993–4	1994–5
Administration costs (£m)	113.4[a]	175.9	162.0
Administration costs as proportion of turnover	9.8%	9.9%	11.0%

[a] 1991–2 figure
Source: Employment Committee (1996).

model employed in other contracting organizations, for example health authorities, and concentrate on administrative expenditure. According to the data returned in TECs' statutory accounts, their spending on administration increased sharply in the early 1990s and then reduced during 1994–5. During the same period, however, annual TEC budget levels declined by about 50 per cent and therefore it is more meaningful to consider administration as a proportion of turnover. This shows an upward trend over the three years (Table 7.5). These figures should be treated as indicative since TECs are no exception to the general rule that it is almost impossible accurately to compile aggregate or comparative data on the costs of administration. Even within accepted accounting practice, costs can be allocated in a variety of ways. The Department for Education and Employment's *Efficiency Scrutiny* (1995: para 4.9) concluded that the variety of ways in which administration costs were dealt with by TECs 'makes it impossible to assess with confidence what TECs are actually spending either on particular programmes, or on non-programme related expenditure'. The Employment Committee (1996: para 107) regarded this as 'highly unsatisfactory' and recommended that clearer information on management costs should be available in a comparative form for individual TECs as a basis for making judgements about value for money.

In considering administrative value for money the Employment Committee followed a path explored two years earlier by Robert Bennett (1994). Bennett argues that the question of TECs' cost-efficiency is important in terms of their accountability for public money, particularly given their role in the Single Regeneration Budget process and status as 'main private sector partners' for the newly created Government Offices for the regions (Department of Employment 1994). Bennett approaches the problem of estimating TECs' administrative costs by positing a 'model' or 'reformed' TEC. This is a TEC which demonstrates best practice by having:

- removed tiers of administration;
- shifted from seconded Civil Servants (who TECs were originally required to accept) to direct employees;
- devolved power and responsibility to programme directors;
- instituted tighter financial control over budgets within cost centres.

Between two and five of the then eighty-two TECs fit this model, depending on the interpretation of the criteria. An expenditure budget consisting of 17 items was constructed for the model TEC and for the hypothetical 'unreformed' TEC, enabling comparison to be made. Bennett concludes that management costs as a proportion of total budget for the model TEC is 15 per cent less than that for the unreformed TEC. From an analysis of the detailed figures, he identifies two contributory factors. First, the unreformed TEC contains Civil Service cultures and working practices that lead to overstaffing and over-administration, especially due to excessive tiers of management. Secondly, there are low volumes of usage for some TEC activities which therefore bear a disproportionately high proportion of overheads. Structural rigidities within the organization prevent change to address this problem.

The analysis is developed through a comparison of TECs with Chambers of Commerce on common areas of activity. Bennett concludes that the unit cost of programme activities is three to four times higher in TECs and twice as high in the area of central management costs. The data do not permit him to identify the main contributory factors. A significant one, however, is likely to be costs associated with the complex regulatory environment within which TECs operate (see Chapter 2). However, he does argue that many TECs do not cover a sufficiently large population and that greater efficiency could be achieved by amalgamation to a total of only 40 or 50 organizations. On the basis of the three components of his analysis – the model TEC, comparison with Chambers of Commerce and amalgamation – Bennett estimates that TECs could achieve efficiency gains of £225 million. This is a figure with which Guy and Howells (1994) – both writing as TEC chief executives – take issue. They argue that the calculations rest on limited evidence and questionable method, and that expenditure reductions of this order would have to be met from a reduction of the unit costs of providers on whom most of TECs' budgets are spent. Parker and Vickerstaff (1996), from their analysis of TEC and LEC provision for small firms, also question whether size is a significant factor in accounting for their performance. Bennett's analysis and the observations of the Employment Committee therefore highlight the case for a more robust means of comparing TECs' cost-efficiency in line with that expected of other public service agencies, quango or not.

Grant-maintained (GM) schools: improving performance through institutional autonomy

GM schools are a product of the Education Reform Act 1988. This substantial piece of legislation introduced significant changes to the principles that had guided state education at primary, secondary and tertiary levels since the Butler Education Act of 1944. The post-1945 settlement within the British political system had accepted the predominance of state-provided education which was planned, managed and accountable through LEAs to a central department of education and, ultimately, a Secretary of State. All schools were required to have governing bodies, but these had limited roles in the management of what tended to be a relatively centralized system. Power in this system was effected in two main ways. First, through centralized resource allocation which required individual schools to engage in regular processes of request and negotiation with the LEA. Secondly, by the strategic planning of provision which – as declining birth rates worked through the demographic profile of the population – led to school reorganizations and closures. The 1988 Act was designed to change this system by delegating power to individual schools, stimulating diversity of provision and increasing parental choice. As the quasi-market in educational provision developed, so competition between schools was expected to improve standards of performance (Department for Education 1992).

The introduction of GM status was one of the key innovations in the Act. It enabled primary, middle and secondary schools within the LEA remit to 'opt-out'. Such schools remain in the state sector, but become independent of the former LEA. The request to attain GM status requires a simple majority of parents in a secret ballot, the decision then being made by the Secretary of State. Within the context of a Trust Deed, the relevant land and buildings are transferred to the governing body of the GM school. Funding was initially provided directly by the then Department for Education, but in 1994 this responsibility was transferred to the new FAS, a non-departmental public body now sponsored by the DfEE. GM status places considerable responsibilities on the governing body, whose role had already been somewhat enhanced following the Education (No. 2) Act 1986. The new responsibilities include the management of financial and other resources, including staff and property, as well as matters to do with admissions, curriculum and assessment. The governing body is also accountable to the FAS for the management of the public funds allocated to it.

A considerable number of schools have opted successfully for GM status, although fewer than the Conservative Government had hoped. By 1996, there had been some 1100 opt-outs from a total population of almost 25,000 schools (Department for Education and Employment/Welsh Office 1996). Nevertheless, parents in many localities have a theoretical choice between sectors, although in practice the admissions policies of both LEA and GM schools may constrain this. Yet what is striking in the evaluations of this new form of provision is how little difference it appears to make. One obvious area for comparison is in terms of examination achievement. While apparently an ideal indicator of the performance of an individual school, these indicators suffer the disadvantage of failing to take into account the ethnic or socio-economic background of pupils – an important predictor of achievement (Gray 1995). Thus crude exam results need to be treated with caution. However, as a recent OECD study commented, 'in spite of the . . . inadequacy of examinations in summing up the real learning achievements of a student, or the performance of a school, they are currently the best performance indicator available' (OECD 1995: 30).

In 1993, the Chief Inspector for Schools produced a review of GM schools and commented that 'examination results in grant maintained schools have improved . . . as they have in [LEA] maintained schools in general'

(Ofsted 1993: 9). He went on to observe that a 'striking feature' was the
variability in examination results from the selective GM schools, some comparing unfavourably with non-selective GM and LEA schools. These findings
were produced from data for 1989 to 1992. Annual tables of individual school
performance were first published in 1992. These tables include data on examination results, which overall have improved year on year. In 1996, 45 per cent
of all pupils reached the benchmark of at least five A*–C grade passes at GCSE
while for GM schools the figure was 52 per cent. However, the best performing schools are generally those with some form of entry selection system and
these are over-represented in the GM sector (Hackett 1996). As Power *et al.*
(1994: 223) observe: 'As long as the GM sector is disproportionately comprised
of schools with academically selective admissions policies . . . it would be
surprising . . . if [their] standards were not rather higher.' It is selection rather
than the fact of GM status that differentiates the sectors in terms of pupil
achievement. Increased organizational autonomy is coincidental. In other areas
of performance, the Ofsted report finds a broad equivalence in standards between GM and LEA schools, for example:

> Careful comparison was made between standards in the grant maintained
> schools and in the LEA maintained schools inspected over the same
> period, but the results were inconclusive.
>
> (1993: 10)

> The quality of teaching could not be said with any confidence to be
> either better or worse in grant maintained than LEA maintained schools.
>
> (1993: 10)

> The pattern of attendance did not differ significantly from that in the
> LEA maintained sector.
>
> (1993: 11)

In reality, GM schools only had significantly more autonomy than their LEA
colleagues for a short period following the 1988 Act. This is because of the
somewhat slower introduction of Local Management of Schools (LMS) in the
local authority sector. Under LMS the majority of a school's budget and the
responsibility for managing it, together with the appointment and promotion
of staff, were devolved to a reconstituted governing body. This shift in resource
control significantly changed the relationship with the LEA and offered the
prospect for schools to exercise greater discretion in their spending. From being
supplicants at the LEA's table, schools were sometimes now in the position of
negotiating to purchase services from them. LMS introduced a managerial
revolution into local authority schools – much as Trust status did for directly
managed units within the pre-1990 health authorities – and put them in much
the same position as GM schools (Levačić 1995). The advantage that GM
schools initially had over those in the LEA sector was finance. This resulted
from the way in which the funding system redirected resources towards them,
despite a governmental commitment to parity (Bush *et al.* 1992). However, as

time has gone on, even GM schools have experienced the impact of public expenditure constraint and the financial benefits available to the early opt-outs are no longer available. This, together with LMS, helps explain the reduction in applications for GM status. Essentially, therefore, what was perceived as a divergent policy on educational provision has come to be a convergent one. This pattern was apparent even in the early 1990s. Writing in 1991, Halpin *et al.* observe:

> We have been struck, not so much by how *different* they are from LEA schools of similar status and size, but by how *like* them they are . . . GM schools are distinguished . . . not so much by what and who they teach (which in most cases has not changed that much, if at all), or even by how they are managed, but by the manner and size of their funding.
>
> (Halpin *et al.* 1991: 417, emphasis in original)

Deleting 'and size' from the last line neatly sums up the position today.

The evidence on the performance of GM schools, therefore, suggests that when social class factors and academic selection are taken into account, they are broadly as effective educationally as those in the LEA sector. This is not a surprising finding, since the literature on school effectiveness accords most importance to factors such as a positive climate, the active involvement of parents and leadership by the headteacher (Gray 1995). Even headteachers in GM schools adopt a pragmatic line and view the benefits in terms of inputs – enhanced resourcing – rather than outputs (Fitz *et al.* 1993). It is perhaps in this way that the performance of the early GM schools has been most differentiated, since unlike LEA schools they were able to gain additional financing in a period of general public expenditure constraint. This gain, however, has more to do with the then Government's desire to reduce the role of LEAs than any value inherent in the organizational form of GM schools.

The performance of quangos reconsidered

This chapter has examined the proposition that the organizational form of the quangos will give performance advantages in the delivery of public programmes. The difficulty in examining this view is not just the technical problem of performance assessment but also the absence of suitable comparators with the elected sector. It is only in the primary and secondary educational sectors that there is the possibility of a comparison, but even here the structural differences between GM and LEA schools are now marginal. GM and LEA school governing bodies have almost identical structures and powers, the key differences being the slightly greater financial delegation to the former and the local authority representative on the latter. And the apparently stronger accountability of LEA schools is questionable since the authority's nominee to the governing body will not necessarily be an elected councillor. The performance of both types of school is broadly equivalent. Having taken account of selection and social class factors, the overall exam performance of LEA schools is very similar to that of GM schools. The Ofsted report revealed little difference in other respects.

The other bodies examined – UDCs and TECs – both show performance achievements and limitations. In the absence of comparators, it is not possible to adduce evidence to judge whether there is a direct or indirect causal relationship between their organizational status as quangos – albeit of different types – and their performance. However there are other lessons to draw. What both cases illustrate are the interdependencies of these bodies on other agencies and processes. Despite the business ethos with which they were designed to be imbued, the performance of both depends largely on external factors over which they have varying degrees of control. Changes in the wider economy are particularly important in shaping their performance. Cycles of boom and slump are reflected in the capacity to UDCs to attract development and employment. These changes in the economy also correlate closely with some of the TECs' performance indicators. These are the influences at the macro level. More immediately, both types of body have to work with and through other organizations to deliver their objectives. Consequently, it is perhaps more appropriate to consider the overall performance of the system – the particular arrangement of agencies, processes and relationships – than to try to isolate one individual component.

The absence of firm data about the performance of quangos, and therefore the inability to develop solid conclusions regarding the impact of this organizational form on the efficiency or effectiveness of public programmes, has echoes in other studies. The work of Dunsire et al. (1991) on the relationship between ownership and performance came to the conclusion that little connection could be made. They compared ten organizations whose ownership structure had changed, evaluating performance in terms of productivity, employment and financial ratios, but could find no clear pattern. More recently, Pollitt et al. (1997) have considered the performance impact of self-management in education, housing and healthcare. They conclude that:

> data on quality and effectiveness was often hard to [obtain]. What frequently did exist was evidence for increasing *activity levels*. However, whether this was due to better management or to other pressures is by no means clear.
>
> (Pollitt et al. 1997: 3, emphasis in original)

In this context the discussion about quangos is driven back to the matter of values. If it is not possible to claim that this organizational form has performance benefits in terms of delivering public programmes, then the debate resolves itself into questions of the performance of democracy. It becomes a question of whether it is preferable to have a society in which public institutions are directly controlled by elected politicians or by appointed individuals.

8

An agenda for reform

The British governmental system is intermittently shaken by a critique of the status quo. The world of quangos has not escaped. The periods 1978–82 and 1993–7 have both been characterized by extensive discussion of the role and governance of appointed bodies and the presentation of proposals for reform. Countless tracts, pamphlets, articles and reports were produced by the media, think-tanks of the centre, left and right, and academic commentators. Questions were asked in the House of Commons, ministerial statements made and official reports produced. The Conservative Party victory in the 1979 general election resulted in some culling of quangos, a process assisted by the official review of NDPBs undertaken by Sir Leo Pliatsky. The final years of the Conservative period of government, prior to Labour's success in the 1997 general election, witnessed further investigations of the appointed sector by the Committee on Standards in Public Life – chaired at that point by Lord Nolan.

The Committee's creation was announced in October 1994 following a series of scandals associated with accusations of improper behaviour by ministers, Members of Parliament and others, including quango appointees. These incidents included MPs receiving cash and other benefits from lobbyists, the 'revolving-door syndrome' in which former ministers and senior Civil Servants moved rapidly from Westminster and Whitehall into business directorships, allegations of partisan placement to quango boards, failures of financial control in quangos, ministries and other public bodies and questions about the financing of the Conservative Party by business and overseas sources. Although the Nolan Committee's terms of reference concern standards of conduct in public life beyond those associated with quangos, one chapter of its first report and the

---

Box 8.1   The Nolan Committee's Seven Principles of Public Life

Selflessness
Holders of public office should take decisions solely in terms of the public interest. They should not do so in order to gain financial or other material benefits for themselves, their family, or their friends.

Integrity
Holders of public office should not place themselves under any financial or other obligation to outside individuals or organizations that might influence them in the performance of their official duties.

Objectivity
In carrying out public business, including making public appointments, awarding contracts, or recommending individuals for rewards and benefits, holders of public office should make choices on merit.

Accountability
Holders of public office are accountable for their decisions and actions to the public and must submit themselves to whatever scrutiny is appropriate to their office.

Openness
Holders of public office should be as open as possible about all the decisions and actions they take. They should give reasons for their decisions and restrict information only when the wider public interest clearly demands.

Honesty
Holders of public office have a duty to declare any private interests relating to their public duties and to take steps to resolve any conflicts arising in a way that protects the public interest.

Leadership
Holders of public office should promote and support these principles by leadership and example.

Source: Committee on Standards in Public Life (1995a).

---

whole of its second are devoted to this issue. It is also undertaking a review of the extent to which appointed bodies have adopted its recommendations. The Committee's seven principles of public life relate directly to the issues facing the appointed sector (Box 8.1).

There is considerable support for a programme of reform. A March 1994 ICM poll commissioned by Channel 4 asked respondents which type of body

Table 8.1   Public attitudes (in percentages) to elected and appointed bodies' responsibilities

Who should run . . . ?	Elected bodies	Mixed bodies	Appointed bodies	Majority for wholly or partially elected bodies
Rented homes	78	6	9	69
Schools	64	13	16	48
Further education	53	15	25	28
Health authorities	50	18	25	25
Hospitals	50	18	24	26
Employment training	49	11	29	20
Police forces	39	13	40	−1

Source: Dunleavy and Wear (1994).

should run each of seven services where local authorities had lost complete or partial responsibility since 1979. The choices were between local councils/locally elected committees, mixed bodies which were part elected and part appointed and wholly appointed boards. Only in the case of the police force was there a balance in favour of appointed rather than elected bodies (Table 8.1).

A MORI survey in April–May 1995, immediately prior to the first Nolan report, tested public attitudes to the openness and accountability of quangos (Table 8.2). It revealed very strong support for public access to board

Table 8.2   Public attitudes (in percentages) to how quangos should be run

Attitude	Agree	Disagree	Neither	Net agree
'Quangos should hold their board meetings in public and make all their board papers available to the public, subject to protection of commercial confidentiality and people's privacy'	81	3	17	+78
'There should be clear legal rules to ensure that all quango boards are balanced in their composition'	80	2	17	+78
'All appointments to quangos should be subject to scrutiny by parliamentary committee'	72	7	21	+65
'The general public should have a say in appointing some people to each quango'	71	10	20	+61
'Government ministers should have the right to appoint whoever they think is most suitable to run quangos'	26	50	25	−24

Source: Dunleavy, Wear and Subrahmanyam (1995).

Table 8.3 The process of quango reform

Date	Event	Comment
1975	Creation of Public Appointments Unit in Cabinet Office	This follows from Civil Service report on *Key Appointments in the Public Sector* (1974) which examined appointments to nationalized industry boards.
1978	Conservative Political Centre publish Holland and Fallon's pamphlet *The Quango Explosion*	Calls for curbing of the number of quangos, clearer accountability to Parliament and greater openness in appointments process.
1979	Holland publishes *Quango, Quango, Quango*	First comprehensive list of quangos, but includes other bodies to which government appoints at least one member.
	What's Wrong With Quangos? published by Outer Circle Policy Group	Analysis of accountability and patronage issues. Recommends greater openness, improved accountability, limitations on patronage and legal controls.
	Election of Conservative Government	Prime Minister Thatcher requests ministers to identify quangos to be culled. Lack of response leads to Pliatzky review.
1980	*Report on Non-Departmental Public Bodies*, Cmnd 7797	The Pliatzky Report leads to modest reduction in numbers.
1989	*Review of Public Appointments Procedures* published	Draws contrast between informal patronage and transparent appointments procedures for Civil Servants. Recommends use of standard employment recruitment and selection techniques. Draws attention to gender and ethnic imbalance on quangos.
1992	*The Financial Aspects of Corporate Governance* published	The Cadbury Report, focused on the private sector but putting corporate governance on the public service agenda.
1993	*The Growth of Government by Appointment* published	Davis and Stewart produce first mapping of quangos operating at the local level.
	The Democratic Deficit: A Guide to Quangoland published	Morgan and Roberts' analysis of quangos in Wales.

Table 8.3 *Continued*

Date	Event	Comment
1994	*Ego-Trip* published	Weir and Hall develop first comprehensive review of quango numbers and critique of their status and operation since changes of 1980s and 1990s.
January	*The Proper Conduct of Public Business* – The Eighth Report of the Public Accounts Committee, HC 154	Reviews poor financial management, impropriety and other failings in public bodies and recommends tighter controls.
October	Committee on Standards in Public Life (the Nolan Committee) appointed	First round of hearings include consideration of non-departmental public bodies and NHS bodies.
1995		
January	*Review of Guidance on Public Appointments* published	Report by the Public Appointments Unit. Promises greater openness in appointments process.
May	*Standards in Public Life: First Report of the Committee on Standards in Public Life*, Cm 2850	Recommends merit appointment, Public Appointments Commissioner, improved codes of conduct and audit arrangements.
July	*The Government's Response to the First Report of the Committee on Standards in Public Life*, Cm 2931	Broadly accept recommendations.
	TEC National Council publish *A Framework for the Local Accountability of Training and Enterprise Councils in England and Wales*	Initiative by TECs to overcome criticisms of their lack of local accountability.
December	Appointment of Sir Len Peach as first Commissioner for Public Appointments and Commissioner for Public Appointments in Northern Ireland	Implementation of government commitment following first Nolan Report, although Commissioner's powers not as strong as Nolan suggested.
1996		
March	*Spending Public Money: Governance and Audit Issues*, Cm 3179	Green Paper following Nolan recommendations, with proposals to strengthen audit and governance arrangements.

Table 8.3 *Continued*

Date	Event	Comment
April	*Code of Practice for Public Appointments Procedures and Guidance on Appointments to Executive Non-Departmental Public Bodies and NHS Bodies published*	First guidance from the Commissioner for Public Appointments.
May	*Local Public Spending Bodies: Second Report of the Committee on Standards in Public Life*, Cm 3270	Considers further and higher education, GM schools, TECs and housing associations. Recommends improvements in member appointment, codes of conduct, financial management and local accountability.
November	Department of Health *Public Appointments Annual Report 1996*	First departmental listing of appointments and self-identification of political party allegiance.
1997		
January	*Guidance on Codes of Practice for Board Members of Public Bodies*	Cabinet Office issue model code of practice for board members.
February	*The Governance of Public Bodies: A Progress Report*, Cm 3557	White Paper arising from Cm 3179 together with response to Cm 3270. Recommendations in relation to public appointments, accountability, propriety, openness and audit.
May	Election of Labour Government	Steps to increase quango accountability and advertisement of board positions.

meetings and papers and for the introduction of rules on balanced board composition. There was opposition to the right of government ministers to decide who to appoint to boards and support for Parliamentary scrutiny of appointments that were made. Subsequent research by Miller and Dickson (1996) confirms this finding. When respondents were asked where account-ability for local quangos should lie, 64 per cent said with local councils. This compared with 18 per cent in favour of central government and 12 per cent believing that they should be left to operate like local companies.

These public and political pressures stimulated a more rapid and active process of reform in the closing years of the Major Government, subsequently continued by the Labour administration elected in 1997 (Table 8.3). A central feature of these reforms has been the desire to moderate the democratic deficit identified in Chapter 2. However, governments have sometimes been unwill-ing to regulate and legislate to any great extent, preferring more limited changes that give the appearance of reform whilst retaining the discretion of ministers and boards, especially in matters of appointment. Overall, the pro-posals for reform of quangos can be grouped into four categories. These cover:

- the appointment of members;
- the governance of quangos;
- strengthening accountability; and
- regulating the system.

The proposals associated with each theme are discussed in detail below. There are also wider political and constitutional questions that bear on the future of the appointed sector. These are considered in the concluding chapter.

Appointing members

Opening up the process

Opening up the appointments process and introducing procedures that would be regarded as good practice in the recruitment and selection of senior public managers has been high on the reform agenda. This would remove the pa-tronage and informality that has characterized appointments to date and intro-duce greater rigour, clarity and transparency into the process. Reformers were intent on turning the tide of tradition which, in the words of a 1974 review of appointments to nationalized industry boards, justified ministers' freedom 'to choose a means of selection suitable to circumstances without commitment to any fixed procedure' (quoted in Wright 1995: 12). As Holland and Fallon (1978) observed:

> . . . no objective criteria are being . . . applied at all . . . The whole process is cloaked in secrecy. Nobody knows, or will say, how lists of 'the great and the good' are compiled, or how worthy people can get onto them.
>
> (Holland and Fallon 1978: 22)

Holland and Fallon argued for the ending of appointment on political grounds and its replacement by advertising and short-listing of suitable candidates, from which the minister could make the final choice. In the case of nationalized industries and commercial boards, the minister's nomination should be subject to the approval of the appropriate select committee.

Despite Holland and Fallon's pamphlet emerging under the imprint of the Conservative Political Centre, one of the Party's think-tanks, and the accession of a Conservative administration the following year, it was not until 1989 that their thinking began to be reflected in government circles. The Cabinet Office's *Review of Public Appointments Procedures* (1989) introduced a radically new official perspective on public appointments. While not directly challenging the notion that appointments should be made by the minister, it did highlight the clear dichotomy between this 'unfettered patronage' and the requirements for 'fair and open competition' in the recruitment and selection of Civil Servants and the staff of public bodies. The report went on to identify that one consequence of the informal appointments process was the predominance of white, male and middle-aged men on boards. It concluded that application of conventional employment recruitment techniques such as advertising, executive search and positive action would be of benefit and proposed that the Public Appointments Unit, established in 1975 to compile and collate lists of potential appointees for use by departments, could play a more active role. Some of this thinking is reflected in the *A Guide for Departments* (Cabinet Office/HM Treasury 1992: para 10.2.2) which recommended that they 'ensure that a good field of candidates, regardless of gender, is considered. It should also include, where possible members of ethnic minority groups . . . as well as other candidates with managerial and commercial skills'. The strength of the informal patronage tradition is revealed by the absence of any discussion of public advertisement in this document. It is also noteworthy that the four paragraphs devoted to 'selection and recruitment' are dwarfed by the thirteen which advise on the intricacies of remuneration, travel and subsistence expenses, injury benefit and the related financial arrangements for board members.

The re-emergence of quangos on to the political agenda in 1993 and the need for the Government to present a positive picture to the first round of the Nolan hearings resulted in rapid action to reform the appointments system. The *Review of Guidance on Public Appointments* (Public Appointments Unit 1995) drew on the philosophy of the 1989 report and proposed a system for NDPBs that included a presumption in favour of advertising and codified the elements of the process that would be required (Box 8.2). New arrangements for appointments to NHS bodies were announced at the same time, including a local panel of three chairmen or non-executives from different boards to sift applications (Department of Health 1995). More recently, William Hague, then Conservative Welsh Secretary, created an independent assessment panel to interview potential governor appointments to the BBC and S4C (the Welsh language TV channel) and advise him accordingly. One of the panel's decisions

Box 8.2   Summary of recommendations from *Review of Guidance on Public Appointments*, 1995

- The aims of an effective public appointments process should be endorsed by Ministers and set out in central and departmental guidance.
- Best practice in making appointments including agreed, clear and documented details of: the job to be done; the qualities and experience sought; the length of the appointment; termination and reappointment procedures; remuneration if any; performance monitoring; the code of conduct required; induction and training required. All mandatory on departments subject to test of proportionality.
- More open advertising, easier access to information, ensuring propriety and proper disclosure of interests.
- Departments should consider systematically the use of advertising, search consultants and databases (with a presumption in favour of advertising).
- Reasons for decisions by Ministers and officials should be recorded and can, where appropriate, be disclosed.
- Departments should ensure that, for each public body, the identity of appointees is available on demand to anyone who wishes to know.
- Work be undertaken to establish the feasibility and cost of providing access through a database linked to the Internet.
- Party political affiliations should not normally be relevant to appointments decisions.
- Chief Whip only to be consulted in circumstances of political sensitivity, as set out in *Questions of Procedure for Ministers*. Whips of all parties to be consulted as part of a regular search for names.
- Screening processes should be carefully examined by departments. For short-listed candidates written references should normally be taken up and interviews undertaken.
- Arrangements should be put in place to ensure that candidates match standards of probity required and that there are no problems with conflict of interest, including those arising from multiple appointments.
- Departments should sustain vigorously the programmes to promote and deliver equal opportunity principles.
- Departments should regularly benchmark their processes against the best in the Civil Service.

Source: Public Appointments Unit (1995).

was not to recommend the re-appointment of Gwyn Jones, a businessman who held seats on a number of prominent Welsh quangos (Hencke 1996).

Elsewhere in the public service, the Department of Employment created an Assessors' Committee, part of whose role was to advise on eligibility criteria for TEC directors and the composition and calibre of TEC boards (Department of Employment 1993). The TEC National Council's *Framework for Local Accountability* (1995) provides guidance to individual TECs on the principles that should underlie selection of directors. An alternative approach was recommended by the Further Education Funding Council (1994: 32) in its guidance to colleges. It proposed that 'formal arrangements' are instituted, which might include 'carrying out a skills and experience audit to establish the ideal profile' for the governing body taking into account 'the needs of the college, the desirability of ensuring an appropriate gender balance and reflecting in the membership the ethnic make-up of the community'. The FEFC guidance does not have a strong line on advertising, merely inviting governors 'to consider' whether this approach should be used.

Such a flurry of activity in clarifying and making transparent the appointment process to NHS bodies and NDPBs looked slightly strange when viewed from Scotland. There, political bias in appointments had been relatively limited. However, Scottish ministers considered that 'a little too much patronage was exercised in the Thatcher years' (Midwinter 1995: 5) and Conservative Secretary of State Michael Forsyth committed the Scottish Office to appointing from more diverse backgrounds. Some quangos already sought applications by advertisement, for example Highlands and Islands Enterprise, and this process was extended to NHS bodies. In 1994 a five member panel was created, chaired by a Scottish National Party member, to assess applications and advise the Secretary of State on appointments. Midwinter concludes that both the composition of the panel and the subsequent appointments show 'little hard evidence of political bias' (1995: 5).

The impact of the PAU *Review* (1995) has been to open up the appointments process and provide greater information of the appointments that are made. Advertisements seeking applications from individuals interested in positions on public and NHS bodies are now found in newspapers. The Annual Reports produced by each central government department have contained, since 1996, details about their appointments including the name of each appointee and occasionally brief biographical details. There is an Internet site at www.open.gov.uk/pau/paupoint.htm providing information on appointments. Departments have internal targets to increase the proportion of women and ethnic minority members on the boards they sponsor.

An independent appointments commission

Weir and Hall sound a note of caution regarding the PAU *Review* (1995). They see it as a 'thoughtful response' to public concern and believe it will advance 'openness and propriety and encourage a more representative diversity of appointees' (Weir and Hall 1995: 1), yet are concerned that it fails to address the more fundamental question of ministerial accountability to Parliament. In other words, the proposed reforms to the appointments system are only *guidance* – however strongly the statements may be worded – and thus rely on the goodwill of individual ministers for its implementation. Weir and Hall propose that the appointments system should be taken out of 'the informal domain of ministerial discretion' (1995: 1) and placed on a statutory basis. They argue that there should be an external means of compliance monitoring, rather than relying on internal departmental audit, and suggest that this might be a role for the Committee on Standards in Public Life (subject to its remit being so redefined) or a House of Commons Select Committee. Such a Public Appointments Commission might incorporate all aspects of the process, from recruitment through appointment to monitoring post-holders' performance. Tony Wright proposes that this body should be the creation of Parliament, reflecting a desire to wrest the appointments process away from ministers and return it to the House of Commons. It would consist of individuals 'chosen by agreement of the parties with the Speaker presiding. They would be persons of distinction and sturdy independence – and certainly not drawn from the ranks of senior politicians and privy councillors' (Wright 1995: 21).

The Nolan Committee were unimpressed by the case for an independent commission. They concluded that ultimate responsibility for appointments should remain with ministers. This, they argued, provided a clear accountability link to Parliament. An independent body, they felt, might not be widely accepted or seen as authoritative when called upon to make appointments to politically controversial posts. However, the Committee did not believe that the safeguards set out by the Government in their evidence were 'sufficiently robust' and recommended the provision of independent checks and balances (Committee on Standards in Public Life 1995a):

1 Legal safeguards, especially ensuring that ministers comply with equal opportunity legislation.
2 Clear principles for selection, based on merit criteria.
3 The recognition that effective board members will be committed to the achievement of the body's objectives, but that this should not exclude appointment of people with no strong political views.
4 The need to appoint boards comprising individuals with a balance of backgrounds and outlooks.
5 That appointments to NDPBs and NHS bodies should be made after advice from a panel which includes an independent member or members.
6 An independent Commissioner for Public Appointments to scrutinize and monitor the system.
7 Greater openness, including job descriptions and the advertising of appointments and decisions.
8 Declaration of any significant political activity undertaken during the last five years.

9 A code of practice to cover the appointments process and the acceptance of the test of 'proportionality' – that, on the grounds of cost-efficiency, variations from the procedure may be permitted where the post is a minor and unpaid one.

Public hearings and scrutiny

The demands of public accountability in appointments can be met through a hearings system. One model would require nominated individuals to appear before a panel in order to have their fitness for appointment assessed. The principle of proportionality would apply, with only those nominated for key positions nationally or locally being subject to a hearings process. The panel could consist of parliamentarians for national posts and councillors and relevant MPs for local posts. Independent assessors would advise the panel. Sir John Banham, himself the former chairman of two quangos – the Audit Commission and the Local Government Commission – proposed an alternative method suitable for local appointed bodies in evidence to the House of Lords Select Committee on central–local government relations:

> Where there are major agents delivering services to local people, there would be a great deal to be said for the person appointed to chair these bodies to be subject to confirmation by the relevant local authority in an open vote after a public hearing.

> (Banham cited in Evans 1996)

The process of public hearings would have the advantage of enabling public checks and balances to be introduced in terms of the individual's experience and qualities, as well as requiring the public expression of a vision for the organization and set of objectives they intended to pursue. This would increase the possibilities for public accountability.

Hearings systems are well developed in the USA, with nominees for selected posts at federal, state and local level being required to appear before a panel. Confirmation of the nomination is subject to the panel's recommendation. Hearings make the nominee's experience, business and political connections and views a matter of public record. Fisher (1993) notes that:

> Senate committees are examining more carefully the financial backgrounds of nominees . . . looking for potential conflict-of-interest. The committees also create public record of the nominee's depth of knowledge, previous policy commitments and . . . philosophy.

> (Fisher 1993: 128)

Yet for all its openness and apparent rationality the system has some major limitations. In the first place it divides power between the nominator and the assessors. In the US political system, this reflects the wider constitutional and political balance of power between President and Congress at federal level, governor and state legislature at state level and – in some types of local government – mayor and council. Consequently the panel's assessment of and decision about one particular nominee can be the manifestation of a more general contest between the parties – 'nominees are frequently caught in a political cross-fire' (Fisher 1993: 6). The political context thus limits the usefulness of such hearings (Comisky 1994). Secondly, hearings are frequently oriented towards seeking grounds for rejection. There is a tendency to focus 'relentlessly on a nominee's *disqualification* rather than *qualification*' (Carter 1994: 20, emphasis in original) arising in part from a lack of clear standards on which to assess individuals. Democrat President Clinton's nomination of Anthony Lake as CIA director provides a recent example. He withdrew his nomination in March 1997, accusing Senate members of 'nasty and brutish treatment' in the confirmation hearings. The Republican chairman of the hearing responded that 'they were simply rigorous' (Thomas 1997).

The adoption of such a system into the British context would bring benefits but also add new complexities. It would mark a major change from the conventions of discrete apolitical public service on quango boards. It therefore raises the question of whether potential appointees to key posts would be willing to endure such a public examination. Alternatively, it could separate out those wishing to make a significant contribution from others who see appointment as an honorary and less demanding activity. The strength of the principles underlying hearings thus conflict with the likely practical outcomes. However, such an innovation would redress the balance from the pragmatism that has dominated for so long.

Governing quangos

Codes of conduct

A considerable number of codes of conduct have been directed at the world of quangos, some focused on a specific type of body while others have a more general audience (Box 8.3). They provide guidance on a range of issues, from the provision of public information to the way in which probity is to be safeguarded. Several codes have emerged from government, but there are other sources. One is the umbrella bodies representing classes of quango, an example being the TEC National Council's document. This arose from recognition of a gap in the TECs' accountability structure. Graham (1995: 279) comments that 'neither the requirements of parliamentary accountability (in the TEC operating contract) nor the Companies Acts prescriptions are sufficient to demonstrate local accountability. As TECs are geographically defined . . . they must demonstrably meet their responsibilities to those communities'. The *Framework* states the importance of three principles – openness, integrity and accountability. It translates these into five themes for TECs:

1 They demonstrate clarity and openness in the selection of well-qualified and trained board members.

Box 8.3   Examples of codes of practice applying to quangos

- *Code of Practice on Open Government* (Cabinet Office 1994)
- *Corporate Governance in the NHS: Code of Conduct; Code of Accountability* (Department of Health 1994)
- *Guide for College Governors* (Further Education Funding Council 1994)
- *Code of Best Practice for Board Members of Public Bodies* (HM Treasury 1994)
- *Framework of Democratic Good Practice for Public Services* (Associations of County Councils, District Councils and Metropolitan Authorities 1995)
- *Review of Guidance on Public Appointments* (Public Appointments Unit 1995)
- *Guide for Members of Governing Bodies of Universities and Colleges in England and Wales* (Higher Education Funding Council for England 1995)
- *A Framework for the Local Accountability of Training and Enterprise Councils* (TEC National Council 1995)
- *Code of Practice on Openness in the NHS* (NHS Executive 1995)
- *Guidance on Codes of Practice for Board Members of Public Bodies* (Cabinet Office 1997)

---

2 They ensure that their board is seen to act effectively in the best interests of the local community.
3 They will be open about their performance and about their employment and financial policies.
4 Dealings with customers are on a basis of openness and high quality service with a robust complaints procedure.
5 In dealings with partners and suppliers they seek to be trustworthy, transparent and follow fair commercial practice.

A further source for codes of conduct are third parties. In 1994 Painter *et al.* undertook a review of the policies and operation of appointed bodies in the West Midlands and produced a recommended code of conduct. This was formally adopted by the joint committee of the seven metropolitan district councils, who requested its adoption by local appointed bodies operating in their area (West Midlands Joint Committee 1994). The (then) three local authority associations also produced a *Framework of Democratic Good Practice for Public Services* which formed part of its evidence to the second Nolan inquiry (Associations of County Councils, District Councils and Metropolitan Authorities 1995).

A code of conduct provides a means of introducing an element of guidance into a system. It enables proposals to be made about the approaches that quangos adopt to particular issues, but in a way that apparently does not constrain the discretion of these arm's-length bodies. However, there is a question about the extent to which codes should be mandatory and their implementation monitored and enforced if necessary. The Nolan Committee, for example, took a strong line on enforcement and recommended that 'board members and staff should be required on appointment to undertake to uphold and abide by the relevant code' (Committee on Standards in Public Life 1995a: 87). In the case of TECs, they proposed that compliance with the *Framework* be mandatory for the award of an operating contract or licence. The Nolan Committee's stance on adherence to codes of conduct reflects the findings of the Public Accounts Committee (1994: v) who, having reviewed numerous failures in the proper conduct of public business, concluded that 'almost every case we have examined involved breaches of existing rules or guidance'.

Whether or not codes are mandatory, variation and discretion in appointed bodies will inevitably lead to differences in implementation and compliance. This is illustrated in a review of practice in a small sample of four NHS bodies two years after the NHS corporate governance codes on conduct and accountability were published. The study found that there had been an adoption of the technical procedures required in the codes, but that corporate governance was seen as a board issue rather than one affecting the whole organization. Progress on the technical aspects of probity and acceptability were not matched by developments on other aspects of governance, such as 'openness, dialogue with the community [and] social responsibility' (Morris 1996: 25).

Regulating conflict of interest

A common element in corporate codes of conduct is the avoidance of conflict of interest, long accepted as a central principle in the operation of elected governmental bodies. Two approaches can be employed to regulate conflict of interests. One is to compile a register of members' interests. The Select Committee on Members' Interests defined the purpose of a register as:

> to provide information of any pecuniary interest or other material benefit which a Member receives which might reasonably be thought by others to influence his or her actions, speeches or votes in Parliament, or actions taken in his or her capacity as a Member of Parliament.
> (Cited in Committee on Standards in Public Life 1995a: 27)

Such cataloguing of board member's business and other interests, including employment, directorships, consultancies and investments, would enable the public and other interested parties to assure themselves of the partiality or otherwise of individual board members. The second approach is the declaration of interests at a meeting. The interest could be pecuniary or personal, direct or indirect. Members declaring an interest would retire from the meeting while the matter was discussed and a decision reached. In that way, in theory at least, the members considering the matter will be impartial with respect to the

Table 8.4 Provisions on conflicts of interest applying to members of NDPBs, NHS bodies and local authorities

Body	Register of interests	Disclosure of interests at meetings
Executive NDPBs	Required to declare personal or business interests which might conflict with their responsibilities. Register suggested as mechanism to achieve this. Some NDPBs covered by more specific guidance.	No guidance.
NHS bodies	Required to declare 'material and relevant interests' on appointment. Declarations to be entered into publicly available register. Any change to be declared within four weeks (England & Wales) or when they occur (Scotland). Declaration of directorships and significant interests in annual report.	Required to disclose direct or indirect pecuniary interest when conducting NHS business. Required to withdraw from discussion and decision making on that item.
Local authorities	Required to provide prescribed information on direct and indirect pecuniary interests for publicly available register. Declare any change within one month. Failure so to do is criminal offence.	Councillors with direct or indirect pecuniary interest prohibited from speaking or voting on the relevant issue. May apply to Secretary of State for a dispensation. Any breech is a criminal offence. General requirement that councillors with private and personal non-pecuniary interest will withdraw from the meeting.

Source: Adapted from *Spending Public Money* (1996).

outcome of their deliberations and so be able to act in the best interests of the community.

Spending Public Money (Cm 3179) reviewed the conflict of interest arrangements applying to members of executive NDPBs, NHS bodies and local government. The non-recognized quangos, where some major issues have appeared, are excluded. The White Paper's analysis (Table 8.4) illustrates that the looser the ties between central government departments and the type of body, the stricter the conflict of interest requirements. Local authority councillors, for example, are threatened with sanctions under the criminal law in regard to matters that are not even covered in guidance to NDPB members. It is tempting to speculate that the informal and personal networks which operate in selecting NDPB members leave ministers and their Civil Servants with a sense of comfort at having appointed 'one of us' and a belief that their choice will know how to behave properly. In contrast, local councillors come from more diverse socio-economic backgrounds and hold political authority independently of the government of the day.

The Parliamentary 'Register of Members' Interests' illustrates some of the difficulties of applying this approach in the absence of regulations requiring the full disclosure of the individual's assets and income. These include the problem of defining the level of detail that is required and the discretion available to individuals in deciding what to include and what to exclude. More generally, the positive value of a register must be offset by the potential confusion it causes – the Nolan Committee commented that it 'has tended to create a false impression that any interest is acceptable once it has been registered' (Committee on Standards in Public Life 1995a: 27). Nevertheless, the significance of probity and good governance in public services mandates the development of registers of members' interests across the appointed sector – including non-recognized bodies – together with regulations covering withdrawal from meetings. Some steps are being made in this direction. Highlands and Islands Enterprise in Scotland requires members to make an annual written declaration of interests, updated as necessary, which is available for public inspection. The TEC National Council's *Framework* recommends maintenance of an up-to-date register of directors' and employees' interests, including 'all paid employment, appointments and directorships, equity interests over 10 per cent and other interests (including those of close family which may be relevant to the business of the TEC)'. The phrase 'may be' is important in enabling registers to provide a comprehensive and relevant picture of members' interests, although it is also one that is difficult to interpret and regulate. The *Framework* also recommends TECs develop procedures for resolving conflicts of interest in business, including declarations and minuted decisions of whether the director or employee may take part in the discussion and decision, or see relevant papers. However, it is important to consider whether, in the light of the findings of the PAC and Nolan reports, voluntary codes of practice are sufficient. There is a strong case for applying the legal framework regulating councillors' conflict of interests to all appointed bodies.

Audit arrangements

There are several limitations in the audit arrangements for quangos, in particular the partial coverage of NDPBs and non-recognized quangos by the National Audit Office, the Audit Office for Northern Ireland, the Audit Commission and the Accounts Commission in Scotland (see Chapter 2). In addition the Comptroller and Auditor General was appointed as auditor for some NDPBs but only had inspection rights for others. Some of the inspection rights were statutorily based while others had to be agreed with the individual public body. These and related issues were investigated by the Nolan Committee, who took evidence from the NAO and Audit Commission to the effect that all appointed bodies should be subject to best practice public audit, covering financial, regularity, probity, value for money and governance matters. The NAO and Audit Commission were also concerned that considerable numbers of institutions were able to appoint their own auditors, arguing that a better quality product was achievable where auditors were commissioned by a third party. The implication was that the NAO and Audit Commission should be responsible for overseeing the audit of all quangos. The Nolan Committee was sympathetic to the philosophy underlying this view. Its first report noted the differences in relation to NDPBs and NHS bodies, and observed that while 'there may be good reason for maintaining differences in the audit regimes for different public bodies . . . the current variation seems to be the result of the introduction of measures on an *ad hoc* basis' (Committee on Standards in Public Life 1995a: 90). The Committee proposed that the external audit arrangements of public bodies be reviewed 'with a view to applying the best practices to all of them' (p. 90).

Nolan's recommendation led to a study by the Cabinet Office which was published as *Spending Public Money* (Weekes 1996). This Green Paper rejected the notion of integrated audit across the appointed sector. It concluded that it was appropriate for the structure of audit to take account of the differences between types of quango, and thus rejected the notion of oversight by the Audit Commission and NAO. However it did suggest some detailed changes. Of particular relevance are:

1 That those undertaking public audit should place greater emphasis on regularity issues and questions about how well and properly public funds are used.
2 That the Government would ensure inspection rights for the Comptroller and Auditor General over all executive NDPBs and companies wholly or mainly owned by them.
3 That the Audit Commission should be able to publish public interest reports on NHS bodies, a power that applied to local authorities but not NHS bodies.

The subsequent White Paper *The Governance of Public Money: A Progress Report* Cm 3557 (1997) reiterated these points. It also proposed that the responsibility for external audit of health bodies in Northern Ireland should be transferred from the Department of Health (Northern Ireland) to the Northern Ireland Audit Office.

Although the first part of the Nolan recommendation was implemented, a patchwork of audit responsibilities remains. Cm 3179 and Cm 3557 produced little change to the status quo, rather than taking the opportunities provided by the momentum for reform of the appointed sector. The underlying rationale for this strategy was rooted in the arm's-length principle (Chapter 3) and the desire of appointed bodies to maximize their autonomy in managing their finances. The Nolan Committee, for example, reported that there was 'a constant complaint' from local appointed bodies 'that they are subjected to excessively detailed monitoring, requiring a disproportionate amount of time to be spent in collecting management information' (Committee on Standards in Public Life 1996: 14). Up to six levels of financial audit were identified in the case of TECs in England and Wales and local enterprise companies in Scotland. Nolan recommended that central control of such bodies should be limited to ensuring an 'effective audit framework' (p. 15). However, it should be remembered that quangos spend considerable amounts of public money and are the sector where there has been the most concern about financial management and probity. Consequently the ability of the public's independent audit bodies – the NAO and Audit Commission – to oversee arrangements and take a strategic perspective is essential. Yet this is only part of the answer – most of the 26 serious failings identified in the Public Accounts Committee's report *The Proper Conduct of Public Business* were in bodies already subject to public audit.

This finding highlights the importance of internal mechanisms to promote probity and to audit performance. One approach is to create an audit committee which, the Chartered Institute of Public Finance and Accountancy (CIPFA) (1996) argued, would enable non-executive board members to provide an independent check on the organization's financial management. It would promote internal control, focus audit resources and monitor audit performance. In this respect, the proposal reflects the thinking behind the Cadbury Report from the Committee on the Financial Aspects of Corporate Governance (1992). The Audit Commission supports this approach, since they found that the governance of audit tends to be distributed across service, finance and performance review committees (Table 8.5).

The final element in the reform of audit arrangements for quangos is the proposal that board members and senior managers should be held accountable for the consequences of poor financial control and lack of probity. This

Table 8.5   The role of the Audit Committee

Role	Activity
Promoting internal control	Systematic appraisal of internal controls
	Develop an anti-fraud culture
	Review financial procedures
Focusing audit resources	Agree audit plans
	Monitor audit delivery
Monitoring audit performance	Secure auditor/officer collaboration within agreed timescales
	Secure timely preparation and response to audit reports
	Monitor the finalization of annual accounts
	Ensure the implementation of audit recommendations

Source: Audit Commission (1996).

reflects the inequity between the treatment of local councillors who are liable for surcharge if expenditure is incurred *ultra vires* or through wilful misconduct (although changes to this regime have been recommended by the Nolan Committee) and members of quango boards who are protected from individual liability. Board members responsible for poor management or lack of probity are either left in place, quietly removed or receive a financial settlement in return for resignation or retirement. Where they are appointed by and accountable to ministers, their poor behaviour reflects on the judgement and oversight of the minister concerned and thus there is a political limitation on disciplinary action. Select committees, however, have been willing to identify and censor particular individuals and Lord Nolan has called for changes in the rules of ministerial accountability in order to make senior managers and boards openly answerable (Nolan 1996).

Strengthening accountability

Transferring quangos to the elected sector of government

The most radical proposal for reform of executive quangos is that they should be transferred – or in some cases returned – to the elected sector of government. This proposal particularly concerns the non-recognized quangos with their significant democratic deficit and challenge to the lead role of the local authority in local service delivery and community governance. In contrast there has been little debate about election for national appointed bodies. Ministers see no problem in exercising their power to appoint and governments have maintained the principle that there is a direct line of accountability from quangos through the minister to Parliament. The new Labour Government, however, has linked democratic oversight of quangos to its proposals for devolution to Scotland and Wales, although this does not necessarily involve direct election to boards.

   Stewart (1995a) has identified two criteria that may be employed in determining whether an area of public activity should be subject to direct democratic control. The first is where a body has a significant responsibility for determining policy that affects the community. Stewart takes the health authority as an example, noting that it is 'debating and clarifying values rather than . . . technical issues' (1995a: 9). The exercise of judgement on matters of value, therefore, creates a predisposition for the body to be in the elected sector. The second criteria is whether 'interests are at stake beyond those immediately concerned' (p. 10). Stewart draws a distinction between the body's responsibility to those who use its services and its responsibilities to the wider community and into the future. In the former case mechanisms other than direct election can provide for consumer rights, for example charters of service standards, complaints systems or the provision of places for user representatives on the governing body. Where a body has wider responsibilities, however, it is necessary to integrate it into the democratic process as a means of facilitating the representation and consideration of broader concerns and interests.

If an appointed body is to be transferred to the elected sector, issues arise about the means to be employed. The choices include:

1 *The incorporation model*: Incorporating the appointed body into a local authority or regional assembly. It could also be incorporated into a central government department.
2 *The direct election model*: Separate elections to the appointed body itself.
3 *The indirect election model*: Indirect election to the appointed body through local authority rights to place councillors on the board.

The incorporation model has appeal to local authority eyes. The appointed body could be reconstituted as a committee of the local authority and its staff transferred to an existing or new department. Health authorities are the most obvious candidates for this solution. They already have a significant interrelationship with social services, especially in the commissioning and joint planning of services. Integration of the two functions could produce efficiencies through the removal of political and operational differences between the two bodies, as well as increasing accountability for the commissioning and purchasing of the social care and health function by giving it a single point of focus (National Association of Health Authorities and Trusts 1993; Association of Metropolitan Authorities 1994; Clarke *et al.* 1995). Wandsworth London Borough Council unsuccessfully applied to the Secretary of State to have certain health responsibilities transferred to it, justifying the move on the grounds of efficiency and accountability (Cooper *et al.* 1995). Hunter (1995) reviews the case for transfer and suggests that it may solve the problem of legitimacy faced by health managers serving a non-elected board. However, he sounds a note of caution, arguing that local political choice may lead to greater disparity in standards and that the greater size and bureaucracy of local authorities may constrain sensitivity to users.

The Scottish and Welsh regional assemblies provide an alternative means of increasing direct electoral control of quangos. The proposals for the Welsh Assembly foresee some quangos, especially those requiring independence from the executive, being maintained. Others would either be transferred to the responsibility of the Assembly or to local authorities. There may also be a reduction in the number of NHS trusts and TECs in Wales. The White Paper on Scotland is more circumspect, noting that the Scottish Parliament will have an oversight of public bodies and that further details will be developed.

Direct elections to the board provide one alternative to the incorporation model. They can be justified where the body serves a well-defined community or constituency. Schools are an example, and direct election to governing bodies is already undertaken for the minority of seats reserved for parent governors. This principle could be extended to all or most places on the governing body. Direct election to a single-purpose body is well established in the USA, for example in the special districts where single-purpose bodies such as school boards operate alongside multipurpose local government. In the USA, however, it has been associated with privatism – interest groups creating specific public bodies in order to gain advantages in the nature and type of services provided (Davis and Hall 1996). Despite this, however, electoral turn-out for special districts is often much lower than that for local government elections in the UK (Burns 1994). Any board proposed for direct election should therefore pass a test of electoral viability so that it is able to claim legitimacy (Stewart 1995a).

The third model for securing democratic control is through indirect election – the placing of MPs, regional assembly members or local authority councillors on quango boards. They may be allocated to all or a proportion of seats. This model has been employed for the joint boards created in the metropolitan counties following the abolition of the county councils in 1986. These statutory bodies have a membership of councillors nominated by the constituent district councils. The police authorities, which have now been superseded by new arrangements under the Police and Magistrates Courts Act 1994, also had magistrate members. Leach *et al.* (1991) argue that the accountability component of the indirect election system might be expected to meet five criteria:

1 Local authority nominees' receive an expert briefing from one or more of the authority's officers on issues arising on the joint board's agenda.
2 There is a forum at which the local authority's stance on these issues is decided.
3 Joint board members receive instructions on voting requirements.
4 The nominees report back to the local authority.
5 Matters relating to the joint board are discussed at committee or full council.

Their research into the operation of the system reveals that in general these conditions fail to be fulfilled. They found that the accountability of joint board members to their own local authorities is limited and tends to come into play only when major policy or financial issues arise in which the authority has an interest. Otherwise these indirectly elected members are left to their own devices and as a result have a tendency to become captured by the service professionals at joint board level. Thus rather than developing and making policy on the basis of the constituent district councils' interest, they tend to become advocates for the joint board. This process is accentuated because of the lack of direct accountability to the electorate. Appointments to joint boards are chosen through each local authority's normal political processes. Therefore it is difficult for individual councillors to make promises in their election addresses about matters covered by the boards since they have no idea whether or not they will be on them. Overall, therefore, indirect election raises as many problems as it solves. It does improve the accountability relationship in theory, yet in practice the political independence of the body is maintained. Effectively, one set of appointees is replaced by another.

The Association of Metropolitan Authorities (AMA) undertook a review of local appointed bodies and examined preferred methods of increasing local

Table 8.6 Reforming local appointed bodies – the AMA view

Body	Proposal	Rationale
Health authorities	Abolish. Transfer commissioning function to local authority and integrate with social services.	To enhance democratic accountability and greater integration of commissioning and purchasing.
NHS trusts	Reform board composition to include councillors, local GPs and trust employees.	Variety of types of trusts suggests incorporation into local government not feasible.
GM schools and city technology colleges	Abolish. Return to local education authority.	Oligarchic governing bodies and lack of accountability to community.
Sixth form and further education colleges	Reform governing bodies to enable broader representation and integration of planning for 14–19 and adult education provision.	Oligarchic governing bodies and lack of accountability to community, but incorporation not feasible due to special nature of the institutions.
Training and enterprise councils	Require TECs to work within policy framework developed by local authority in partnership with other local bodies. Appointments to be made by local authority in consultation with local business community. Possibility that private sector interests could elect their members.	Involvement of business essential. Arm's-length principle acceptable provided accountability link to local authority.

Table 8.6 *Continued*

Body	Proposal	Rationale
Urban development corporations	Statutory duty to work in partnership with local authority; 50% board places from local authority and 50% from employer, trade union and community.	Most now in exit phase due to having a limited life. New board structure will facilitate this exit process.
Housing action trusts	No change. No further HATs to be created.	Little purpose served in change.
Housing Corporation	Abolish. Divide funding functions between government offices for the regions and local authorities. Regulatory functions transferred to Audit Commission.	To increase local accountability for public expenditure on local housing need.
Environment Agency	Reform board to include local authority nominees. Local authority members to form significant proportion of membership of regional environmental protection advisory committees.	Accept case for arm's-length body in this field, but propose alternative model.
Audit Commission	Reform so that significant proportion of Commission's members are serving councillors or officers with extensive local government experience.	To increase ownership of the Commission by organizations who use its services.

Source: Association of Metropolitan Authorities (1995).

government's influence at board level (Table 8.6). Only in two cases did they recommend the complete transfer of the activity to local government – health authority commissioning and purchasing and GM schools/city technology colleges. It believed that part of the Housing Corporation's funding function should also come into local government. In the main, however, the AMA opted for increased local authority nomination rights to boards. This was justified principally on the grounds of the particular or special circumstances of the body. Consequently, the radical option of transferring appointed bodies to the elected sector is not one that local government regards as feasible or desirable for most types of local appointed body. Instead, nomination rights for local authorities are adopted as the main mechanism for reducing the democratic deficit.

Contestability

The idea of contestability provides an alternative to the option of turning appointed bodies into elected authorities. Mulgan (1993) argues that direct election does not necessarily ensure that the best or most representative individuals are elected. Further, because appointed bodies are effectively local monopolies, their boards can survive almost regardless of their performance.

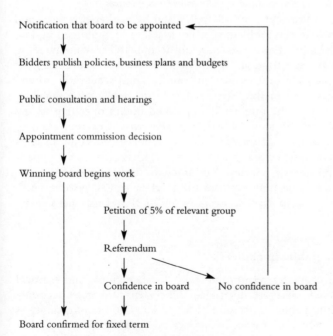

Figure 8.1 The process of contestability.
Source: Adapted from Mulgan (1993).

He proposes that quangos are likely to perform at their optimum when their boards face the threat of dismissal, presenting the principle that 'wherever in public life there is a deficit of competitive pressures, mechanisms need to be devised which create them' (p. 5).

The principle of contestability would involve the creation of an appointment commission comprising representatives from the democratically elected institutions having an interest in the particular body (Figure 8.1). The commission would announce the appointment of a new body, or of a new board, six months prior to their date of commencement. Appointment would be for a fixed term. Groups or coalitions would bid to become the board, submitting details of their policies, a business plan and indicative budget. All submissions would be available for public scrutiny. The appointment commission would assess the bids and select the preferred one. Mulgan suggests that such a model has several virtues: it would encourage coalition-building across ranges of interests; it would make the selection procedure and criteria public; the public could be involved through representation to the appointment commission; and it would make explicit the criteria that would be used to assess the board's performance. The possibilities for public evaluation of performance are linked to a dismissal process. A petition by 5 per cent of the population of the area covered by the body would trigger a referendum of confidence in the board. Failure in the referendum by a simple majority would lead to the dismissal of the board and the instigation of new appointment procedures.

Mulgan's model provides a novel application of market principles and competitive tendering to the problem of accountability in appointed bodies. He suggests that it achieves greater efficiency and accountability while avoiding the twin problems of patronage and inadequate democratic procedures. Its main virtue is in making clear the evaluation criteria against which a board will be judged and suggesting a method for linking this to public accountability. One difficulty arises from the number of appointed bodies operating in any locality. There is a question about whether citizens would be motivated to monitor and initiate actions against each individual appointed body. In contrast, the advantage of the electoral system is that it offers citizens the opportunity to discuss a package of policies to be implemented through a range of institutions and at the same time evaluate the local or central government's previous performance, all in a single event – the local and national general election.

Involving the public in choices

Independently of a changing relationship with local, regional and national government, appointed bodies are able to take other steps to increase accountability and involve the public in decision making. The critique of quangos as closed and unaccountable institutions has combined with the growth of consumerism and renewed interest in citizenship to create a climate in which new democratic practices are emerging, especially in relation to local appointed

bodies who feel these pressures most keenly. HATs and many health authorities, for example, have taken considerable steps to develop a richer engagement with their communities. The 'Local Voices' initiative in the NHS was
designed to 'give people an effective voice in the shaping of health services
locally [and] will call for a radically different approach from that involved in the
past' (NHS Executive circular cited in Cooper et al. 1995: 46). Despite criticisms of tokenism, 'Local Voices' demonstrated that citizens could be involved
in examining and advising on complex matters of judgement involving widely
differing value positions. The technique employed to develop this process was
citizens' juries (Stewart et al. 1994). A citizens' jury is a small group of individuals selected to be representative of the community. They meet to consider a
particular policy issue, receiving evidence from a range of witnesses who they
can cross-examine. They examine the facts of the situation, consider underlying causes and investigate choices and their consequences. They present the
findings from their deliberations to the health authority or other body. The
evidence to date is that 'jurors become confident lay experts, thinking not just
for themselves but for the public at large, changing their minds in the course of
deliberation and reaching decisions which command the respect of experts'
(Cooper et al. 1995: 68). Citizens' juries can be supplemented by a variety of
other democratic practices (Stewart 1995b). Together they provide an important means of developing a constructive dialogue between appointed bodies and
their community or constituency and in the process begin to overcome some
of the problems created by the growth of the quango state.

Registers and scrutiny

The paucity of information about quango members has resulted in the compilation of unofficial registers at national and local level. The Parliamentary
Questions asked by Peter Kilfoyle MP and Alan Milburn MP were consolidated
and published in the BBC Political Research Unit's directory (BBC 1994d).
This provided the first comprehensive list of names of members of quango
boards (see Chapter 5). Subsequently some official directories have appeared,
most notably that for the NHS. A number of local authorities enthusiastically
compiled registers to increase public information about the quangos operating
in their locality. These registers typically list the names and addresses of the
bodies, information on their board members, expenditure details and information on how citizens can make representations or complain. They are available
at libraries and other local information points and have also, as in the case of
Stevenage Borough Council, been published in local newspapers (Local Government Information Unit 1994a). Besides the public information basis of this
work, the compilation of registers demonstrates the local authority's legitimate
concern with the operation of appointed bodies as part of its wider community
governance role.

Having gained an overview of quangos in their area, local authorities
such as Oxford City Council and Watford Borough Council developed

arrangements to monitor and scrutinize their activities. This involved inviting members and officers of quangos to present and discuss reports on their activities at council committees, the creation of special committees at which local authority members are able to monitor the activities of appointed bodies in their area individually and collectively and liaison arrangements between the various parties. Collaborative working has also developed with a number of local authorities establishing partnership forums together with appointed bodies and other interested parties to explore joint plans in the context of the needs of the locality. Finally, local authorities have taken steps to raise issues of concern to citizens with the relevant bodies and to seek change (Local Government Information Unit 1994b). Such monitoring and scrutiny activities illustrate at a local level what could be implemented at the national level. They model the role that could be performed by a Select Committee on Appointed Bodies within the House of Commons (see below). It is local authorities' closeness to the community and the activities of an individual quango that are their strength, enabling relevant and appropriate questions to be asked and a form of local accountability to be developed.

Regulating the system

Select committee on quangos

Proposals that the House of Commons should have stronger mechanisms to monitor appointed bodies and hold them to account have been suggested over a considerable period of time. In the current select committee system, quangos are investigated either by the Public Accounts Committee, on matters of probity and the efficient use of public money, or by the relevant select committee for those quangos sponsored or funded by the department that it oversees. Only in the case of Northern Ireland, Wales and Scotland is an overall national perspective possible. As a result, Parliament lacks the capacity to gain an oversight of the appointed sector in England or the UK as a whole, to monitor trends and performance or to take appropriate action (Chapter 2). This contrasts with the 'Next Steps' agencies created since the early 1990s. Here the Public Service Committee, formerly the Treasury and Civil Service Committee, has the potential to take such an overview.

Holland and Fallon (1978: 24) suggested that 'a [new] Select Committee should be given the power to examine any non-industrial body that has not been investigated by any other Committee of the House within the last five years'. An alternative would be to establish a Select Committee on Appointed Bodies reflecting the stance developed towards nationalized industries in the 1950s. Then, there was considerable debate about the nature of ministerial accountability for and Parliamentary oversight of these new and significant public corporations (Coombes 1966). The Morrisonian model was predicated on the distinction between general political direction and matters of specific management. Ministers were accountable to Parliament for the former while the board of the corporation was accountable to the minister for the latter. Great efforts to hold this line were made by Morrison himself and by the chairmen of the newly nationalized industries. Morrison and the chairmen argued that the idea of a select committee:

> was not only contrary to the spirit and intention of the legislation, but contrary to the British constitutional tradition. The nationalisation statutes clearly intended Parliament to abstain from interfering in the details of management. If a select committee were appointed the lines of responsibility would become blurred; and in any case they thought Parliament is not a suitable body to investigate the managerial efficiency of a complex industrial undertaking.
>
> (Robson 1962: 185)

Similarly vibrant efforts to re-assert Parliamentary scrutiny were made by various MPs and eventually the Select Committee on Nationalized Industries was created. Its investigations, however, tended to be of individual bodies rather than of the system as a whole. This reflected its rather constrained terms of reference – 'to examine the reports and accounts of the nationalised industries established by statute' (ibid.: 189–90) – as much as the political context of the time and the Select Committee's lack of technical support. The Committee undertook a number of investigations, but was abolished in 1979 when a new select committee system was created. Nevertheless, the principle of a select committee to monitor and review the activities of a class of public bodies has been established, and it is that principle which could again be adopted in relation to quangos. Such a select committee would operate in parallel with the departmental select committees much as the PAC does at present. Its remit would be to monitor, assess and make recommendations on matters concerned with appointed bodies, taking the strategic perspective that it is not possible for departmental committees or the PAC to adopt. It would, for example, be able to consider the extent to which the Nolan recommendations related to quangos had been implemented. To be effective, however, the remit of such a body would need to include all quangos, including those that are – in Weir and Hall's terms – not recognized.

Sunset provisions and administrative law

The 1979–97 Conservative Governments adopted the recommendation of the Pliatzky Report that NDPBs be subject to quinquennial review. This process had two stages. The first was a 'prior options' review designed to test the suitability of the body or its individual functions for market testing, privatization or transfer to another organization. If the NDPB survived this stage, a further review was undertaken to examine its cost-effectiveness and internal financial management. The process, therefore, related to the market-led strategy of the previous government. The criteria employed in the review process are likely to change under the new Labour administration.

A more radical proposal to regulate the appointed sector comes from practice in the USA. 'Sunset' legislation adopted by a large number of states provides that various types of public bodies are given a fixed term of operation. They are automatically abolished at the end of this period unless a procedure to renew leads to a positive outcome (Holland 1994). Such legislation arose in the context of movements to reduce the scale of government and its financial demands on the population, a value more strongly rooted in the US political culture than that of the UK. However, it would be particularly effective in regulating the advisory quangos and ensuring that their purpose was meeting public rather than private ends (Weir and Hall 1995). More importantly, such provision would require clarification of the presently confused legal basis for appointed bodies. Existing quangos have been created by Royal Charter or Warrant, Act of Parliament, ministerial administrative act, a Treasury minute notifying Parliament or through Companies Act or charitable trust registration. There is no clear logic to the choice of mechanism.

In some countries, government institutions are governed and regulated by systems of administrative law and have bodies whose role is to exercise an oversight of the whole system. Most European states have a body of administrative law as do the Scandinavian nations and the USA. France, for example, has a system of administrative courts at the pinnacle of which is the Council of State. This arrangement derives from the tradition of Napoleonic rationality and is supported by a written constitution codifying the relationship between the individual and the state (Stevens 1996). Australia and the USA both have agencies charged with reviewing administrative activity by government. In Australia, the Administrative Review Council's role is to advise the Attorney General on ways in which practice can be built on consistent principles rather than *ad hoc* developments as in the UK. A number of bodies feed into the Council, including the Administrative Appeals Tribunal which monitors the application and development of discretionary decision making on the part of government (Weir and Hall 1994). To be effective, 'sunset' legislation and the introduction of administrative law would require the definition of the appointed sector to be clear and for government to accept that it includes the non-recognized bodies.

The changing agenda of reform

Prior to the 1997 general election, the debate about quango reform was charged with a particular saliency. Then, the Conservative Party had been in power for more than a decade. Improper and impolitic behaviour of quango board appointees was associated with a general decline in standards on the part of Conservative ministers and MPs. The growth of non-recognized bodies and actual or claimed political patronage in the appointments process was seen as part of the Conservative Party's strategy to retain the reins of power at national level and extend its influence into the regions where Labour and Liberal Democrats had been making local electoral gains. Advocates of reform, therefore, were as much concerned with halting the tendency to monopolistic Conservative power as with

Table 8.7 Reforming appointed bodies

Proposal	Comment
● Appointing members	
Opening up process of appointment through advertising, selection criteria, etc.	Creates opportunity to draw on whole population; increases clarity and openness; greater use of advertising since mid-1990s; impact of openness on recruitment yet to be identified.
Independent Appointments Commission	Reduces possibility of ministerial patronage; problem of acceptability of members and decisions; possible reduction in accountability to Parliament.
Public hearings for key quango posts	Creates public record of experience and views; problems of dividing responsibility for appointment; would involve major change in British convention, possibly reducing individuals' willingness to serve.
● Governing quangos	
Codes of conduct	Provides clear principles and good practice; likelihood of variation in compliance; difficulties of monitoring.
Regulating conflict of interest	Varying requirements at present; success depends on full disclosure; possible legal sanctions.
Audit arrangements	Variation before and after Nolan; partial acceptance of wider NAO/Audit Commission roles; development of audit committees; sanctions on board members where poor financial management and lack of probity.

Table 8.7 *Continued*

Proposal	Comment
● **Strengthening accountability**	
Transferring quangos to the elected sector	Possible in a few cases; alternative models permit regional assembly or local authority influence and greater local accountability; problems with indirect election.
Contestability	Competitive bidding to run organization; clear performance criteria; process for dismissal; requires active public scrutiny.
Involving the public in choices	Draws on innovations in democratic practice; application in practice; develops dialogue between community and board.
Registers and scrutiny	Some national registers; local authority compilation of registers of quangos in locality; increases public information; basis for scrutiny via local select committees; collaborative planning arrangements.
● **Regulating the system**	
Select committee on appointed bodies	Provides strategic overview; operate in parallel with departmental select committees; role in monitoring implementation of Nolan.
Sunset provisions and administrative law	Requires formalization of legal basis of quangos; facilitates development of consistent principles; clearer basis for citizens to argue grievances.

creating appropriate forms of public governance and management. The four themes for reform provide different strategies to achieve these ends (Table 8.7).

As the Major Government faced crisis after crisis in the era of sleaze, so it accommodated some of the demands of the reformers. This particularly applied to the publication of information about appointees and the introduction of advertising for board positions. The creation of the Nolan Committee enabled a public airing of concerns and reasoned consideration of proposals for change, but also performed the classic and inevitable function of distancing the issue from the government of the day. Quango reform became a matter on which Lord Nolan's Committee would report in due course. The Committee's recommendations appeared quite quickly and trod a middle path between the established position on quangos and the demands of critics. On some issues it supported the status quo (for example, ministerial accountability to Parliament for quango board appointments and the arm's-length principle), while on others (such as strengthening audit) it was more radical. Some proposals were accepted by government; others were rejected or compromised. *Spending Public Money* provides a case in point (see above). There has been further movement on the reform agenda since the new Labour administration took power. More use is being made of advertisements to recruit potential board members to NDPBs and NHS bodies, greater objectivity is being introduced into the appointment process in some ministries and the proposals for regional assemblies in Scotland and Wales promise a greater level of democratic oversight. Where changes have been introduced by either party they have tended to follow the British tradition of incremental change. And the result is that ministerial power in the appointments process to public bodies has not weakened and the fundamental problems of the non-recognized bodies remain untouched.

The result of the 1997 general election has led to a weakening of popular pressure for quango reform, despite the continuing need for it to occur. The movement of the Conservatives into opposition has defused the sleaze debate and, as a result, disassociated the question of quasi-government from 'cash for questions', politicization of the senior Civil Service and abuse of public office. Although the problems of the democratic deficit remain and effective public governance and regulation of the appointed sector is still lacking, the events surrounding the general election of May 1997 have pushed the discussion of quangos down the political agenda. It is almost as though quangos as an organizational form are now acceptable and it was only their manipulation by the Conservative Government that created problems. This parallels the situation around the time of the 1979 general election, when the roles of the two parties with respect to quangos were reversed. However, it is dangerous to fall into the trap of believing that the limited reforms to date and the change of national government have resolved the problems of the appointed sector. If the recent debate about quangos has shown anything, it is that the institutions of British government remain rooted in a set of inconsistencies and lack an integrating logic. In this way the analysis of quangos casts light on a wider reform agenda and one which is pursued in the concluding chapter.

9

Assessing quasi-government

The rapid growth of the appointed sector and its close association with party political patronage and questionable standards of governance produced a flood of criticisms and rebuttals during the mid-1990s. Now that the waters have calmed a little, it is possible to construct a more considered assessment of this major change to the way in which Britain is governed. The nature of this movement should not be underestimated. There has been a substantial transfer of power from the elected to the appointed sector of government, and particularly to the non-recognized quangos – Nolan's 'local public spending bodies' – where new board members are appointed by those already in post. Here the ministerial writ is weak and the personal accountability of board members limited. Yet, however much one may support the principle of direct democratic control, the complexity of the modern state and the nature of its functions mean that there will always be a place for appointed bodies. Indeed, the creation of several new quangos was amongst the Labour Government's early actions.

A balance sheet for quasi-government can be created (Box 9.1). This contains justifications for the creation of quangos but also questions that should be asked. In a society that has struggled over several centuries to create and extend the franchise and build institutions for sound central and local government, the passing of power to non-elected bodies should be subject to critical debate. Hard-won democratic rights must not easily be lost to those who prefer to exercise their will through patronage, private decision making and a limited role for citizens. Beyond this balance sheet, the debate about quangos raises wider questions concerning the governance of Britain. These link to the

---

Box 9.1   Quasi-government – A balance sheet

The case for

- Particular expertise can be brought into government.
- Design of board structure enables key stakeholders to be incorporated into public policy process.
- Potential to achieve desired socio-economic pattern of board membership.
- Single-purpose boards offer potential for focus on specific policies and tasks.
- Judgements about application and interpretation of public policy best made by individuals who are independent of government.
- Implementation of public policy enhanced where it is undertaken by individuals who are committed or sympathetic to it.
- Delegation of authority reduces demands on ministers and other centres of elected decision making.

The case against

- Democratic deficit undermines legitimacy of elected central and local government.
- Problems of accountability for public programmes.
- No requirement for elected politicians to have particular expertise.
- Role of directly elected politicians constrained by distancing them from particular fields of governmental decision making.
- Claimed independence of bodies undermined by potential for party political patronage in appointment.
- 'Congested state' arising from increase in numbers of single-purpose bodies, causing problems of strategic governance and coordination and creation of meso-level quasi-governmental 'partnership' agencies.
- Lack of rationale for allocation of executive functions between elected and appointed bodies.

---

developing analysis of citizenship and accountable government. They are to do with the way in which society governs itself and the ideas and principles that inform democratic practice.

A balance sheet for quangos

Expertise, independence and responsive competence: the case for quangos

Government by appointment is not *per se* undesirable. There are positive justifications for the use of this mechanism. One of the main benefits is that particular patterns of membership can be created. The ability to appoint has the potential to bring into the core of government expertise that would otherwise be peripheral. The advisory quangos demonstrate this feature. They provide a means by which relevant knowledge and informed opinions on specific matters can be utilized by Whitehall within the public policy process. Advisory quangos inject particular expertise, especially on technical and scientific matters, and act as a confidential sounding-board for politicians and their officials. The existence of expertise does not mean that a consensus view exists, and in public policy there are inevitably differences of opinion about the weighting of values and prediction of outcomes. The ability of ministers to structure a quango board's composition enables various interests and stakeholders to be incorporated into the process of deliberation and decision. The decision-making forum itself, therefore, can consist of representatives from the parties affected rather than elected politicians who may have little direct understanding or experience of the issue in question. This is illustrated in some NDPBs in the agriculture and urban regeneration fields as well as non-recognized bodies in the training and education sector. Bringing such stakeholders into government offers the prospect of decisions that are better informed and built on consensus. The power to determine the structure of the board can also be used to create a membership having a desired socio-economic composition. It can be employed to overcome the under-representation of ethnic minorities, women, working class and younger people in government. This is more a potential than a reality, as the analysis in Chapter 4 illustrates, for there is little evidence of such positive appointment strategies other than in the NHS.

A cornerstone of the appointed sector is the arm's-length principle – that boards are given overall direction by ministers and then left to implement policy in ways they judge to be preferable. This suggests that quangos are relatively independent of the party political world of elected government. Consequently, it can be argued that quango members are more 'objective' than elected politicians and thus better able to make decisions that are in the general public interest. This is the counter-democratic notion of benign rule by those who are above the tensions and contests of day-to-day affairs. However, distance from elected government is important in cases where quasi-legal judgements are being made, especially where the matter in dispute is a decision of another public body. The independence of appointees is a matter of principle when the rights of the citizen are set against the coercion of the state. There are an extensive series of tribunals that undertake this role. Their task is to weigh evidence and reach a judgement, yet their membership is appointed by government. It is unclear whether this causes role tensions on the part of members in reaching their decisions.

The delegation of authority to quangos reduces the demands on central and local authorities. Politicians can give strategic guidance without having to be concerned with the detail of implementation – unless it causes major political problems. Such delegation is not cost-free, since implementation involves the interpretation of guidance and exercise of discretion. Boards may make judgements that are not in line with the wishes of the elected government on

whose behalf they act. This raises the general problem of responsive competence (Chapter 5). The exercise of patronage enables the selection of board
members who are sympathetic, or at least not opposed, to government policy.
Informal linkages and reciprocity facilitate compliance on the part of bodies
with delegated authority. The rhetoric of arm's-length independence is compromised by the criteria and process of appointment. In this way, the business
of politics is facilitated.

Democratic deficit, managerialism and the congested state: the case against quangos

The democratic deficit is central to the critique of appointed bodies. The
weaker accountability, audit and governance standards applying in general to
quangos undermine the legitimacy of elected government. If appointed bodies
can run public services quite well without a panoply of election, party politics
and regulation, one may ask, should all remaining public provision be removed
from central and local government? More broadly, is there a case for maintaining the range of democratic institutions now found in the UK? This challenge
to elected government arises from the ideology of managerialism that has
informed the recent growth of quangos. It reflects a narrow view of the public
realm as being about the efficient production of goods and services for public
purpose in which the primacy of the consumer is emphasized. The concern
with service provision, important as it is, distracts from the more fundamental
role of government in arbitrating the competing values and demands of citizens
in society. The mechanisms for undertaking this – election of citizens, opportunities for expression of view, transparency of decision process, means of
appeal – are largely absent in quangos. The democratic deficit reflects a fundamental weakness in the ability of citizens to be involved in the structures with
which society governs itself.

One of the characteristics of the British political system is that candidates
for election need offer no particular expertise. Government is undertaken by
informed lay-people advised by officials, rather than by experts. This offers the
prospect of judgements that combine informed opinion with an awareness of
public preferences. The structuring of some quango boards to accommodate
particular expertise combined with their members' lack of a public profile and
constituency base limits the capacity for these bodies to incorporate popular
views and preferences. Conversely, the creation of quangos distances the elected politicians who bring this perspective from decisions on a range of public
services. Not only are they less able to contribute as policy makers, but their
role in representing, advocating and trouble-shooting on behalf of constituents
is reduced. Popular perceptions of party political patronage in quango appointments together with the closed nature of the process compounds public mis-
trust of elected politicians and of the governmental system more generally.

The case against the current scale of the appointed sector must also be
considered in terms of its impact on the overall governmental system. The

substantial number of single-purpose quangos is limiting the capacity for the strategic guidance and coordination of public policy and programmes and is resulting in the phenomena of the *congested state*. The congested state denotes an environment in which high levels of organizational fragmentation combined with plural modes of governance require the application of significant resources to negotiating the development and delivery of public programmes. Congestion is overcome by building coalitions of organizations, which may be of a temporary nature, around particular missions. In the urban regeneration field, for example, the interconnections between central government and local authority departments, TECs, voluntary and business organizations, project-oriented quangos such as HATs, UDCs and City Challenge, further education corporations and other agencies are such that new quasi-governmental partnership bodies are being created to manage the complexities involved. These multi-agency partnerships are frequently focused on bidding competitions for government funds, for example Single Regeneration Budget. Meso-level quasi-government structures are therefore emerging from the complexities of existing elected and appointed sectors. In the process, the democratic deficit is increased and the capacity for elected politicians to exercise governmental action reduced. The very flexibility offered by the British administrative and governmental system's basis in convention rather than law accentuates this problem. The absence of a rationale for the allocation of functions and activities between elected and appointed bodies enables ministers to manipulate the arenas in which public policy is developed and implemented with a modicum of approval and oversight by the legislature.

Towards a new public governance

The issue of quangos is a manifestation of wider problems in the political forms that predominate in the UK. To see the solution to the quango problem as a return to traditional forms of accountability, warns Hirst, is to miss the bigger question. There is now 'a serious issue about the degree to which representative institutions can render government in general accountable' (1995: 342) and thus the matter of quangos should be set in the context of a wider debate about the nature of democracy in the UK. This is an important point since there is a danger, especially when viewing the growth of appointed bodies from a local government perspective, to see them as an aberration needing to be returned to the elected fold. As Wright (1994: 101) observes: 'the fact of election has traditionally been offered as a fact of accountability . . . he who says election says accountability'. Such a position ignores the problems of accountability in the UK's electoral systems, including low turn-out and under-representation of third and minority parties. Similarly, the comparison between the auxiliary precautions of elected and appointed bodies (see Chapter 2) can easily – but wrongly – be translated into the prescription that if only the latter were more like the former all would be well. Yet to draw this conclusion is to ignore the poor standard of freedom of information and open government provisions applying to elected bodies, the constraints on ombudsmen and systems of legal remedy and the general problem of scrutiny and oversight of the executive by the legislature. Resolving these problems is seen by Birkinshaw (1993) as the mark of an advanced democratic society:

> the existence of [freedom of information and open government] legislation, or its absence, is an insight into how seriously a society takes democracy. The view that the democratic process begins and ends with the ballot box is acceptable if a society has recently progressed from a state of affairs where even that safeguard was not present. It is a poor realisation of democracy, however, if that is the only justification and legitimisation for the exercise of power over others.
>
> (Birkinshaw 1993: 44)

Hirst locates the problem of rendering government accountable by drawing a distinction between the political constitution and the social constitution. The former defines the power of the state and sets its limits. Essentially, it encapsulates the rights and obligations of state and citizen. The social constitution, in contrast, is 'a complex of laws, practices and procedures that defines the ways in which the political institutions and the wider society interact' (Hirst 1995: 348). It expresses the dynamics of the state's role and particularly its degree of intervention into the operation of the institutions of civil society including enterprises, trade unions, voluntary associations and media organizations. Hirst suggests that both the political and social constitutions of the UK are now exposed as fundamentally flawed. The former has not stood the shocks of conviction politics in the 1980s nor the loss of legitimacy and credibility arising from one party government and the sleaze episode. The latter has been undermined by the collapse of bipartisanship, the failure of self-regulation by private interests and the informal power exercised by a small élite within society. The issue of quangos, therefore, are part of a wider problem to do with the relationship between state and civil society: 'Despite nostalgia for Britain's old social constitution, its informal arrangements and unwritten understandings were no longer adequate in a world that demands openness and has rejected deference' (Hirst 1995: 355). The task, therefore, is not specifically to reform quangos but to arrive at a new settlement between state, citizen and the intermediate institutions of civil society and, as part of this, to resolve the problems of accountability inherent in the present system.

In their normative exploration of management for the public domain, Ranson and Stewart (1994) present the question of accountability as one of ensuring relations of control and consent (holding to account) and of discourse within the polity (giving an account). Reconstructing such a system of governmental accountability, within which quangos would be subsumed, will require the flexibility and innovation shown by individual parts of the public service during the past two decades but applied on a wider scale. It will require the constitutional and political change necessary to offer new democratic possibilities. Models of new democratic practice are available and begin to address the two requirements set by Ranson and Stewart. But by themselves these are not sufficient. Stone (1995) draws attention to a further meaning of account-ability – taking into account: the means through which the welfare of others is incorporated into the process of decision making. This suggests the need for governmental bodies to be open to dialogues about accountability relationships as a permanent feature of the way they operate in addition to the *post hoc* arrangements which can be read into the idea of 'holding to' and 'giving an' account. Such dialogues go beyond the current fashion for consultation and involvement of consumers and other stakeholders in the decisions of govern-ment. They are about the nature of the relationship between the parties. 'The question to put about institutions,' Day and Klein (1987: 244) point out, 'is whether or not they promote the process of argument about what should be the criteria of judgement [of accountability]'. Few quangos, let alone other types of government body, have engaged in this dialogue. This is the agenda for the future.

References

Aglietta, M. (1979) *A Theory of Capitalist Regulation*. London: Verso.

Amenta, E. and Skocpal, T. (1989) 'Taking exception: explaining the distinctiveness of American public policies in the last century', in F.G. Castles (ed.) *The Comparative History of Public Policy*. Cambridge: Polity Press.

Anstis, G. (1985) *Redditch: Success in the Heart of England*. Stevenage: PC Publications.

Ashburner, L. and Cairncross, L. (1993) 'Membership of the "new style" health authorities: continuity or change?', *Public Administration*, 71(3): 357–75.

Ashburner, L., Ferlie, E. and Cairncross, L. (1993) *Boards and Authorities in Action*, Research for Action paper 11. Warwick: Centre for Corporate Strategy and Change, Warwick Business School.

Association of Metropolitan Authorities (1994) *Local Authorities and Health Services: A Discussion Document*. London: AMA.

Association of Metropolitan Authorities (1995) *Changing the Face of Quangos: Proposals for the Reform of Local Appointed Bodies – A Policy Statement on Behalf of Metropolitan Local Government in England*. London: AMA.

Associations of County Councils, District Councils and Metropolitan Authorities (1995) *Local Public Spending Bodies – The Perspective from Local Government: Nolan Committee on Standards in Public Life – Evidence from the Local Authority Associations*. London: AMA.

Audit Commission (1993) *Annual Report and Accounts 1992/93*. London: HMSO.

Audit Commission (1995) *Taken on Board: Corporate Governance in the NHS – Developing the Role of Non-Executive Directors*. London: HMSO.

Audit Commission (1996) *Called to Account: The Role of Audit Committees in Local Government*. London: HMSO.

Baines, P. (1995) 'Financial accountability: agencies and audit', in P. Giddens (ed.) *Parliamentary Accountability: A Study of Parliament and Executive Agencies*. Basingstoke: Macmillan.

Barnett, S. and Curry, A. (1994) *The Battle for the BBC*. London: Aurum.

Barron, J., Crawley, G. and Wood, T. (1989) 'Drift and resistance: refining models of political recruitment', *Policy and Politics*, 17(3): 207–19.

BBC (1994a) ' "Here and Now" publishes comprehensive quango list', *News Release*, 1 November 1994.

BBC (1994b) 'Tory Party donors get top quango jobs reveals "Here and Now" ', *News Release*, 28 November 1994.

BBC (1994c) 'Top bank's quango jobs and £600 000 Tory Party donation', *News Release*, 29 November 1994.

BBC (1994d) *'Here and Now' Quango Directory*. London: Political Research Unit, BBC.

Bennett, R.J. (1994) 'TECs: are they cost-efficient?' *Policy Studies*, 15(1): 42–55.

Bennett, R.J., Wicks, P. and McCoshan, A. (1994) *Local Empowerment and Business Services: Britain's Experiment with Training and Enterprise Councils*. London: UCL Press.

Birkinshaw, P. (1993) 'Citizenship and privacy', in R. Blackburn (ed.) *Rights of Citizenship*. London: Mansell.

Blau, P (1964) *Exchange and Power in Social Life*. London: John Wiley.

Boddy, M. (1995) *TECs and Racial Equality*. Bristol: School for Advanced Urban Studies, University of Bristol.

Bourne, J. (1994) 'The National Audit Office: a force for change', in N. Flynn (ed.) *Change in the Civil Service: A Reader*. London: CIPFA.

Briggs, A. (1979) *Governing the BBC*. London: British Broadcasting Corporation.

Brindley, T., Rydin, R. and Stoker, G. (1996) *Remaking Planning: The Politics of Urban Change*, 2nd edn. London: Routledge.

Brownhill, S. (1993) 'The Docklands experience: locality and community in London', in R. Imrie and H. Thomas (eds) *British Urban Policy and the Urban Development Corporations*. London: Paul Chapman.

Buchanan, J.M. (ed.) (1978) *The Economics of Politics*. London: Institute of Economic Affairs.

Burns, N. (1994) *The Formation of American Local Governments: Private Values in Public Institutions*. Oxford: Oxford University Press.

Burns, T. (1977) *The BBC: Public Institution in a Private World*. London: Macmillan.

Bush, T., Coleman, M. and Glover, D. (1992) *Managing Autonomous Schools: The Grant-Maintained Experience*. London: Paul Chapman.

Butler, D. and Kavanagh, D. (1992) *The British General Election of 1992*. Basingstoke: Macmillan.

Cabinet Office (1989) *Review of Public Appointments Procedures*. London: Cabinet Office.

Cabinet Office (1994) *Code of Practice on Open Government*. London: HMSO.

Cabinet Office (1996) *Public Bodies*. London: HMSO.

Cabinet Office (1997) *Guidance on Codes of Practice for Board Members of Public Bodies*. London: Cabinet Office.

Cabinet Office and HM Treasury (1992) *Non-Departmental Public Bodies: A Guide for Departments*. London: Cabinet Office.

Cabinet Office, Privy Council and Parliament (1996) *The Government's Expenditure Plans 1996–97 to 1998–99*, Cm 3220. London: HMSO.

Cairncross, L. and Ashburner, L. (1992) *NHS Trust Boards: The First Wave – The First Year*, Research in Action paper 6. Warwick: Centre for Corporate Strategy and Change, Warwick Business School.

Cannon, T. (1994) *Corporate Responsibility: A Textbook on Business Ethics, Governance, Environment: Roles and Responsibilities*. London: Pitman.

Carter, N., Day, P. and Klein, R. (1992) *How Organisations Measure Success: The Use of Performance Indicators in Government*. London: Routledge.

Carter, S.L. (1994) *The Confirmation Mess: Cleaning-Up the Federal Appointments Process*. New York: Basic Books.

Chartered Institute of Public Finance and Accountancy (1996) *Corporate Governance – A Framework for Public Service Bodies*. London: CIPFA.

Cherry, G.E. (1988) *Cities and Plans: The Shaping of Urban Britain in the Nineteenth and Twentieth Centuries*. London: Edward Arnold.

Chumrow, J. (1995) 'HATs: a possible role model', *Parliamentary Affairs*, 48(2): 254–70.

Clarke, J. and Newman, J. (1997) *The Managerial State*. London: Sage.

Clarke, M., Hunter, D. and Wistow, G. (1995) *Local Government and the National Health Service: The New Agenda*. Luton: Local Government Management Board.

Cochrane, A. (1991) 'The changing state of local government: restructuring for the 1990s', *Public Administration*, 69: 281–302.

Comisky, M. (1994) 'The usefulness of Senate Confirmation Hearings for Judicial Nominees: the case of Ruth Bader Ginsburg', *Political Science and Politics*, 27(2).

Committee on the Civil Service (1968) *Report of the Committee on the Civil Service*, Cmnd 3538. London: HMSO.

Committee on the Financial Aspects of Corporate Governance (1992) *The Financial Aspects of Corporate Governance: The Code of Best Practice*. London: Gee.

Committee on Standards in Public Life (1995a) *First Report*, Cm 2850(I). London: HMSO.

Committee on Standards in Public Life (1995b) *Local Public Spending Bodies: Issues and Questions*. London: HMSO.

Committee on Standards in Public Life (1996) *Second Report: Local Public Spending Bodies*, Cm 3270(I). London: HMSO.

Committee of University Chairmen (1995) *Guide for Members of Governing Bodies of Universities and Colleges in England and Wales*. Bristol: Higher Education Funding Council for England.

Coombes, D. (1966) *The Member of Parliament and the Administration: The Case of the Select Committee on Nationalised Industries*. London: Allen and Unwin.

Cooper, L., Coote, A., Davies, A. and Jackson, C. (1995) *Voices Off: Tackling the Democratic Deficit in Health*. London: Institute for Public Policy Research.

Coulson, A. (1993) 'Urban development corporations, local authorities and patronage in urban policy', in R. Imrie and H. Thomas (eds) *British Urban Policy and the Urban Development Corporations*. London: Paul Chapman.

Crail, M. (1994) 'Time and tide', *Health Service Journal*, 20 October 1994.

Crowley-Bainton, T. (1993) *TECs and Employers: Developing Effective Links – Part 2: TEC–Employer Links in Six TEC Areas*, Research Series No. 13. Sheffield: Employment Department.

Cullingworth, J.B. (1979) *Environmental Planning 1939–1969: Volume III. New Towns Policy*. London: HMSO.

Davis, H. (1993) *A First Guide to Appointed Bodies in the West Midlands*, Birmingham City Council/University of Birmingham Partnership Paper. Birmingham: Institute of Local Government Studies, The University of Birmingham.

Davis, H. and Hall, D. (1996) *Matching Purpose and Task: The Advantages and Disadvantages of Single and Multi-Purpose Bodies*. York: YPS/Joseph Rowntree Foundation.

Davis, H. and Stewart, J. (1993) *The Growth of Government by Appointment: The Implications for Local Democracy*. London: Local Government Management Board.

188   The appointed state

Day, P. and Klein, R. (1987) *Accountabilities in Five Public Services*. London: Tavistock.
Department for Education (1992) *Choice and Diversity: A New Framework for Schools*, Cm 2021. London: HMSO.
Department for Education and Employment (1995) *Efficiency Scrutiny: The TEC Contract and Management Fee*. London: DfEE.
Department for Education and Employment (1997) *The Government's Expenditure Plans 1997–98 to 1999–2000*, Cm 3610. London: HMSO.
Department for Education and Employment/Welsh Office (1996) *Self-Government for Schools*, Cm 3315. London: HMSO.
Department of Employment (1993) 'TEC Comparison Tables Published', *Press Notice*, 181/93, 13 September.
Department of Employment (1994) ' "TECs have key role in local economic development" says Employment Secretary David Hunt', *Press Notice*, 5/94, 27 January.
Department of Environment (1996) Annual Report 1996: *The Government Expenditure Plans 1996–97 to 1998–99*, Cm 3207. London: HMSO.
Department of Health (1994) *Corporate Governance in the NHS: Code of Conduct; Code of Accountability*. London: DoH.
Department of Health (1995) 'Virginia Bottomly announces strengthened national procedures for appointments to NHS organisations', *Press Release*, 95/67, 14 February.
Department of Health (1996) *Public Appointments Annual Report 1996*. London: DoH.
Docklands Consultative Committee (1990) *Ten Years of Docklands: How the Cake Was Cut*. London: AMA.
Doig, A. (1977) 'Public bodies and ministerial patronage', *Parliamentary Affairs*, 30 (Winter).
Dudley, G. (1994) 'The Next Steps agencies, political salience and the arm's-length principle: Barbara Castle at the Ministry of Transport 1965–68', *Public Administration* 72: 219–40.
Dunleavy, P. (1991) *Democracy, Bureaucracy and Public Choice*. London: Harvester Wheatsheaf.
Dunleavy, P. and Weir, S. (1994) 'Democracy in doubt', *Local Government Chronicle*, 29 April 1994.
Dunleavy, P., Weir, S. and Subrahmanyam, G. (1995) 'Public response and constitutional significance', *Parliamentary Affairs*, 48: 602–16.
Dunsire, A., Hartley, K. and Parker, D. (1991) 'Organisational status and performance: summary of the findings', *Public Administration*, 69(1): 21–40.
Eisenstadt, S.N. and Roniger, L. (1984) *Patrons, Clients and Friends: Interpersonal Relations and the Structure of Trust in Society*. Cambridge: Cambridge University Press.
Emmerich, M. and Peck, J. (1992) *Reforming the TECs: Towards a New Training Strategy*. Manchester: Centre for Local Economic Strategies.
Employment Committee (1989) *Third Report: The Employment Effects of UDCs*, Session 1988–89, HC 327. London: HMSO.
Employment Committee (1996) *The Work of TECs*, First Report, Session 1995–96, HC 99. London: HMSO.
Environment Committee (1993) *The Housing Corporation*, Second Report, Session 1992–93. HC 466. London: HMSO.
Evans, A. (1996) 'Banham reveals the pain of being sacked', *Local Government Chronicle*, 22 March 1996.
Fainstein, S. (1994) *The City Builders*. Oxford: Basil Blackwell.

Ferlie, E., Ashburner, L. and Fitzgerald, L. (1995) 'Corporate governance and the public sector: some issues and evidence from the NHS', *Public Administration*, 73(3): 375–92.

Ferlie, E., Ashburner, L., Fitzgerald, L. and Pettigrew, A. (1996) *The New Public Management in Action*. Oxford: Oxford University Press.

The Financial Times (1993) 'Patronage dictates who serves at the top', 14 January 1993.

Finch, W. (1994) 'Life on the board', *NATFHE Journal*, Summer.

Finer, S. E. (1952) 'Patronage and the public service', *Public Administration*, 30(4): 48–67.

Fisher, L. (1993) *The Politics of Shared Power: Congress and the Executive*, 3rd edn. Washington DC: CQ Press.

Fitz, J., Halpin, D. and Power, S. (1993) *Grant-Maintained Schools: Education in the Market Place*. London: Kogan Page.

Flynn, N. (1986) 'Performance measurement in public sector services', *Policy and Politics*, 14(3): 389–404.

Freedman, A. (1994) *Patronage: An American Tradition*. Chicago: Nelson Hall.

Fry, G. (1979) *The Growth of Government: The Development of Ideas about the Role of the State and the Machinery and Functions of Government in Britain since 1780*. London: Frank Cass.

Further Education Funding Council (1994) *Guide for College Governors*. Coventry: FEFC.

Game, C. and Leach, S. (1993) *Councillor Recruitment and Turnover: An Emerging Precipice?* London: Local Government Management Board.

The Governance of Public Money: A Progress Report (1997) Cm 3557. London: HMSO.

Graham, A. (1995) 'The TECs and accountability', *Parliamentary Affairs*, 48(2): 271–83.

Gray, A. and Jenkins, A. (1985) *Administrative Politics and British Government*. Brighton: Wheatsheaf.

Gray, J. (1995) *Good School, Bad School: Evaluating Performance and Encouraging Improvement*. Buckingham: Open University Press.

Graystone, J. (1991a) *The New Governing Bodies in FE: Size and Composition*. Bristol: The Staff College.

Graystone, J. (1991b) 'Just white, male and business-like', *Education*, 23 August 1991.

Greer, A. and Hoggett, P. (1995) 'Non-elected bodies and local governance', in J. Stewart, A. Greer and P. Hoggett *The Quango State: An Alternative Approach*, Commission for Local Democracy Research Report 10. London: CLD.

The Guardian (1994) 'Tories "pack" schools quango', 23 February 1994.

The Guardian (1996) 'Heritage minister asks Sir Jocelyn not to resign over cuts in funding', 22 November 1996.

Guy, R. and Howells, D. (1994) 'TECs: are they cost-effective?', *Policy Studies*, 15(2): 19–36.

Hackett, G. (1996) 'Results show rise in standards is slowing', *Times Education Supplement*, 22 November 1996.

Hague, D.C., Mackenzie, W.J.M. and Barker, A. (1975) *Public Policy and Private Interests: The Institutions of Compromise*. London: Macmillan.

Hague, R., Harrop, M. and Breslin, S. (1992) *Comparative Government and Politics*, 3rd edn. London: Macmillan.

Hall, W. and Weir, S. (1995) *National Executive Quangos*. [Mimeo.] London: Democratic Audit.

Hall, W. and Weir, S. (1996) *The Untouchables: Power and Accountability in the Quango State*, Democratic Audit Paper 8. London: The Scarman Trust.

Halpin, D., Power, S. and Fitz, J. (1991) 'Grant-maintained schools: making a difference without being really different', *British Journal of Educational Studies*, 34(4): 409–24.

Haywood, S. and Ranade, W. (1985) 'Health authorities: tribunes or prefects?', *Public Administration Bulletin*, 47, April.

Haughton, G., Hart, T., Strange, I., Thomas, K. and Peck, J. (1995a) *TECs and Their Non-Employer Stakeholders*, Research Series No. 46. Sheffield: Employment Department.

Haughton, G., Peck, J., Hart, T., Strange, I., Tickell, A. and Williams, C. (1995b) *TECs and Their Boards*, Research Series No. 64. Sheffield: Department for Education and Employment.

Health Service Commissioner (1996) *Selected Investigations – Access to Official Information in the NHS, First Report, Session 1996–97*, HC 62. London: HMSO.

Health Service Journal (1996) 'Managers doubt Trust fed political affiliation survey', 30 March 1996.

Hencke, D. (1996) 'Nolan reforms oust quango man', *The Guardian*, 4 December 1996.

Hencke, D. (1997) 'Ex-college head faces fraud inquiry', *The Guardian*, 31 January 1997.

Hickson, D.J., Butler, R.J., Cray, D., Mallory, G.R. and Wilson, D.C. (1986) *Top Decisions*. Oxford: Basil Blackwell.

Hirst, P. (1995) 'Quangos and democratic government', *Parliamentary Affairs*, 48(2): 341–59.

Hodges, R., Wright, M. and Keasey, K. (1996) 'Corporate governance in the public services: concepts and issues', *Public Money and Management*, 16(2): 7–13.

Hoggett, P. (1987) 'A farewell to mass production', in P. Hoggett and R. Hambleton (eds) *Decentralisation and Democracy: Localising Public Services*. Bristol: School for Advanced Urban Studies, University of Bristol.

Hoggett, P. (1996) 'New modes of control in the public service', *Public Administration*, 74(1): 9–32.

Holland, P. (1994) *The Hunting of the Quango*. London: Adam Smith Institute.

Holland, P. and Fallon, M. (1978) *The Quango Explosion: Public Bodies and Ministerial Patronage*. London: Conservative Political Centre.

Housing Corporation (1994) *Performance Standards for Housing Associations*. London: The Housing Corporation.

Housing Corporation (1996) *The Housing Corporation Review, 1995/96*. London: The Housing Corporation.

Howells, D. J. (1980) 'The Manpower Services Commission: the first five years', *Public Administration*, 58: 305–31.

Hunter, D.J. (1995) 'Accountability and local democracy', *British Journal of Health Care Management*, 1(2): 78–81.

Imrie, R. and Thomas, T. (eds) (1993) *British Urban Policy and the Urban Development Corporations*. London: Paul Chapman.

The Independent (1994) 'The sleazy state: how the web of patronage works', 17 March 1994.

Jones, M. (1996) 'Resolving the TEC crisis: why easing financial controls isn't the answer', *Working Brief*, May.

Judge, D., Stoker, G. and Wolman, H. (eds) (1995) *Theories of Urban Politics*. London: Sage.

Kearns, A. (1994) *Going by the Board: Unknown Facts about Housing Association Membership and Management Committees in England*. Glasgow: Centre for Housing Research and Urban Studies, University of Glasgow.

Keith-Lucas, B. (1980) *The Unreformed Local Government System*. London: Croom Helm.
Kristinsson, G.H. (1996) 'Parties, states and patronage', *West European Politics*, 19(3): 433–57.
Labour Research Department/GMB (1994) *Who Runs our Health Service?* London: The Labour Party.
Lane, J-E. (1995) *The Public Sector: Concepts, Models and Approaches*, 2nd edn. London: Sage.
Leach, S. (1996) 'The indirectly elected world of local government', *Local Government Studies*, 22(2): 64–76.
Leach, S., Davis, H., Game, C. and Skelcher, C. (1991) *After Abolition: The Operation of the Post-1986 Metropolitan Government System in England*. Birmingham: Institute of Local Government Studies, University of Birmingham.
Levačić, R. (1995) *Local Management of Schools*. Buckingham: Open University Press.
Lindley, P.D. (1982) 'The framework of regional planning 1964–1980', in B.W. Hogwood and M. Keating (eds) *Regional Government in England*. Oxford: Clarendon.
Lipietz, A. (1987) *Mirages and Miracles: The Crises of Global Fordism*. London: Verso.
Local Government Information Unit (1994a) *Quango Registers, The Quango File No. 7*. London: Local Government Information Unit.
Local Government Information Unit (1994b) *Scrutiny and Partnership, The Quango File No. 8*. London: Local Government Information Unit.
Lowndes, V. (1996) 'Varieties of new institutionalism: a critical appraisal', *Public Administration*, 74(2): 181–97.
Lowndes, V. and Skelcher, C. (1998) 'The dynamics of multi-organizational partnerships: an analysis of changing modes of governance', *Public Administration* (forthcoming).
Marsh, D. (1992) 'Youth employment policy 1970–1990', in R.A.W. Rhodes and D. Marsh (eds) *Policy Networks in British Government*. Oxford: Clarendon.
McEldowney, J. (1993) 'Administrative justice', in R. Blackburn (ed.) *Rights of Citizenship*. London: Mansell.
Midwinter, A. (1995) 'Quangos in Scotland: briefing paper for Nolan Committee Quango Group', *Briefing Papers for the Nolan Committee*. Birmingham: Institute of Local Government Studies, University of Birmingham.
Miller, W.L. and Dickinson, M.B. (1996) *Local Governance and Local Citizenship: A Report on Public and Élite Attitudes*, Local Governance Programme Working Paper 1. Swindon: Economic and Social Research Council.
Millward, R. (1995) 'Industrial organisation and economic factors in nationalisation', in R. Millward and J. Singleton (eds) *The Political Economy of Nationalisation in Britain 1920–1950*. Cambridge: Cambridge University Press.
Mintzberg, H. (1983) *Power in and Around Organisations*. London: Prentice Hall.
Morgan, G. (1997) *Images of Organisation*, 2nd edn. London: Sage.
Morgan, K. and Osmond, J. (1995) 'The Welsh quango state', *Briefing Papers for the Nolan Committee*. Birmingham: Institute of Local Government Studies, University of Birmingham.
Morgan, K. and Roberts, E. (1993) *The Democratic Deficit: A Guide to QUANGOland*. Cardiff: University of Wales.
Morris, K. (1996) 'Remorse codes', *Health Service Journal*, 17 October 1996.
Morris, R. (1990) *Central and Local Control after the Education Reform Act 1988*. Harlow: Longman.

192   The appointed state

Mulgan, G. (1993) *The Power of the Boot: The Case for Contestable Institutions.* [Mimeo.] London: Demos.

National Association of Health Authorities and Trusts (1993) *Securing Effective Public Accountability in the NHS: A Discussion Document.* Birmingham: NAHAT.

National Association of Health Authorities and Trusts/King's Fund Centre (1993) *Equality Across the Board.* Birmingham: NAHAT.

National Audit Office (1993) *The Achievements of the Second and Third Generation Urban Development Corporations, Report of the Comptroller and Auditor General, Session 1992–93,* HC 898. London: HMSO.

National Audit Office (1994) *The Sports Council: Initiatives to Improve Financial Management and Control and Value for Money, Report by the Comptroller and Auditor General, Session 1993–94,* HC 131. London: HMSO.

National Audit Office (1995a) *Department of Employment: Financial Controls in Training and Enterprise Councils in England, Report of the Comptroller and Auditor General, Session 1994–95,* HC 361. London: HMSO.

National Audit Office (1995b) *London Docklands Development Corporation: The Limehouse Link, Report of the Comptroller and Auditor General, Session 1994–95,* HC 468. London: HMSO.

National Audit Office (1996) *Department for Education and Employment: Financial Control of Payments made under the Training for Work and Youth Training Programmes in England, Report by the Comptroller and Auditor General, Session 1995–96,* HC 402. London: HMSO.

National Audit Office (1997a) *Wind Up of Leeds and Bristol Urban Development Corporations, Report by the Comptroller and Auditor General, Session 1996–97,* HC 292. London: HMSO.

National Audit Office (1997b) *Governance and Management of Overseas Courses at the Swansea Institute of Higher Education, Report by the Comptroller and Auditor General, Session 1996–97,* HC 222. London: HMSO.

National Audit Office (1997c) *Waltham Forest Housing Action Trust: Progress in Regenerating Housing Estates, Report of the Comptroller and Auditor General, Session 1996–97,* HC 207. London: HMSO.

National Health Service Executive (1995) *Code of Practice on Openness in the NHS.* Leeds: NHS Executive.

Natzler, D. and Silk, P. (1995) 'Departmental Select Committees and the Next Steps Programme', in P. Giddens (ed.) *Parliamentary Accountability: A Study of Parliament and Executive Agencies.* Basingstoke: Macmillan.

Nevin, B. 'Developer-led land use strategies: the Black Country Development Corporation', in R. Imrie and H. Thomas (eds) *British Urban Policy and the Urban Development Corporations.* London: Paul Chapman.

Newman, J. and Clarke, J. (1994) 'Going about our business: the managerialisation of public services', in J. Clarke, A. Cochrane and E. McLaughlin (eds) *Managing Social Policy.* London: Sage.

Newton, K. (1976) *Second City Politics.* Oxford: Clarendon.

Niskanen, W.A. (1971) *Bureaucracy and Representative Government.* Chicago: Aldine-Atherton.

Nolan, Lord (1996) *The Executive,* Second Radcliffe Lecture, Warwick University, 21 November 1996. [Mimeo.]

Norton-Taylor, N. (1997) 'More women for quangos', *The Guardian,* 10 January 1997.

The Observer (1994) 'Tory peers pile aboard the quango gravy train', 6 February 1994.

OECD (1995) *Schools Under Scrutiny*. Paris: Centre for Educational Research and Innovation, OECD.

Ofsted (1993) *Grant Maintained Schools 1989–92: A Report from Her Majesty's Chief Inspector of Schools*. London: Ofsted.

O'Gorman, F. (1989) *Voters, Patrons and Parties: The Unreformed Electoral System of Hanoverian England 1734–1832*. Oxford: Clarendon.

O'Malley, T. (1994) *Closedown? The BBC and Government Broadcasting Policy*. London: Pluto Press.

Osborne, D. and Gaebler, T. (1992) *Reinventing Government*. Reading, MA: Addison-Wesley.

Painter, J. (1995) 'Regulation theory and post-Fordism', in D. Judge, G. Stoker and H. Wolman (eds) *Theories of Urban Politics*. London: Sage.

Painter, C., Isaac-Henry, K. and Chalcroft, T. (1994) *Appointed Agencies and Public Accountability: Proactive Strategies for Local Government*. West Midlands Joint Committee/Institute of Public Policy and Management, University of Central England Business School, Birmingham.

Painter, C., Isaac-Henry, K. and Rouse, J. (1997) 'Local authorities and non-elected agencies: strategic responses and organisational networks', *Public Administration*, 75(2): 225–46.

Parker, K.T. and Vickerstaff, S. (1996) 'TECs, LECs, and the small firms: differences in provision and performance', *Environment and Planning C: Government and Policy*, 14: 251–67.

Parkinson, M. (1996) 'Twenty-five years of urban policy in Britain: partnership, entrepreneurialism or competition?', *Public Money and Management*, 16(3): 7–14.

Payne, T. and Skelcher, C. (1997) 'Explaining less accountability: the growth of local quangos', *Public Administration*, 75(2): 207–24.

Peck, E. (1995) 'The performance of an NHS Trust Board: actors' accounts, minutes and observation', *British Journal of Management*, **6**: 135–56.

Peck, J. (1993) 'The trouble with TECs . . . A critique of the Training and Enterprise Councils initiative', *Policy and Politics*, 21(4): 289–305.

Peele, G., Bailey, C.J. and Cain, B. (1992) *Developments in American Politics*. London: Macmillan.

Peters, B.G. (1995) *The Politics of Bureaucracy: A Comparative Perspective*, 4th edn. New York: Longman.

Peters, T. and Waterman, R.H. (1982) *In Search of Excellence*. New York: Harper Row.

Pettigrew, A. and McNulty, T. (1995) 'Power and influence in and around the boardroom', *Human Relations*, 48(8): 845–73.

Pfeffer, J. (1981) *Power in Organisations*. Marshfield, MA: Pitman.

Pifer, A. (1975) 'The quasi-non-governmental organisation', in D.C. Hague, W.J.M. Mackenzie and A. Barker (eds) *Public Policy and Private Interests: The Institutions of Compromise*. London: Macmillan.

Pliatzky, L. (1980) *Report on Non-Departmental Public Bodies*, Cmnd 7797. London: HMSO.

Pollitt, C. (1993) *Managerialism and the Public Services: Cuts and Cultural Change in the 1990s*, 2nd edn. Oxford: Basil Blackwell.

Pollitt, C., Birchall, J. and Putman, K. (1997) *Opting-out and the Experience of Self-Management in Education, Housing and Health Care*, Local Governance Programme Working Paper 2. Swindon: Economic and Social Research Council.

Power, S., Halpin, D. and Fitz, J. (1994) 'Parents, pupils and grant-maintained schools', *British Educational Research Journal*, 20(2): 209–26.

Public Accounts Committee (1993) *Wessex Regional Health Authority: Regional Information Systems Plan, Sixty-third Report, Session 1992–93*, HC 658. London: HMSO.

Public Accounts Committee (1994) *The Proper Conduct of Public Business, Eighth Report, Session 1993–94*, HC 154. London: HMSO.

Public Accounts Committee (1995a) *Value for Money at Grant-maintained Schools in England: A Review of Performance, Twenty-third Report, Session 1994–95*, HC 225. London: HMSO.

Public Accounts Committee (1995b) *Severance Payments to Senior Staff in the Publicly Funded Education Sector, Twenty-eighth Report, Session 1994–95*, HC 242. London: HMSO.

Public Accounts Committee (1995c) *London Docklands Development Corporation: The Limehouse Link, Fourty-seventh Report, Session 1994–95*, HC 574. London: HMSO.

Public Appointments Unit (1995) *Review of Guidance on Public Appointments*. London: Cabinet Office.

Ranson, S. and Stewart, J. (1994) *Management for the Public Domain: Enabling the Learning Society*. Basingstoke: Macmillan.

Rhodes, R.A.W. and Marsh, D. (eds) (1992) *Policy Networks in British Government*. Oxford: Clarendon.

Richards, P.G. (1963) *Patronage in British Government*. London: George Allen and Unwin.

Roberts, S. and Pollitt, C. (1994) 'Audit or evaluation? A National Audit Office VFM study', *Public Administration*, 72: 527–49.

Robinson, F. and Shaw, K. (1994) *Who Runs the North?* London: UNISON.

Robinson, F., Lawrence, M. and Shaw, K. (1993) *More Than Bricks and Mortar: Tyne and Wear and Teesside Development Corporations – a mid-term report*. Durham: Department of Sociology and Social Policy, University of Durham.

Robson, B.T. *et al.* (1994) *Assessing the Impact of Urban Policy*. London: HMSO.

Robson, W.A. (1962) *Nationalised Industry and Public Ownership*, 2nd edn. London: George Allen and Unwin.

Rolfe, H., Bryson, A. and Metcalfe, H. (1996) *The Effectiveness of TECs in Achieving Jobs and Qualifications for Disadvantaged Groups, Research Studies RS4*. London: Department for Education and Employment, HMSO.

Scott, W.R. (1994) 'Institutions and organisations: towards a theoretical synthesis', in W.R. Scott and J.W Meyer (eds) *Institutions, Environments and Organisations*. London: Sage.

Scottish Affairs Committee (1994) *The Operation of the Enterprise Agencies and the LECs, First Report, Session 1994–95*, HC 339. London: HMSO.

Select Committee on the Parliamentary Commissioner for Administration (1997) *Report of the Health Service Commissioner for 1995–96, First Report, Session 1996–97*, HC 93. London: HMSO.

Shattock, M. (1994) *Derby College, Wilmorton*. Coventry: Further Education Funding Council.

Shaw, K. (1993) 'The development of new urban corporatism: the politics of urban regeneration in the North East of England', *Regional Studies*, 27: 251–9.

Shaw, K., Robinson, F. and Curran, M. (1996) 'Non-elected agencies and the new quangocrats: a profile of board membership in the North East of England', *Regional Studies*, 30: 295–310.

Singleton, J. (1995) 'Labour, the Conservatives and nationalisation', in R. Millward and J. Singleton (eds) *The Political Economy of Nationalisation in Britain 1920–1950*. Cambridge: Cambridge University Press.

Skelcher, C. and Stewart, J. (1993) *The Appointed Government of London: A Study for the Association of London Authorities*. Birmingham: Institute of Local Government Studies, University of Birmingham.

Skelcher, C. and Davis, H. (1995) *Opening the Board-Room Door: The Membership of Local Appointed Bodies*. London: LGC Communications/Joseph Rowntree Foundation.

Skelcher, C. and Davis, H. (1996) 'Understanding the new magistracy: a study of characteristics and attitudes', *Local Government Studies*, 22(2): 8–21.

Skelcher C., Lowndes, V. and McCabe, A. (1996) *Community Networks in Urban Regeneration*. Bristol: Policy Press.

Sohpal, R. and Muir, C. (1995) 'Survey of councillors', *Facing the Challenge: A Report of the First All-Party Convention of Black, Asian and Ethnic Minority Councillors*. London: Local Government Information Unit.

Spending Public Money: Governance and Audit Issues (1996) Cm 3179. London: HMSO.

Starkey, K. (1995) 'Opening up corporate governance', *Human Relations*, 48(8): 837–44.

Stevens, A. (1996) *The Government and Politics of France*, 2nd edn. Basingstoke: Macmillan.

Stewart, J. (1995a) 'Reforming the new magistracy: choices to be faced and criteria to guide', in J. Stewart, A. Greer and P. Hoggett *The Quango State: An Alternative Approach*, Commission for Local Democracy Research Report 10. London: CLD.

Stewart, J. (1995b) *Innovations in Democratic Practice*. Birmingham: Institute of Local Government Studies, University of Birmingham.

Stewart, J. and Davis, H. (1994) 'A new agenda for local governance', *Public Money and Management*, 14(4): 29–36.

Stewart, J., Kendall, E. and Coote, A. (1994) *Citizens' Juries*. London: Institute of Public Policy Research.

Stewart, J. and Stoker, G. (1995a) 'Fifteen years of local government restructuring 1979–1994: an evaluation', in J. Stewart and G. Stoker (eds) *Local Government in the 1990s*. Basingstoke: Macmillan.

Stoker, G. and Mossberger, K. (1995) 'The post-Fordist local state', in J. Stewart and G. Stoker (eds) *Local Government in the 1990s*. Basingstoke: Macmillan.

Stone, B. (1995) 'Administrative accountability in the Westminster democracies: Towards a new conceptual framework', *Governance*, 8(4): 505–26.

Taylor, A. (1995) 'How political is the Arts Council?', *Political Quarterly*, 66: 184–96.

TEC National Council (1995) *A Framework for the Local Accountability of Training and Enterprise Councils*. London: TEC National Council.

Thody, A. (1994) 'Practising democracy: business community representatives in the control of English and Welsh Schools', *Research Papers in Education*, 9(3): 339–67.

Thomas, I.C. (1994) 'The relationship between local authorities and TECs in metropolitan areas', *Local Government Studies*, 20(2): 275–305.

Thomas, R. (1997) 'Lake drops out of CIA race after "brutish" grilling by Senate', *The Guardian*, 19 March 1997.

Treasury (1994) *Code of Best Practice for Board Members of Public Bodies*. London: HM Treasury.

Vaughn, P. (1993) *TECs and Employers: Developing Effective Links – Part 1: A Survey*. Sheffield: Employment Department.

Vile, M. J. C. (1983) *Politics in the USA*. London: Hutchinson.

Walsh, K. (1995) *Public Service and Market Mechanisms*. Basingstoke: Macmillan.

Weekes, T. (1996) 'Dodging the detectives', *Public Finance*, 15 March 1996.

Weir S. (1996) 'From strong government and quasi-government to strong democracy', in P. Hirst and S. Khilnani (eds) *Reinventing Democracy*. Oxford: Basil Blackwell.

Weir, S. and Hall, W. (1994) *EGO-Trip: Extra-Governmental Organisations in the United Kingdom and their Accountability*. London: Charter 88.

Weir, S. and Hall, W. (1995) *Appointments to Public Bodies: Comments on the PAU Review and the Government's Evidence to the Committee on Standards in Public Life: Supplementary Working Brief for the Committee on Standards in Public Life*. [Mimeo.] Colchester: Democratic Audit of the United Kingdom, University of Essex.

Welsh Affairs Select Committee (1997) *Morriston Hospital NHS Trust: A Case Study in the Workings of the Internal Market, First Report, Session 1996–97*, HC 166. London: HMSO.

Welsh Office (1996) *Departmental Report 1996: The Government's Expenditure Plans 1996–97 to 1998–99*, Cm 3215. London: HMSO.

West Midlands Joint Committee (1994) *Appointed Agencies and Public Accountability: West Midlands Code of Good Practice*. Dudley: West Midlands Joint Committee.

The Western Mail (1993) 'Shortening the leash on power plays', 20 August 1993.

Wilson, D. and Game, C. (1994) *Local Government in the United Kingdom*. Basingstoke: Macmillan.

Wright, T. (1994) *Citizens and Subjects: An Essay on British Politics*. London: Routledge.

Wright, T. (1995) *Beyond the Patronage State*. Fabian Pamphlet 569. London: Fabian Society.

Young, K. and Rao, N. (1994) *Coming to Terms with Change: The Local Government Councillor in 1993*. London: LGC Communications/Joseph Rowntree Foundation.

Index

UNDERSTANDING GOVERNANCE
POLICY NETWORKS, GOVERNANCE, REFLEXIVITY
AND ACCOUNTABILITY

R.A.W. Rhodes

Understanding Governance asks:

- What has changed in British government over the past two decades, how and why?
- Why do so many government policies fail?
- What does the shift from government to governance mean for the practice and study of British government?

This book provides a challenging reinterpretation which interweaves an account of recent institutional changes in central, local and European Union government with methodological innovations and theoretical analysis. It emphasizes: the inability of the 'Westminster model', with its accent on parliamentary sovereignty and strong executive leadership, to account for persistent policy failure; the 'hollowing out' of British government from above (the European Union), below (special purpose bodies) and sideways (to agencies); and the need to respond to the postmodern challenge, rethinking the methodological and theoretical assumptions in the study of British government. Professor Rhodes makes a significant and timely contribution to our understanding of government and governance.

Contents

256pp   0 335 19727 2 (Paperback)   0 335 19728 0 (Hardback)

THE STATE UNDER STRESS
CAN THE HOLLOW STATE BE GOOD GOVERNMENT?

Christopher D. Foster and Francis J. Plowden

This is a comprehensive account of the changes that have taken place in British government in recent years – since 1979 but, more especially, since 1988. It argues that (and explains why) there has been a general decline in competence and ability to deliver good government. Ministers are increasingly overloaded, their long-standing relationships with civil servants have altered and the power of Parliament has declined. And the machinery of government has been transformed, at one level, by changes in the use of Cabinet and at another by privatization, contractorization and the creation of executive agencies. Any new government will find government transformed to a point where most memories of how it used to work in the 1970s are irrelevant. *The State Under Stress* argues that, while the clock cannot be turned back, urgent reforms are needed if democracy is not to be further undermined.

Contents

The causes of fiscal crisis – The politics of fiscal crisis – New public management examined – Separating provision from production – Complete separation: social objectives and regulation of privatization – Impermanent separation: contractorization – Decentralization: empowering local communities – The agency: incomplete separation – Ministers and agencies: separation as metaphor? – The role of minister – What future for politics? – Conclusion – References – Index.

288pp   0 335 19713 2 (Paperback)   0 335 19714 0 (Hardback)